THE JAPANESE SCHOOL

Lessons for Industrial America

Benjamin Duke

PRAEGER

PRAEGER SPECIAL STUDIES • PRAEGER SCIENTIFIC

New York • Westport, Connecticut • London

Permission to reprint the materials in this book is gratefully acknowledged. A complete list of grantors begins on page 237.

Library of Congress Cataloging-in-Publication Data

Duke, Benjamin
   The Japanese school.

   "Praeger special studies. Praeger scientific."
   Bibliography: p.
   Includes index.
   1. Education—Japan—Aims and objectives.
2. Education—United States—Aims and objectives.
3. Labor and laboring classes—Education—Japan.
4. Labor productivity—Japan. I. Title.
LA1312.D85 1986   370'.952   86-5002
ISBN 0-275-92053-4 (alk. paper)
ISBN 0-275-92003-8 (pbk. : alk. paper)

Library of Congress Catalog Card Number: 86-5002
ISBN: 0-275-92053-4 (alk. paper)
ISBN: 0-275-92003-8 (pbk. : alk. paper)

First published in 1986

Praeger Publishers, 521 Fifth Avenue, New York, NY 10175
A division of Greenwood Press, Inc.

Printed in the United States of America

The paper used in this book complies with the Permanent Paper Standard issued by the National Information Standards Organization (Z39.48-1984).

10 9 8 7 6 5 4 3 2 1

THE JAPANESE SCHOOL

Dedicated
to

Susan, Kim, and Chris

whose experiences in the Japanese school
provided many of the insights for this book

Contents

Forewords from America

The central theme of this careful and balanced study is that the "challenge to industrial America lies primarily in the Japanese classroom rather than in the factory." It is the school that trains the Japanese work force and plays such an essential part in "bringing up the future Japanese worker." The Japanese school produces "a loyal, literate, competent, and diligent worker with whom we are competing"; and it is the school "where the ultimate challenge from the Japanese lies."

This is not the only view of the "ultimate challenge" from Japan that confronts the United States. Others have argued that the challenge lies in the style of labor-management relations or in the high rate of savings and investment or in government guidance of industrial policy in a future-oriented direction or in the cultural traditions of a nation based on the Confucian ethic. I know of no way to prove which challenge is the more ultimate or whether they must all be taken together to constitute an ultimate challenge as they reinforce each other. If I were to choose one, and only one, it would be the Confucian ethic still going strong. But, whether or not the school in and by itself is the ultimate challenge, Benjamin Duke makes a very strong case that, without it, the industrial system would be far less effective. With this observation nearly all observers would agree; I most certainly do.

Duke sets forth most forcefully the strong points of the Japanese school. These include the emphasis on excellence in all subjects all the time; on the basics of reading, writing, and arithmetic; on concern for discipline; on the high social status of schools and of school teachers; and on intense competition in every form that competition can take. And the results are impressive. High school graduates score higher in mathematics than graduates do anywhere else in the world, and 95 percent of young people are graduated from high school. The Japanese, as a consequence, have the highest rate of literacy and of numerical competence in the world. This is an enormous achievement in building human capital never matched before in the history of civilization.

But all is not lost. The United States has advantages, too, as Duke well states. The U.S. system is better at emphasizing individual initiative and creativity, at providing an environment for more balanced growth of young people, and at testing performance in a more humane, fairer manner that is also more conducive to learning than is rote memorization. And at the level of higher education, the educational system in the United States is far superior. The United States, thus, has its triumphs, too, in the quality of its educated elites. As Duke notes, the United States has had 30 times more Nobel Laureates than Japan has. The United States fails worst in what it contributes to the competence of the average and to the less than average student; this is exactly where the Japanese do their best.

Thus, "we can learn something, a great deal from the Japanese"; but they also can learn a great deal from us. Both countries must "learn what to adapt and what not to adapt" from each other. One great strength of this study is to analyze what each country can learn from the other by way of selective adaptation. Another great strength is the clear description of how the Japanese school really works – the best description I have ever seen; and we cannot afford not to know – otherwise we might really become a "nation at risk."

Clark Kerr
Professor
University of California
Berkeley
Former President
University of California

Among foreigners living in Japan, no subject gets more attention than how the Japanese, only a century after their opening to the West, have adapted so successfully to the needs of a modern industrial economy. I know because I lived in Tokyo from 1975 to 1980. Frequently I found myself in discussions about how the Japanese had developed so many of the virtues of the work ethic we have traditionally associated with America's economic strength.

Professor Duke is exceptionally well qualified to explain how Japanese schools produce loyal, literate, competent, and diligent industrial workers and how those schools contrast with those in the United States. He is a specialist in comparative education who has taught in both countries and whose children have attended Japanese schools. Using his professional knowledge and detailed observations in both countries, he has brought into vital juxtaposition two subjects of urgent concern to Americans today: the problems of our schools and the competitive strengths of Japanese industry.

Tradition accounts for much of Japanese behavior, but it would appear that few countries have been so strongly affected by deliberate social engineering. Over the last century, Japanese schools, under the direction of the Ministry of Education, have undertaken several phases of adaptation to modern conditions while continuing to sustain traditional values. The result is a highly structured educational program that emphasizes certain basic subjects and very specific forms of behavior. By contrast, except for the liberalizing influence of John Dewey and his followers on the practices U.S. schools inherited from the nineteenth century, there has been no such focused effort to produce a set of specific qualities in U.S. students. As a result, there is extraordinary variety in our schools and in the young people who emerge from them. This study compares the strengths and weaknesses of these two systems clearly and convincingly.

Professor Duke has thought hard about what the future holds for both Japan and the United States and about what Japanese and U.S. schools might learn from each other. He is obviously a loyal and concerned

American and a strong friend of Japan. At a time when the United States has profound needs to improve both its schools and its industrial efficiency, and when Japan must face equally profound questions about its future, he has used his intimate knowledge of both countries to raise timely questions, and he has done so with insight and passion.

James M. Hestor
President
The New York Botanical Garden
Former President
New York University
Former Rector
United Nations University
Tokyo

Foreword from Japan

The initial encounter between Japan and the West, which took place in the sixteenth century, involved only the Spanish and Portuguese who first came to our country. One of the early results of this meeting was the compilation of a Portuguese-Japanese dictionary. The purpose was not, however, for the Portuguese to learn about Japan through a knowledge of the Japanese language, but rather to enable the Portuguese to promote Catholic Christianity in Japan.

During a later period a number of distinguished Western scholars came to Japan, not to teach the Japanese about the West, but instead to study Japanese history, literature, and the arts searching for the distinctive non-Western character of the cultural traditions of Japan. The translation into English of *The Tales of Genji* by Arthur Waley and George Samson, in their cultural history of Japan, is an outstanding example of this approach.

From 1868, following the Meiji Restoration Western analysts evaluated Japanese efforts to modernize the country primarily from the viewpoint of Japan imitating the West. Even today this perspective is rather widespread. Until recently relatively few studies have focused on what can be learned from Japan as a modern industrialized society.

However, from the 1960s, Japan's economic and technical achievements gained international recognition and admiration. Accordingly Western scholars undertook research on what Japan can teach the West. The most prominent example of this approach was Dr. Ezra Vogel's *Japan as Number One*, which was widely read in the United States, Japan, China, and other countries.

Professor Duke's detailed study of *The Japanese School*, which belongs to a new category, is based on the conviction that the economic growth of modern Japan has depended extensively on the role of the school. The ethical teachings and the basic subject matter of mathematics, reading, and writing, all reflecting the cultural traditions of Japan, are analyzed as major contributing factors in Japan's economic development.

In 1983 a report to the president of the United States, *A Nation at Risk*, received widespread attention. The report rather impetuously concluded that the U.S. school was falling behind the Japanese school. Many Japanese came to the same conclusion. Professor Duke's book takes a different perspective. He analyzes fairly and objectively both the positive and negative features of the Japanese and U.S. school. He also analyzes with clarity the basic differences in educational traditions and in the systems of the two countries. But of utmost importance, Dr. Duke undertakes the challenging new perspective of seeking out what our two peoples can learn from each other.

Today, in contrast to the earlier periods when the Spanish and Portuguese came to Japan to teach us about their culture and religion, followed by the era when Western scholars studied the distinctive traditions of our culture, we have entered a new period of reciprocity. We have begun to recognize the importance of learning from each other. Dr. Duke's book is a good example of this new way of thinking with which I find myself in complete agreement. It is an important contribution in the ongoing relationships between our two countries.

Professor Duke has been teaching at the International Christian University in Tokyo for many years. During this time he has also developed close relations with leaders of the Japanese industrial world. In addition, his three children received their basic education in the Japanese school. Based on this broad perspective, his analysis has great reliability.

The readers of this book, whether they be Americans or Japanese, or Europeans and Asian as well, will gain important insights into the relationships between the school and modern industrial societies. I appreciate Professor Duke's efforts in preparing this excellent study. I sincerely hope that it reaches a wide audience.

Michio Nagai
Senior Advisor to the Rector
United Nations University
Former Minister of Education
Tokyo

Preface

This book is intended primarily to answer questions posed to me by the following Americans I met during my sabbatical in the United States:

A remedial reading specialist in an elementary school in a small community near my hometown:

After listening to a group of sixth grade children, apparently average in intelligence but afflicted with the so-called dyslexia disease, floundering over simple sentences, I casually remarked that dyslexia is not a serious problem in Japan. The teacher looked at me in disbelief. "I don't believe it. At least 25 percent of all our students read at a level two or more years below their grade level, symptoms of dyslexia. How do the Japanese do it?"

A welder for Harley-Davidson, the remaining maker of motorcycles in the United States:

I had asked him why he thought his company had lost the U.S. market in small- and medium-sized bikes to the Japanese and was now being pressured by them for the large-size market, the last one dominated by the U.S. firm. He responded: "We can compete with the imports if we have a chance. If I had my way, I'd keep out all those Jap bikes from America. Do you know that even some of our own guys ride Hondas to work? And we can buy Harley-Davidsons at a discount? How do you explain that?"

A history teacher in an inner-city high school in Washington, D.C.:

I opened his U.S. history book to a random page and asked him how many of his graduating seniors could read the page with a fair degree of understanding. His answer: "About 85 to 90 percent of my class will have great difficulty reading and understanding that page. Therefore, I can't assign it for outside reading unless I go over every paragraph and explain many of the words one by one. It's very difficult to teach American history to our kids these days. Do Japanese history teachers have this problem?"

A local teacher's union representative in a high school in Chicago:

The union official was listing a number of teacher grievances underlying a recent strike that had paralyzed the city's school for several weeks. One of his long-standing complaints was that the class size was too large in many schools. "No teacher should have more than 30 students in a class," though up to 35 was permitted in some instances. I told him that high school teachers in Tokyo public schools would envy Chicago teachers because classes average about 48 in all Tokyo high schools. "My God," he responded. "How can any Japanese teacher handle that many in one class and get anything across? We simply couldn't do it here."

A social studies teacher in one of the leading high schools in southern California:

I had remarked that the vast majority of the students were obviously well qualified, coming almost exclusively from the professional classes of that very prosperous area. Her response: "Our students all read very well. But they read very little. They aren't too concerned about getting into the university. For example, when SAT time (the Scholastic Aptitude Test used by many universities as one measure, and a very critical one in most instances, to select students for entrance) comes around, few make much effort to prepare for it. Almost all will get in somewhere. I heard that Japanese kids study very hard to get into the university. How do they get them to do it?"

The mathematics teacher in a Florida school who happened to come into the room where I was waiting to see the principal:

I noticed the photocopied material he had just prepared for his next class and asked if I could look at it. He explained that it was for the ninth graders. He also said that his school had been selected by the Florida State Department of Education as one of the model schools, or something of that nature, for the teaching of mathematics. "The governor may even come to make a presentation." When I explained that the problems were similar to my son's math problems in the fifth and sixth grades of our local Japanese public schools, he responded in disbelief: "Amazing. Can the Japanese really do that?"

The former factory worker in my hometown, a high school classmate:

We were discussing the troubled local economy that had been dependent upon one large factory, an old established maker of subway and train cars. The local operation had finally dwindled and moved out after years of labor troubles marked by lengthy strikes. I remembered my father at home for weeks, and sometimes months, waiting for the periodic strikes to end. When I asked why the men went on strike so often, explaining that it was not common in Japan, he explained, "The company didn't give a damn about us. And they hated our union. I can't figure about the Japanese workers. Are they crazy?"

Introduction

In the past four decades, Japan has moved in U.S. minds from being an economic basket case to becoming an economic miracle. Interest in Japan has naturally increased, as it came to loom as "A Challenge to Industrial America," in fact, the primary challenge in the whole world. Eager experts have sprung up, like bamboo shoots after a shower, ready to expound the phenomenon by a myriad of explanations, from the "A" of national character, through the necromancy of strange practices, such as singing company songs, to the "Z" of dirty tricks like dumping.

Some of the so-called explanations are not very convincing and become downright silly when asked to carry much of the load. Other explanations have more validity. There can be no doubt, for example, that the Japanese worker, the product of the Japanese educational system, is an extraordinarily hard-working person, strongly oriented to quality work, deeply loyal to his working groups and his company, and superbly educated with the skills he needs for his job. Education undoubtedly plays a central role. Beyond this, the Japanese company is a strongly unified organism, able because of its manner of employment, methods of recompense, and organization of ownership and finance to plan rationally far into the future. And the whole national economy is susceptible to carefully planned guidance toward sensible long-range objectives.

The vastly complex but successful system that makes up Japan's contemporary economy is obviously not the product of any single wonder ingredient or any set of neat tricks. It comprises a high array of interlocking elements, and these in turn stem from long and complex traditions and from recent events. They cannot be reproduced at will in other societies, as Professor Duke clearly explains, though he quite rightly emphasizes that much of Japan's success derives directly from Japan's formal educational system, elements of which could be borrowed by the United States and other nations.

No one who studies Japan can miss the major role that education has played in Japan's economic success, though Dr. Duke is probably correct in asserting that this is an aspect of modern Japan that, has been relatively underplayed by those who have had their eyes focused narrowly on

Japan's economic success. As a U.S. educationalist who has spent the bulk of his career teaching in Japan and has sent his own three children through the basic Japanese schools, Professor Duke's understanding of the situation and of the weaknesses of Japanese schools is hard to match. He draws an intimate and authentic picture of Japanese education, making clear three basic points: the crucial role education has played in the economic success of Japan, the many ways the United States should seek to learn from the Japanese experience, and the various imperfections that continue to flaw the Japanese system.

Japan has undoubtedly outpaced all the other major nations of the world in what should be the fundamental task of schooling, imparting to virtually all students adequately high levels of the basic skills, such as literacy and high competence in mathematics, needed for life in the modern world. Professor Duke devotes two fascinating chapters to these crucial subjects. These are areas in which U.S. schools fail miserably, and, as the Japanese would phrase it, there is much need for Americans to self reflect with the Japanese model in mind.

The general admiration for the results of Japanese education has been accompanied by a growing awareness of its weaknesses. The infamous examination system for entering schools, which rewards rote memory rather than reasoning, is a notably unsatisfactory and inhuman way of sorting out leadership, usually for life, but it is so deeply imbedded in the whole system that it seems almost immovable. The squandering of four years at the college level on poor teaching and very little study seems an incredible waste of time for a nation so passionately devoted to efficiency. Creativity and individualism also appear to be sacrificed to mediocrity and group achievement, but it may be too early yet to write Japan off on this score. Once Japan had adjusted to the shock of Western civilization, it showed no dearth of creative artistic talents, and ingenious modification and adaptation in technology are certainly creativity of a high sort. We should remember that the United States had a long apprenticeship as a technological borrower and adapter before it became a leader in science and technology in the twentieth century. Perhaps Japan's age of great creativeness lies just ahead, despite a formal educational system that does not seem to encourage it.

The inadequate investment in school plant and facilities in Japan is puzzling in such an affluent society, but it may be a blessing in disguise. It may help channel attention and investment into the quality of teachers and ensure the payment of initial salaries more comparable to salaries of those with similar educational achievements, which is definitely not the case in the business-oriented United States where the inequalities in pay between teachers and others are shocking. Perhaps the high regard the Japanese show their teachers and the respect for teaching as a high calling, when backed by the strong supportive attitude for education on the part of Japanese families, account more for Japan's educational success than the educational system itself. Such attitudes in Japanese society certainly give education a strong backing that it lacks in the United States, where the tradition has been that teaching is a tolerable solution for the unmarriageable village spinster or should be assigned to misfits who, lacking the capacities "to do," must settle for teaching. The traditional East Asian emphasis on scholarship and the drive for schooling built up in the late feudal period in Japan should also be mentioned. Both Americans and the citizens of developing countries should note that the quality and morale of persons becoming educators in Japan are far more important than school facilities in explaining Japan's educational success.

Just as Japan's educational achievements are interwoven in an intricate pattern with its economic success, its achievements in both education and business are outgrowths of its traditions. The creation of a strong group spirit, with which Professor Duke starts his analysis, is a key to the whole of modern Japan. It derives from the organization of late feudal times and before that from ancient Confucian concepts. Much the same could be said of the diligence and perseverance of the Japanese and of their pride in perfection in their work. Professor Duke devotes chapters to each of these aspects of modern Japan as crucial elements in its educational and economic success.

Most of the characteristics of Japanese education can be regarded as virtues, but some of these virtues may in the long run prove to be vices. The development of a strong group spirit within a firmly unitary and distinctive Japan has without doubt helped the nation in the past to grow from relative obscurity as an economic cripple to become today's economic *Wunderkind.* But the Japanese should not forget that they did this in an expanding world economy enjoying relatively free trade. In the process, Japan has become dependent for its very life on the continuation of a unified, expanding world economy composed of a great variety of independent national pieces. Japanese, like the other peoples of the world, must recognize that all nations are now interdependent and that they must learn to cooperate effectively if civilization and humanity are to survive.

Japanese education and the society and economy in which it is imbedded, however, do very little to prepare the Japanese for this situation. Their emphasis is on the individual's own groups – the "we" of the classroom, company, or nation as opposed to the "they" of all other groups. It is somewhat frightening to realize that in the uniformity of Japanese education all the children of a given age group are learning precisely the same lesson in much the same way on the same day throughout Japan, emerging with the same distinctive and often exclusive ideas about their own little groups or the large group of Japan. Broader world interests are given lip service, but in reality very little emphasis is given to the essential "we" group of humanity.

It seems significant that, despite the extraordinary amount of time devoted to the study of English in Japanese schools, the results are meager. People are produced who, through painful reading, can acquire knowledge about the outside world and, if required, can develop their abilities into rudimentary speaking skills adequate for necessary economic negotiations in English. But the Japanese educational system turns out few Japanese who can participate actively in the intellectual life of the world. Most knowledgeable people would agree that foreign language instruction has improved the least in Japanese schools during the last 40 years. This may be a symbol of Japan's greatest educational failure and its most serious economic and political danger.

Professor Duke has quite rightly concentrated on the strong points of the Japanese educational system, and one hopes that Americans and others will take note and learn from them. Many aspects of U.S. education desperately need to be improved. For Japanese, however, Professor Duke's comments on the weaknesses of the Japanese educational system may prove more important. They are fully aware of some of the weaknesses. To others they may be more oblivious. Floating happily along, absorbed in the euphoria of the manifold successes of Japanese education and of much else in modern Japanese society, they run the risk of failing to hear the distant roar of the waterfall of world economic or political disaster that may lie ahead unless education, and the society it helps form, undergoes some drastic modifications.

Edwin Reischauer
Professor
Harvard University
Former United States Ambassador to Japan

1

A NATION AT RISK

Our nation is at risk. Our once unchallenged preeminence in commerce, science, and technological innovation is being overtaken by competitors throughout the world . . . one of the many causes and dimensions of the problem . . . is the one that undergirds American prosperity, security, and civility . . . the educational foundations of our society are presently being eroded by a rising tide of mediocrity that threatens our very future as a nation and as a people.
– The National Commission on Excellence in Education

In 1983, barely a decade and a half before the twenty-first century, the U.S. government published this remarkable document starkly warning its citizens that "our nation is at risk." Fortunately a military attack on U.S. shores was not imminent. Rather, the "once unchallenged preeminence" of U.S. industry and commerce was being severely challenged. Our competitors were rapidly overtaking us. In effect, there was a clear and present danger to the republic.

When this controversial document was issued, among the most determined of our competitors stood, nay ran, the Japanese conspicuously in front of the pack. The industrial, commercial, and technical supremacy not only of the United States but of Europe as well had already been boldly defied by the Japanese through their deep penetration of our domestic markets and their rapid advancements into high technology. With extraordinary zeal and enterprise, Japan had thrown down the gauntlet by inviting us into competition on our own home grounds. The challenge to industrial America by industrial Japan was well underway.

But it was not only a challenge to U.S. industry. The National Commission's report to the president of the United States pinpointed the root of the problem underlying America's fall from industrial prominence that placed our nation at risk: the erosion of our educational foundation by a "rising tide of mediocrity." In sharp contrast, and of enormous significance, among the criticisms of the Japanese school by the Japanese themselves (and there are many) educational mediocrity is seldom found. To be sure, our foremost economic and industrial competitors, the Japanese, have not only invited us into competition at the market place, they are also inviting us into educational competition. Few Americans have yet to recognize fully that we are competing not only with the Japanese factory, but with the Japanese school as well.

Several years after the *Nation-at-Risk* report received much attention, another government commission produced an equally disturbing report and reinforced the thrust of the earlier report. The President's Commission on Industrial Competitiveness, chaired by the head of one of America's leading high technology companies, reported in *The New Reality* that the United States by the mid-1980s had virtually lost the international competition in manufacturing. In addition, and of the greatest importance for the United States in the twenty-first century, we risk losing the international competition in high technology. "Seven out of ten American high technology sectors have lost world markets since 1965," according to the report. Once again the Japanese were singled out as aggressively competing with us in the high technology sector where we take pride in leading the world. Japan was reportedly ahead in several areas and threatening to move farther ahead. Although the dire warnings in the *Nation-at-Risk* report had already lost much of their initial force as a new sense of euphoria swept the nation, we are apparently still a nation at risk technologically and industrially, and the Japanese continue as our foremost competitor.

In a unique coincidence, when the *New Reality* report was published in the United States in early 1985, the Asahi newspaper company in Japan circulated a report that reinforced the conclusions of the U.S. study. Their investigations showed that within one area of high technology, telecommunications, figures from the Ministry of Finance proved that in 1983 (the year of the *Nation-at-Risk* report) Japan exported telecommunications equipment worth 186 billion yen to the United States while importing U.S. equipment worth only 28.5 billion yen, a ratio of 6.5 to one. A year later, as the United States emerged from its doldrums during an upbeat presidential election campaign casting aside any so-called "risks" facing the land, Japan increased its telecommunications exports to the United States to 259.4 billion yen. During the same period U.S. firms sold 22.4 billion yen's worth of Made-in-America equipment to the Japanese, a ratio reaching 11.6 to one, almost double the previous year's in favor of Japan.

Unknown to the average American, the sharp increase in Japanese telecommmunications imports was attributed to a great extent to the breakup of AT&T, the U.S. telecommunications monopoly. Under the reorganization plan, the many new independent local telephone companies were no longer bound to purchase their equipment from an AT&T affiliate. With cheaper and more attractive products available from Japan, the newly independent regional managers quickly took advantage of the situation. The result was a surge in sales of fine Japanese telecommunications equipment to the United States. Once again our "unchallenged preeminence" in high technology was being challenged by the Japanese.

But the story is not complete, according to the Japanese study. During the period when Japanese telecommunications equipment flooded into the United States, the Japanese came under intense pressure from the United States to reciprocate and open their domestic markets to U.S. goods. The Japanese equivalent of AT&T, the NTT, responded by dispatching survey missions to the United States in search of U.S. equipment compatible with the Japanese market, even producing English manuals of standards for the convenience of U.S. suppliers. (Needless to say, the newly independent AT&T affiliates did not publish manuals in Japanese for the convenience of Japanese businesses when they expanded their efforts to increase sales in the United States upon the AT&T breakup.) Nevertheless, when NTT imported 50 different types of U.S. telephone equipment on a trial basis, not a single type met the Japanese standards.[1]

The *New Reality* report traced the decline of U.S. competitiveness to the period beginning about a decade and a half ago, long before the advent of the "strong dollar." In fact, it was precisely during the era of the weak dollar when the erosion began. But it was also the very period when Japan aggressively began to challenge America's industrial and technological preeminence. Over the past two decades, for example, Japan's share of free world trade has increased from 3 percent to 8.5

percent. During the same period the U.S. share dropped from 18 percent to 13 percent. Germany and France, in contrast, showed little change (Figure 1.1). In order to appreciate more fully the international trends in economic growth since the 1960s, the New York Stock Exchange published a revealing report, "U.S. Economic Performance in a Global Perspective." Japan's Economic Performance Index, a composite index incorporating real economic growth, consumer price index, and unemployment rates, tells a story in itself.[2]

From the U.S. point of view, some of the most disturbing figures are illustrated by the balance of trade currents between Japan and the United States over the past ten years (Table 1.1), a fair indicator of the competitiveness of Japanese products throughout the United States. Furthermore, Japan has determinedly carved out a substantial share of the

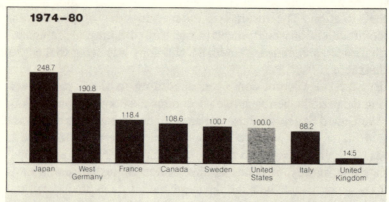

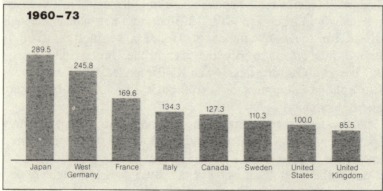

FIGURE 1.1 Comparisons of the Economic Performance Index Relative to the U.S. (United States EPI = 100). *Source*: NYSE.

domestic markets of Europe, as evidenced by the trade patterns during that period. In addition, Japan has been running trade surpluses with Africa, Latin America, Southeast Asia, and the Communist bloc. Unfortunately the statistics cannot show the magnitude of the loss of U.S. markets throughout the world to Japanese products.

In addition to Japan's enormous expansion in exporting manufacturing goods, this tiny nation has now become the world's greatest exporter of capital. During the first four years of the current decade, Japan's net long-term capital outflow reached $90 billion, including $50 billion alone in 1984, a level no other nation rivals.[3] Reflecting the Nation-at-Risk syndrome, the United States has become a net-debtor nation while Japan becomes the world's leading exporter of money. The tables have truly been turned.

The so-called economic miracle of Japan in the postwar period is perhaps best illustrated through the rapid growth of her gross national product (Table 1.2) During the three decades from 1951 to 1982, the GNP in Japan increased by 80 times. During the identical period the U.S. GNP increased nine times. The German, French, and British GNP, incidentally, moved ahead 28-, 19-, and 12-fold respectively. All four major Western powers started out far ahead of Japan in GNP in the early 1950s. By the 1980s, Japan had become a supereconomic power far

TABLE 1.1
Japanese Balance of Merchandise Trade
(US $ millions)

	With the United States	With the European Community
1975	1,690	2,304
1976	5,335	3,611
1978	11,580	5,033
1980	10,410	8,808
1983	19,629	10,403
1984	34,022	
1985	50,000 (Estimated)	

Note: Statistics in this chapter, unless otherwise indicated, are from *Japan, An International Comparison* 1983, 1984, 1985. Keizai Koho Center, Japan Institute for Social and Economic Affairs, Tokyo.

Source: Statistical Abstract of the United States, 1985 ; Bureau of Census, United States Department of Commerce, p. 818.

TABLE 1.2
Gross National Product (1951-83)
(US $ millions)

	Japan	USA	Germany	France	UK
1951	14	328	29	35	41
1960	39	504	71	60	72
1970	203	993	186	146	124
1975	498	1,549	420	340	235
1980	1,040	2,631	821	657	525
1982	1,060	3,059	659		
1983	1,098	3,304			

Note: Statistics in this chapter, unless otherwise indicated, are from *Japan, An International Comparison* 1983, 1984, 1985. Keizai Koho Center, Japan Institute for Social and Economic Affairs, Tokyo.

Source: Statistical Abstract of the United States, 1985 ; Bureau of Census, United States Department of Commerce, p. 818.

outstripping the leading European nations. It is now, with half the population and .04 the land area, second only to the United States in gross national product among the free world nations.

The industrial and technological challenge to the United States by the Japanese, from all indications, is not a temporary phenomenon nor a passing fancy. Their initial entry into the high technology area should not be overlooked. For instance, Japan has quickly moved into the forefront in the application of robots to industrial production, far surpassing the United States. In fact, Japanese industry outpaced competitors by installing more robots than all other Western nations combined (Table 1.3).

In patent applications, a relative indicator of new-product developments, again Japan holds the leading position among all non-Communist nations. For example, at the beginning of the 1980s, the total number of new patent applications in Japan in one year (218,216) reached twice the number applied for in the United States (106,413), the nearest rival. Significantly 13 percent of all applications submitted in the United States were made by Japanese; Americans applied for just 4.7 percent of new patents in Japan. Even in Germany, England, and France, the Japanese applied for about 10 percent of all patents (Table 1.4). The

TABLE 1.3
Operating Robot Installations 1983

Japan	41,265
USA	9,400
Germany, F.R.	4,800
France	2,010

Source: Japan 1985, An International Comparison, p. 28. (Original source: Robot Institute of America).

TABLE 1.4
Patent Applications 1981

Nationality of Applicant	Country of Application				
	Japan	*USA*	*Germany*	*UK*	*France*
Japan	191,645	14,009	4,945	3,852	2,176
USA	10,290	62,404	4,374	5,962	3,688
Germany, F.R.	5,797	9,924	29,841	2,705	3,132
UK	1,556	4,294	712	20,808	636
France	1,614	3,237	877	802	10,945
Total Applications	218,216	106,413	46,579	39,214	24,668
Applications by Japanese (in percent)	87.8	13.2	10.6	9.8	8.9

Note: Statistics in this chapter, unless otherwise indicated, are from *Japan, An International Comparison* 1983, 1984, 1985. Keizai Koho Center, Japan Institute for Social and Economic Affairs, Tokyo.

Source: Statistical Abstract of the United States, 1985 ; Bureau of Census, United States Department of Commerce, p. 818.

reverse flow was negligible. By the mid-1980s, the Japanese had increased their share of American patents to 16 percent of the total.[4]

A new recognition of the Japanese challenge to the United States in high technology comes forth in the U.S. press through a steady stream of mostly critical articles. For example, *Business Week*, bastion of the U.S. industrial world, published a special report dramatically entitled "Chip Wars: The Japanese Threat," in which Japan (Table 1.5) is depicted as the "enemy camp." Let U.S. business speak for itself.

> Competing in the U.S. semiconductor business has never been easy.... But now, American companies are heading straight for their toughest competitive fight ever. The outcome of this battle will be just as important to the nation as it will be to the chipmakers. Integrated circuits launched the second industrial revolution; they are the starting point for much of the U. S. high technology industry. U. S. chipmakers have dominated the world semiconductor market from its inception in the early 1950s.... [Now] the Americans are sweating out competition they once ignored from Japan. Picking up speed rapidly, the Japanese are now a strong No. 2 with about 30% of the world market.[5]

A year and a half later, *Time Magazine* updated developments in the chip war under the bold headline, "Raking in the Chips: U.S.

TABLE 1.5
Japanese Chipmakers Climb the Top 10

1983	1979	Company	Estimated 1983 Integrated Circuit Sales (millions)
1	1	Texas Instruments	$ 1,276
2	2	IBM	1,262
3	3	Hitachi	958
4 ↑	7	NEC	942
5	5	Motorola	842
6	↓ 4	Phillips	805
7	↓ 6	National Semiconductor	793
8 ↑	10	Fujitsu	692
9	↓ 8	Intel	665
10 ↑	11	Toshiba	597

Source: Business Week, May 23, 1983.

semiconductor makers are out of a slump and into their biggest boom." In spite of this declaration, the article, more circumspectly, indicates that the Japanese continue to challenge the U.S. position in this most sensitive industry into the mid-1980s:

> Despite their sophisticated design and awesome powers, semiconductors are not hard to understand. There are basically two kinds: memory chips which hold information, and logic chips which use the data to control what a machine does. . . . U.S. companies dominate the market for logic semiconductors. Japan, however, still holds a commanding lead in memory chips.
>
> What most worries U.S. firms about their Japanese rivals is signs that they plan to move more aggressively into logic chips, a traditional American stronghold. While Japan's manufacturers were once thought to have difficulty in creating innovative and highly successful logic circuits, that view is now changing. Hitachi unveiled a new logic semiconductor that is among the first to combine the features of high speed and low-service use. . . . Technical dominance is no longer the preserve of the U. S. companies.[6]

Echoing the threat from Japan in military technology, a U.S. columnist reported on the Pentagon's concern with the Japanese challenge.

> The United States and Japan are racing to build a new "supercomputer" and the outcome may determine whether America can remain the world leader in military technology, U.S. officials say. Japan recently embarked on a government-backed program to produce by the 1990s a supercomputer 1000 times faster than today's computers, a machine that could "think" like a human, manipulating symbols and making inferences. . . . At issue is not only America's economic stake in the information industry, but also its military security. Supercomputers would be an essential component in the array of futuristic weapons the Pentagon wants to build from space-based lasers to battlefield robots and precision-guided rockets that could make the tank obsolete. The idea that Japan might create the computer technology first and sell it on the international market does not sit well with Pentagon officials.[7]

A surprising aspect of the challenge in high military technology posed by the Japanese was evidenced in the 1983 negotiations between the two countries over U.S. demands for the transfer of high military technology from Japan to the United States. Many Japanese were puzzled at what their military establishment, miniscule in comparison to the powerful U.S. armed forces, could have developed that the U.S. military complex, with its huge industrial base and mammoth budgets, could not develop on its own. An agreement was finally concluded under U.S. pressure provoking considerable opposition in Japan where, according to the "Renunciation of War" clause in the Japanese Constitution promulgated during the American Occupation, "land, sea, and air forces, as well as other war potential, will never be maintained." The first official U.S. request came in 1985. Apparently, the Japanese have even moved into the once-forbidden area of advanced military technology. That move will further aggravate the mammoth trade imbalances between the two countries.

Not only in high electronic technology is the United States seriously being challenged by the Japanese. One analyst said of the controversial G.M.-Toyota automobile production joint venture in California:

> America's largest manufacturer has decided that it cannot compete against the Japanese in small cars ... the ramifications are potentially staggering not only for the American auto industry but also for much of American industry now entering global competition. If G.M. cannot compete against the Japanese in small cars, will it be able to compete in the future in the mid-size cars, where the Japanese are beginning to press their cost and quality advantages? If G.M. cannot compete, is there any reason to think Ford and Chrysler can?[8]

This opinion was reinforced by the initial influence of the sudden strengthening of the Japanese yen in 1985. The strong yen had been cited by many Americans as a major factor enabling the Japanese to export their products from a favored position based on the cheap yen penalizing the Americans and their strong dollar. After a precipitous drop of about 20 percent in the value of the dollar, Ford Motors reported that only $450 had been trimmed from the $2,500 cost advantage Japanese carmakers had enjoyed over American companies in building small cars.[9] Meanwhile, General Motors sold less than 2,000 cars in Japan during fiscal 1985.[10]

We can move down the interminable line past the domestic markets in cameras, videos, and TVs, which are dominated by the Japanese, to such growing imports as grand pianos and fashion and trumpets. For example, in a move which made headlines in the Philadelphia *Inquirer* ("Now from Japan, fine instruments") the Philadelphia Orchestra, one of the premier orchestras in the United States, purchased several trumpets from Yamaha, the leading Japanese manufacturer of musical instruments with a large U.S. distribution.

Why should the Philadelphia Orchestra, an ensemble with enormous wealth and prestige, buy trumpets from Japan, a country with an entirely different musical tradition? "These instruments are first-rate, top-notch," explains the orchestra's principal trumpet player and a devoted user of German-made instruments. "Sure, we considered others. But these new Japanese instruments stay in tune, sound good, and complement the trumpets we already have." The orchestra's musical director, Riccardo Muti, believes that the Yamaha trumpet is appropriate for the works of such 19th century composers as Schumann, Schubert, and Mendelssohn. The Philadelphia Orchestra is not the only ensemble to have discovered Yamaha trumpets. The instrument has also made its way into such leading U.S. orchestras as the Boston Symphony, the Chicago Symphony, and the Los Angeles Philharmonic. Even the Berlin Philharmonic and Vienna Philharmonic, those bastions of musical conservation, use Japanese trumpets along with their venerable German models.[11]

Japanese trumpets appropriate for Mendelssohn? Where will it end? It's worthy of noting that Philadelphia had already experienced another example of Japanese inroads into the local markets when Nissho-Iwai, a major Japanese trading company, outbid U.S. makers for 110 subway cars for the Broad Street Subway in the early 1980s. The remarkable aspect of this agreement was that Nissho-Iwai won the contract against the one remaining subway car builder in the United States, the Budd Company, with its plant in the City of Brotherly Love itself. Although the mayor diplomatically, or politically, announced he would have preferred to award the contract to Budd, in competitive bidding Budd was $13 million over Nissho-Iwai.[12]

As impressive as all of these financial and industrial statistics are, they assume an added dimension when the physical conditions of the challenger, Japan, are contrasted with that of the challenged, the United States. To begin with, Japan's land area is approximately the size of Montana, or a little larger than Finland. The population of 121 million, however, is roughly half that of the U.S. population. Can one conceive of half of the U.S. population moving to Finland, and becoming an economic superpower to boot? Because two-thirds of Japan is covered by forests, mostly in mountainous areas, Japan is the equivalent of half the total U.S. population living in an area one-third the size of Montana.

The situation is even more extreme than these statistics portray. The Japanese population not only exists on four moderately sized islands: the majority of it is heavily concentrated in a tiny area of this tiny land. Approximately 60 percent of the population lives on just 2 percent of the land. The equivalent, then, would find one of every four Americans living on just 2 percent of Montana with that tiny enclave becoming the center of the second most productive nation in the free world. A preposterous idea to say the least, but it depicts the actual status of Japan.

Obviously this nation is incapable of feeding itself under these harshly restrictive conditions with only 14 percent of the land available for agricultural use. Even the United States would find it extremely difficult to feed half its population on 14 percent of the area of Montana. In contrast, the United States has 78 times the arable land that Japan has. In other words, for every acre of precious and egregiously expensive agricultural land in Japan, the United States has 78 acres. Consequently, this tiny industrial giant has become heavily dependent on others, mainly the United States, to provide food. For example, Japan imports 60 percent of all U.S. beef exports and 40 percent of its total exports of citrus fruits. It boggles the mind to imagine the magnitude of our binational imbalances in trade in manufactured goods only, that is, without factoring in America's huge exports of grain, soybeans, and other foodstuffs to Japan.

Fortunately for the United States, Japan's food imports have increased 15 times in the past decade and a half. Unfortunately for Japan, it is self-sufficient only in rice. Consequently it must import 90 percent of the wheat and nearly 100 percent of the corn to keep up with the increasingly Westernized eating habits as bread and meat gradually replace rice and fish as the staple foods. Is it any wonder that plain hamburger in local Japanese supermarkets sells for three to four times its price in the U.S. supermarket?

Not only is this supereconomic power reliant on others for food to sustain its people, it has become even more deeply dependent on other lands for the raw materials necessary to sustain its factories (Table 1.6). Japan must import a staggering 85 percent of its energy supplies to keep its vast industrial sector moving. In sharp contrast, the United States depends on imports for about 14 percent of its energy requirements. An "oil shock" to the United States becomes an "oil calamity" to the Japanese. Again, is it any wonder that regular gasoline in Japan sells at over twice the average price per gallon in the United States? Japan's life line both in foodstuffs and raw materials is tenuous at best.

From any point of view, then, this is a most unlikely challenger from the Orient with whom we find ourselves locked in international industrial competition. But what exactly are we competing with? Japanese management techniques? Company-union relationships? The company

TABLE 1.6
Japan's Overseas Dependency for Natural Resources, 1984

Raw Material	Percent
Oil	99.7
Iron ore	99.8
Copper	96.8
Natural gas	91.4
Coal	81.4
Wood and lumber	64.3
Total energy requirements	82.2

Source: Statistical Abstract of the United States, 1985 ; Bureau of Census, United States Department of Commerce, p. 818.

songs? The morning exercises? The quality control circles? Japanese robots? The Japanese mentality?

Fundamental to our interminable frustration over our burgeoning imbalances of trade with Japan, as high quality Japanese products continually flood the international market place, is the identification of what we are confronting. If we are to meet the Japanese challenge in high or low technology, we obviously must understand the nature of our foremost commercial rivals. Fortunately, and none too soon, that process is finally underway. Since a prolific number of firms throughout the United States has experienced the cold sting of the Japanese invasion into their home markets, responsible Americans, as well as representatives from many other countries, have begun to study seriously the modus operandi of the Japanese company.

As never before the Japanese firm has engaged our attention. Because the massive flow of Japanese products that has captured such an impressive share of many U.S. markets originates in the Japanese factory, conventional wisdom tells us that we must investigate the factory. In order to compete with Japanese corporations, we must learn how they function and how they are managed. Indeed, one of the signs of our times has been the flow of Western industrialists, government missions, union groups, and various specialists to Japan for the singular purpose of deciphering how Japanese industry has achieved an economic miracle.

But how do the Americans perceive the Japanese challenge? A perusal of the U.S. press at any one time, in this case during the writer's sabbatical in the United States, is most revealing. Again, let the Americans speak for themselves. In the prestigious New York *Times*, a fairly representative article on Japan begins:

> A Problem Washington Has Yet to Face:
> Second-Rate Management
> If this nation has learned anything from Japan's successful invasion of American markets and enviable economic performance, it is that long-term productivity growth depends mainly on day-to-day management practices. Managers at every corporate level decide on the allocation of scarce capital and labor resources. These decisions, more than any other single factor, determine productivity.[13]

To attribute Japan's postwar economic resurgence in productivity primarily to day-to-day management practices, "more than any other single factor," surely simplifies a highly complex situation. But this level of understanding of the Japanese challenge has plagued us for years. For example, at the end of the last decade, *Fortune Magazine*, another pillar of the U.S. industrial and commercial world, took its turn in unraveling the Japanese challenge of the 1970s. In a major article entitled "What It Takes to Meet the Japanese Challenge: A Warning from Experts on Japan," the two specialists bearing excellent credentials wrote:

> During the decade, Japan has outshone the U.S. in just about every imaginable measure of economic performance. The Japanese are now close to us in GNP per capita, and will probably be well ahead by the end of the eighties. . . . Unless we compete more effectively with Japan, the worsening economic mismatch will jeopardize our standard of living and erode our national strength. . . . Americans generally must be aware that the Japanese have been running rings around us in economic performance. But not many Americans have a clear idea why. . . . Japan's emergence as a global industrial power is the product of a highly rational and sophisticated economic policy. If there is a single critical difference between Japan's economic performance and ours, it is that: intelligent economic policy.[14]

Intelligent economic policy indeed! What about the skills of the workers? What about the high rate of literacy and of numerary skills of those who produce the mountains of electronic exports sold throughout the United States? What about the attitudes toward work held by the average Japanese worker? Can that be attributed merely to "intelligent economic policy"? To a certain degree, perhaps so. But it barely scratches the surface. What these analyses indicate, more than what they explain, is that the Japanese have once again made us sit up and take notice of them. And this marks the starting point in the long process of not just meeting but benefiting from the challenge Japan presents to industrial America in this century.

Historically, however, the challenge has been the reverse. Industrial America has traditionally posed a challenge to Japan. To many Japanese, it remains so even now. It would be prudent to turn back the pages of history in Japanese-U.S. relations for a moment to see why. Perhaps we can take a lesson from the historical Japanese who began their arduous and highly successful march into the modern world by confronting, and meeting, an American challenge.

There have been two major waves of Japanese reactions to the U.S. challenge. The more recent followed their defeat in World War II. In order to regenerate their devastated land lying in ruin following the massive air raids near the end of the conflict, the Japanese eagerly sought to learn from us. They traveled to the United States as industrialists, government officials, scholars, and students to study everything they could about the United States. At the same time the Americans poured into Japan during the American Occupation of Japan to teach the receptive Japanese everything they could in order to reconstruct Japanese institutions on the U.S. pattern. This recent period in our relationship is rather well known to the Americans.

The postwar, near-slavish admiration by the Japanese of all things Western, especially American, had a parallel in history and has a direct bearing on the contemporary scene. It was, in fact, reminiscent of the latter half of the nineteenth century when Japan was first pried open by Americans and other Westerners after its 300 years of self-imposed isolation. This great event in Japanese history took place during the era when the powerful industrializing Western nations were carving up the backward nations of the world into vast global colonial empires.

Once convinced of Western superiority in matters technical, the Japanese government underwent a monumental shift. In an abrupt turnabout, the new Emperor Meiji, displaying perceptivity of far-reaching consequence, promptly set the compass of his new government on the so-called Charter Oaths of 1868. Prominent among the five declarations was the challenge "To seek knowledge throughout the world." The school was destined to play a prominent role in the reconstruction of Japan. The new body politic was to be grounded in education.

In the 1870s the Japanese government dispatched, among others, the huge Iwakura Mission to North America and Europe to devote several years seeking the source of the West's successful experiments in industrialization. In addition to the several thousand emissaries dispersed by the government before 1900, private individuals by the hundreds also made their unofficial way to the United States and, to a lesser extent, to Europe. All became immersed in the systematic pursuit of the elusive keys to modernization, then locked rather securely in the vaults of the rapidly developing industrial nations of North America and Europe.

Exemplifying remarkable foresight, the early Japanese missions reaped a bountiful harvest by studying the entire gamut of Western societies from the new factories to the post offices to the railroads to the schools. The industrious adventurers from the mysterious East returned home not only with new insights into Western-style capitalism and the modern factory system; they also carried back reams of reports on the entire infrastructure that formed the foundation of the Western societies' burgeoning industrial revolution. The translation task reached monumental proportions ranging from manuals to philosophical treatises to elementary school textbooks. For example, a translation of the American Wilson Readers was used in the elementary schools of Japan at that time.

The enlightened founders of modern Japan held firmly to the conviction that building a modern system of education was fundamental to "catching up with the West" in industrial development. To the Japanese pioneers of modernization, industrial prosperity could not be envisioned without a solid educational foundation. They resolutely set about building the framework of a modern industrial state by first constructing the base, an efficient and effective school system.

When the nineteenth-century Japanese recognized and accepted the challenge from the United States and Europe, they obviously recognized the interrelatedness of the factory and the school. In order to compete industrially with the West, the Japanese, exhibiting an insatiable thirst for learning, began by investigating the various Western traditions in education. Adventurers in every sense of the word, they studied U.S. and European schools and persevered with the alien cultures, the strange languages, customs, and food. But study they did, tirelessly. They learned their lessons well.

Returning to Japan from North America and Europe during the latter half of the nineteenth century amid the great industrial revolution underway in the West, the founders of the modern Japanese state, never wavering in their steadfast determination to apply what they had learned, drew up a plan for a national school system. They extracted from a variety of Western sources that which they felt best fit into their basic traditions and customs. Rather than adopting, they judiciously adapted Western culture and technology. Once a solid educational base was laid, the Japanese girded themselves to meet the industrial challenge of the West.

A number of outstanding figures of the latter half of the nineteenth century and early years of the twentieth century served a catalytic role in transforming Japan from a medieval into a modern state. These early outstanding leaders, many originating from samurai families, recognized the broad ramifications of the challenge of the United States to Japan. They set about promptly to meet that challenge by assiduously studying the challenger. Their experiences have great relevancy for the United States endeavoring to meet the challenge from Japan in the twentieth century, for it was individuals like these who enabled Japan to meet the challenge from America in the nineteenth century. A glimpse into their lives could be instructive.

One of the most important founders of the modern Japanese state was Mori Arinori, possessor of many talents, who was destined to serve as the Minister of Education from 1885-89 during an earlier period of the new government. He first left Japan in 1865 as a boy of 17. Dangerously defying the ban on foreign travel, he surreptitiously left on a British steamer and went to England to study. Later he traveled to the United States where he spent a year before returning to Japan to serve the new Meiji government when the feudal regime was overthrown in 1868. Before Mori was 20 years old he already had had unusual experiences in the West, some rather comically related to his peculiar fascination with a tiny Christian sect in rural New York.

With Mori's unique knowledge of the West and his language proficiency, he was assigned to Washington as Japan's first chargé d'affaires in 1871 at, unbelievably, the age of 23. It was Mori who shepherded the Iwakura Mission around Washington introducing the peculiarly dressed retinue from Japan to President Ulysses S. Grant, a scene that should have been captured on canvas. Later, Mori served as ambassador to the Court of St. James for four years. During this assignment he deliberated the great issues of national education with such figures as the eminent philosopher, Herbert Spencer, then preparing his great philosophical treatise, "Education: Intellectual, Moral, and Physical." Traveling on the European continent, Mori met on a number of occasions with Ito Hirobumi, another pillar of early modern Japan, then studying the German state system and constitution. They, and many other fellow countrymen, witnessed firsthand the immense vitality of Western nations, the cradle of the industrial revolution.[15]

These two governmental figures, preeminently fit to lead Japan in meeting the industrial challenge of the West, returned to their native land with a keen knowledge of Western societies and the Western mentality. Both served Japan well, Mori as Minister of Education and Ito as Prime Minister. Guided by the ultimate aim of developing Japan into a modern industrial nation equal to the United States and other Western powers, these two truly international figures turned to the task of constructing a modern school system and society for Japan. The rest is history. By the turn of the century, Japan had achieved one of the highest standards of mass literacy and mathematics in the world and was well on its way to become a major world power.

Other Japanese of the period, acting mostly in a nongovernmental or semigovernmental capacity, were also motivated by the challenge of America and later made monumental contributions to the modernization of Japan. Among such notable figures as Fukuzawa Yukichi, Niijima Jo and Uchimura Kanzo, stands one of the greatest international literary figures of the time, Nitobe Inazo. His stature stems not only from his deep understanding of the United States and Europe during the turn of the century but also from his remarkable grasp of the English language, which provided him with an unusual literary skill to interpret Japanese history and customs for the Western mind.

Nitobe first went to the United States in 1884 at the age of 22 as a student at Johns Hopkins University where he studied economics, history, and literature for three years. Among his classmates were John Dewey, the father of American Progressive Education and the foremost figure in education in the twentieth century, and Woodrow Wilson, later to become president of the United States. From there Nitobe traveled to Germany where he studied for three years at the universities of Berlin, Bonn, and Halle, the last conferring the Ph.D. in 1890.

Upon completion of his studies in the West, Nitobe returned to Japan to assume professorial duties at several Japanese national universities, bringing with him an American wife of the Quaker persuasion. Among his many contributions to Japanese education was his role as the first president of the Tokyo University for Women, one of the foremost institutions in Japan today. He also served as the principal of the single most prestigious boys' higher preparatory school for Tokyo University for seven years before his appointment to the university faculty.

Nitobe not only recognized the importance of the Western challenge to Japan at that time; he also realized how pathetically little the United States and other Western nations knew about Japan. With an astonishing skill in writing the foreign language of English, unsurpassed by few native writers of English, Nitobe set out to rectify the situation by writing books on Japanese history and culture in English. His most famous work, *Bushido*, published at the end of the nineteenth century, brilliantly analyzed the soul of Japan in terms understandable to the Western mind. No one can fully appreciate Japanese social and cultural history without studying this classic on the Japanese mentality. In one of the most unusual circumstances of the period, this distinguished Japanese figure originally wrote his treatise on Japan in English. It was subsequently translated into Japanese to become a standard work for the Japanese themselves.

Nitobe, later to be appointed under secretary of the League of Nations in Geneva for six years, along with Mori, Ito, and a host of other early notables stand out as foremost examples of the caliber of the Japanese who recognized the importance of the challenge of America and the West to Japan in the 1800s. It required tremendous effort and sacrifice on their parts to study in the West, learn Western languages, and live within Western societies in order to understand the Western challenge. Not only did these pioneers grasp the significance of the challenge to Japan a century ago; they also acted in a decisive manner by turning the Western challenge into Japan's benefit.

The industrialization and modernization of Japan in the latter half of the 1800s under the guidance of such an enlightened leadership was ultimately made possible because of the availability of a stable, capable work force. The new national education system, centered on the rapidly expanded network of elementary schools, provided the impetus. The new schools turned out a literate worker who was not only willing to sacrifice himself through a frugal, somewhat feudalistic life style; he was also motivated with a work ethic infused by a nationalistic spirit focusing on a recognizable national goal, catching up with the United States and the West. A spiritual reformation took place in the classroom challenging the Japanese mentality to compete with the "superior Westerners" by learning from their advanced technology. The basic conditions for Japan's industrial launch, a literate, capable, motivated work force challenged by the United States and other leading Western countries, was thus laid in the Japanese classroom of the last century.

Although about 100 years have passed since that monumental period in Japanese history, we would be dangerously myopic if we did not learn from the experiences of the nineteenth-century Japanese. There is a profound lesson to be learned from the "challenge of America" to Japan of the last century. And that lesson is that a nation's industrial competitiveness cannot be measured merely in terms of factory output, rates of productivity, or day-to-day management practices. Rather, the overall competitiveness of a nation's factories derives from the effectiveness of the entire infrastructure of the society; basic to that is the school system.

Current trends indicate that we have unfortunately learned too little from the experiences of the nineteenth-century pioneering Japanese. U.S. managers and workers, as well as the policymakers at all levels, should learn what makes their counterparts in Japan so frustratingly competitive. Productivity statistics tell the American little. The flood of high quality, reasonably priced Japanese products all around him, in his living room, on his shelves and desk, and in his garage, amply testifies to the competitiveness of the Japanese. The sojourn of Western visitors to Japanese factories and governmental bureaus does little to ease that frustration.

What is essential for an understanding of the Japanese challenge to America in the twentieth century has not been altered significantly from an understanding of the U.S. challenge to Japan in the nineteenth century. The industrial productivity of a nation is intimately related to, as it were, the productivity of its schools. Therefore, in order for us to understand what we are facing, that is, the nature of the Japanese challenge, we must look beyond the factory, beyond day-to-day management practices, and even beyond their "intelligent economic policy." We must probe far more deeply into Japanese society than just the shop floor, be it the factory assembling the attractive cars, the plant producing the fine cameras, or the shop turning out intricately designed robots – all three among a vast range of others capturing impressive shares of U.S. and international markets.

What makes the Japanese auto worker work? What makes him toil for wages considerably lower than those of his U.S. counterpart, if we are to accept the many statistics emanating from all kinds of sources comparing wages and incomes factoring in the relative costs of living? For example, *Time Magazine* reported that a U.S. auto worker earns nearly $23 an hour including wages and benefits, compared with his Japanese counterpart who earns about $12 an hour.[16] What makes a Japanese worker loyal to his employer so that company strikes are infrequent, contentious issues between management and labor? What makes many, perhaps most, administrative staff remain at work after regular hours – until 6:00, 7:00, or even later, five nights each week – and go to work on Saturday mornings, too? In other words, what makes the Japanese work force competitive?

No visit to a Japanese factory to view the workers on line, or to the corporate offices to question executives on management techniques, or to the Ministry of International Trade and Industry to learn about Japan's economic policies can provide the answer. Rather, the answer lies in the social structure of the Japanese community, which is so clearly reflected in the local school. A visit to the public elementary school located several blocks away from a factory will provide far deeper insights into the Japanese economic miracle than will a visit to the plant site itself. A thorough study of the Japanese school will reveal why the typical Japanese worker can be characterized as competent, loyal, diligent, and competitive.

In other words, the challenge to industrial America from Japan lies primarily in the Japanese classroom rather than in the factory. It is the contemporary Japanese school that provides the basic training of the Japanese work force. Likewise, it must be remembered, it is the contemporary U.S. school that provides the basic training of the U.S. work force locked in an international industrial, commercial, and apparently even military competition with the Japanese.

This in no way implies that the United States should model its school system, or factories as well, after the Japanese. That would be misguided and futile. The Japanese school itself reflects the social and cultural patterns of Japan, its customs and traditions, which date back many centuries. The Japanese school certainly has its share of problems, too. In order to compete with the Japanese, we cannot become Japanese. Our schools cannot be modeled on the Japanese school. Our Western Judaic-Christian foundations are simply too different from the Shinto-Buddhist-Confucianist cultural patterns of Japan for us to copy them.

Japanese society is also one of the most homogeneous societies in the world. We are one of the least homogeneous, priding ourselves justifiably as being the great melting pot of the world. We speak many diverse languages in our country. We possess varying colors of skin. We have geographical differences, all rendering us naturally diverse. The Japanese all have black hair, all read and speak, with varying dialects, one language, and nearly all share essentially common historical roots. We cannot become like the Japanese, even if we wanted to. And we do not.

However, certain practices, customs, procedures, and attitudes of the Japanese are not only admirable but are also adaptable in a manner that can fit into our fabric of social, industrial, and educational heritage. At the same time, we would be wise to avoid other Japanese attributes – both in school and without. In other words, we can learn something, a great deal, from the Japanese. And that is inherent in the challenge from Japan: to learn what to adapt and what not to adapt, which is precisely the exercise the Japanese experienced in the 1800s when they encountered, and met, the Western challenge. But if we fail to recognize the nature of the Japanese challenge itself, we cannot adequately meet that challenge and benefit from it during the rest of the twentieth century and into the twenty-first century.

The challenge to industrial America from Japan can be categorized into three levels, the superficial, the fundamental, and the ultimate: the what, the why, and the how. We are currently not much beyond the superficial level with our missions to Japan to study what the shop-floor practices or managerial techniques are like, followed by a series of interviews with responsible officials, both government and private. The morning pep talks, the noontime radio calisthenics, and the quality control circles are some of the conspicuous features that often intrigue foreign observers in many Japanese factories. But they provide only a limited glimpse into the Japanese challenge.

The what, nevertheless, is naturally important. We must obviously learn what the Japanese company is like. We must find out what the well-known quality control circles consist of and what their objectives are. We need to examine what functions the new Japanese robots have in the automobile plants, as well as what type of agreements the auto workers' unions have signed with management providing the increased use of robots on the assembly lines without upsetting amicable labor relations. There is no denying the necessity of examining what the Japanese factory and its management are like. But it's only an initial step in unraveling the challenge from Japan.

Next, we must learn why, for example, blue-collar unions have agreed to more automation in the automobile factories. We must learn why all white-collar employees, nearly all university graduates, of a middle-level financial advisory service remain at their desks until six-thirty or seven o'clock every night, no one leaving before the other. We must also learn why many department or divisional heads of companies place their desks alongside those of staff rather than in secluded private offices. And we must certainly learn why the average workers take considerable pride in their work.

The fundamental challenge we face from Japan is not merely to learn about *zangyo*, the custom of working overtime, or the impressively low incidence of employee absenteeism or employee theft. The fundamental challenge concerns why the Japanese managerial staff feel obligated to remain at their desks long after the office officially closes or why worker absenteeism is not a problem in the Japanese factory. We must learn why a so-called "Monday car" made in Japan is no different from a "Wednesday" or "Thursday car" and is most unlikely to come off the assembly line a lemon. We must also learn why an employee, be he staff or administration, who is highly trained in an electronics company would rarely take his specialized knowledge and skills to a rival company in return for a higher income.

But even at this level of understanding, which is also obviously of great importance, we cannot really get at the very roots not only of the Japanese challenge but of the Japanese postwar economic miracle itself. The final stage, the ultimate challenge from Japan, then, is to determine *how* such attitudes are formed, *how* they are nurtured, and *how* they are being perpetuated in a nation gearing itself for the twenty-first century of high technology. This is the depth of understanding of the United States that the early Japanese pioneers such as Mori and Nitobe achieved when Japan was confronted with the Western industrial challenge a century ago. It is that degree of understanding of Japan we must reach if we are ever to fully understand the Japanese challenge of today.

When we finally reach the level of the ultimate challenge from Japan, the "how" of it all, we encounter the role of the school. It is the Japanese school that functions as one of the major, if not the most critical, instruments within the infrastructure of Japanese society, carefully and painstakingly nurturing and perpetuating the basic qualities of a Japanese worker. The ultimate challenge from Japan, then, concerns the very core of Japanese society, its primary institutions, the schools, which transmit the values, the customs, and the attitudes from one generation to the next.

In order for us to understand the Japanese factory, we must probe into the classroom of the first grade to see how the students all learn to read and write, into the way the seventh graders take lunch, into how third graders clean their rooms, and even on to the stage for the graduation ceremony. It's all part of making a future Japanese worker. It may not be nearly so exciting or glamorous as studying *Theory Z* about the Japanese company, or interviewing managers about their quality control circles, or watching a fully automated robotized automobile factory disgorging its gleaming products, many destined for U.S. highways. It may all be very mundane. But if we are ever to understand our foremost industrial competitors, the Japanese, we must look to the Japanese school for lessons in producing a loyal, literate, competent, and diligent worker. And that is precisely where the ultimate challenge from Japan lies. In order to face up to the new reality as a nation at risk, according to our own governmental reports, we must inevitably turn our attention to the Japanese school to understand and benefit from the twentieth-century challenge to industrial America from the Japanese.

2

THE LOYAL WORKER
Kumi: The Group

Loyalty: the tie binding a person to something; unswerving in allegiance.

– Webster

One of the predominant traits of the Japanese – be it at work, school, or play – is loyalty to the group. It transcends all layers of the society. It is the stuff of "being Japanese." Company loyalty, a peculiarity of labor practices in Japan, typifies the allegiance that binds workers to their company. Although group loyalty has become a cultural element of the society, it must be systematically transmitted from one generation to the next. The Japanese school stands out as a major instrument in that process undergirding the tradition of one-company employment to retirement among the Japanese work force.

The course for developing group loyalty begins in school with the very first day of grade one when every Japanese child enters his kumi. Although the Japanese kumi outwardly resembles a first grade class in any U.S. school, the differences are critical. The first grade kumi represents the beginning of the formal process of group training, Japanese style, that is, developing ties that bind the individual to his group in order to achieve the ultimate goal, group harmony. It is, in every sense, the initial stage in school in the long task of preparing the future Japanese worker for the harmonious adjustment of employer-employee relationships characteristic of labor relations within Japanese industry.

Each kumi consists of 40 to 45 first graders in one class assigned to one teacher, often for a two-year period or until the end of second grade. The teacher has the heavy responsibility of molding this large number of children, especially by U.S. standards, into a harmonious unit. The techniques are neither imaginative nor innovative, but rather arduous and tedious. Most of all they reflect the practical necessities of this nation. A comparison with a U.S. elementary classroom can be most revealing.

Typically the Japanese public school teacher at all levels arranges the classroom into four or five straight rows of double desks that remain fairly stationary throughout the year. Each child is then assigned at random to his seat, a row of boys beside a row of girls, for several months at a time. A third or so of the way through the year, the kumi seating arrangement is revised and *sekigae*, the changing of the seats, takes place, a moment of considerable excitement. The children who were near the window side are scattered closer to the hallway. Those who were in front are shifted more to the rear. In contrast, seldom is a U.S. first grader assigned to one spot within his homeroom for months at a time.

The ramifications of the kumi seating pattern in Japan should not be overlooked because the activities of the kumi occupy a child's life throughout his entire schooling. He is perpetually in a kumi. The regular school day is long, running from 8:30 to 3:00 or 3:30 with a short lunch break. Afterschool activities frequently keep the elementary child in his kumi until 4:00 and even 4:30. In addition, every Japanese child attends Saturday classes from 8:30 to 12:30 each week. The Japanese child attends school from September 1 to July 20 for a total of 230 school days each year. A U.S. child attends school five days a week, for only about 180 days each year. In comparison, a Japanese child spends a total of 460 days over a two-year period in the same kumi.

Every day, six days a week, often for two years in a row, the Japanese child enters the same kumi, greets the same teacher, chats with the same students, and sits at the same desk for two or three months at a time before moving across the room to another seat for several months. Consequently the Japanese child learns naturally to relate very closely to his kumi. Often when an adult neighbor first meets a child after the beginning of a school year, the child is asked what kumi he is in. He invariably replies with considerable pride, "Ninen san kumi," the third class of grade two.

And that is precisely the point. The second grader belongs to a set group, his kumi. His existence is constantly under its shadow. His seat is set. It changes infrequently. It represents his home away from home. He becomes bound to his kumi and his teacher. And he is frequently reminded by the teacher that the kumi depends on him, either through praise when he is successful or through shame when naughty. His life revolves around his school kumi. He becomes, in effect, dependent on his kumi. It is his closed society at school.

Belonging is the sine qua non of Japanese society. One's seat, that is, one's place, one's school, or one's company is of vital importance to the individual Japanese. To restate the often stated, Japanese society reflects a group orientation. Japanese exist most comfortably within the group. They are nervous and ill at ease when confronting a situation alone. The school perpetuates this trait with its rigid organization into kumi and the extended seating arrangement in one place resulting in prolonged unity with that kumi, which itself often continues as a self-contained unit for two-year periods during elementary school.

The child learns his place, its relative permanence, its security, and the sanctity as well as the restrictions of belonging to a group through the kumi. He devotes most of his waking hours within his kumi from first grade. Close personal relationships are formed between the individual and the other members of the group. For example, students of the same kumi usually play together during recess, study together during the long class time, and even eat together during lunchtime in their assigned seat, all within the four walls of the kumi for two years in a row. Deep bonds of personal friendship are thus firmly established among members of the same kumi at school. One of the unique but more understandable characteristics of this society is the life-long reunions of kumi members.

The kumi mentality obviously builds within its members a strong feeling of "we and them." Them, the outsiders, are just that, those outside the group. Japanese children often use a special phrase during play, *nakama hazure*, to distinguish between those outside the group and those inside. Nakama hazure has the special feeling of not being part of the intimate group and, therefore, of being rejected by it. It is often used in a taunting manner. Few children want to be rejected by their peers. Most make maximum efforts to be accepted by the group and remain securely within it.

The closed nature of the Japanese elementary classroom or kumi stands in sharp contrast to a number of educational concepts employed in various communities in the United States. The ones which come to mind most readily include the open classroom, the classroom without walls, the ungraded class, or team teaching. All of these innovations in the U.S. scene are incongruous with Japanese education. The diametrically opposite viewpoints not only reflect the closed nature of Japanese society in contrast with the open character of U.S. society but also play an important role in international industrial competition between the two, to be considered later.

The elementary teacher in Japan, the *tannin no sensei* or kumi teacher, plays a very special role in the life of every Japanese child. In many schools, as mentioned previously, the kumi teacher remains with the same class for two years, that is, first and second grades, third and fourth grades, and finally the same teacher for both the fifth and sixth grades. It is often this last teacher that the Japanese remember so well. During these very impressionable ages the kumi teacher, over a two-year period broken only by a 40-day summer vacation, builds a strong sense of group loyalty and affection for the tannin no sensei that is never forgotten.

The tannin no sensei employs consciously or otherwise a variety of methods both formally and informally to develop a keen sense of kumi loyalty. Teaching methods, for example, play an important role in developing and nourishing a group feeling among the kumi students. The overwhelming number of Japanese teachers at all levels of the school devote most of their teaching time treating the kumi as a single group, moving along at a single pace, teaching the group as one. All students are following the lesson on the same page in identical textbooks. The teacher makes a Herculean effort to keep the whole class progressing in concert. The typical teacher thus stands before the class with book open, directing her teaching to all the students, asking questions here and there, and calling everyone's attention as a group to the examples on the board.

The teaching of reading, considered in some detail in Chapter 3, is a good example of teaching methods in Japan in contrast to the methods used in a typical U.S. classroom. For example, many U.S. elementary school teachers divide their 20 or 30 students homogeneously into reading groups with graded readers assigned according to each group's level of reading ability. The teacher circulates among the groups trying to provide as much individualized instruction as possible, frequently moving the children from one group to another as they show signs of progress or slackness. The Japanese teacher keeps her reading class, all 40 of them, together using the same book and teaching the same lesson to all at the same time.

Many assignments also have a group approach rather than a concern for individuality. For example, many elementary classes throughout

Japan will have adorning their walls row upon row of specimens of calligraphy. Foreign visitors often note that every specimen is of the same character, such as bright or house. And what the teacher has tried to achieve, as far as possible, is uniformity of the group. She wants as close a replica of the model of the character as possible. This is often extended into art work when every child draws exactly the same picture, all posted in neat straight rows on the wall. Everyone, although working individually, has drawn the same scene. The kumi has once again functioned as a single unit.

Ironically, although the kumi operates most of the time during the regular class hours as a single unit, the Japanese teacher also nourishes group loyalty by dividing the large kumi of 40 to 45 students into smaller groups called the *hans*, which remain intact often for prolonged periods of time for specific purposes. These small intimate groups within the larger umbrella group are reminiscent of, and preparation for, the well-known factory circles in the Japanese company. Although U.S. elementary teachers often divide their classes into small groups, the groups rarely remain together for long periods of time. Usually their small groupings relate to reading groups according to ability, mentioned earlier, or to interest groups for short-term projects in social studies. The Japanese han has a definite structure and covers a broad area of activities over a fairly long time.

The activities of each han begin by the election of the *han-cho*, who becomes the leader of the small group. All members participate as equals in selecting their leader. The han-cho, as well as the elected head of the kumi, assumes a unique position and must learn the subtleties of Japanese leadership, which are passed down in varying degrees by the teacher and often reinforced at home. Although he or she has been chosen as a leader, that child learns early that every effort must be made to lead without leading too much because humility is cherished in Japanese society. The leader soon learns that he cannot stand out too much from the group, for, as the Japanese saying goes, "The nail that sticks out gets knocked down."

The leader of the han or the kumi, then, must learn not to get out too far ahead of the group. He must listen carefully to his group and act compatibly with the general will of the group. He must patiently endeavor to persuade members of his group, often through lengthy discussions, to support a certain action. As leader his responsibility is primarily to harmonize the group attitude by forging a general consensus through reconciling various opinions into a resolution. A sense of fairness must prevail. Through this process the loyalty of each child to the group is strengthened and leadership, Japanese style, is developed.

Although the group leader is recognized as such, the members must feel that they are part of the decision-making process through mutual understanding. In other words, han and kumi decisions should be made in a consensuslike procedure in order to achieve harmony. This behavior forms the very basis of the decision-making process in Japan. And, even though it is indicative of modern Japanese-style democracy, be it in the classroom, on the shop floor, or in the executive offices, it harks back to a very old precept expounded by Japan's most famous early statesman, Prince Shotoku Taishi. This colorful figure, well known to every Japanese because his likeness has been portrayed on local currency until recently, is accredited with greatly influencing events on the path toward national unification. In his so-called Constitution of A.D. 604, he recognized the value of group participation accordingly:

> Decisions on important matters should not be made by one person alone. They should be discussed with many. But small matters are of less consequence. It is unnecessary to consult a number of people. It is only in the case of the discussion of weighty affairs, when there is a suspicion that may miscarry, that one should arrange matters in concert with others, so as to arrive at the right conclusion.[1]

That this traditional decision-making process in modern Japanese society plays such an important role in its industrial competitiveness makes further analysis of it necessary. To many Americans, and other Westerners as well, the process of arriving at a consensuslike decision, Japanese style, is too time consuming, inefficient, and downright frustrating. We commonly arrive at a decision, once the various points of view have been put forth, by letting the chips fall where they may by calling for the vote. Once the conflicting points of view are on the table, we see little value in going over the issues again and again. We simply vote. The ayes have it. The matter has been settled.

Not so in Japan. When a Japanese group holds a meeting to discuss some controversial proposal, the conflicting opinions will slowly come forth, often couched in vague terms, depending on the nature of the group. The discussion continues and continues and continues as the various points of view are repeated and repeated. Still, the vote is not called for. A decision is not made. A consensus is obviously not formed. The discussion continues. The same opinions are repeated.

The leader of the group is seeking some compromise whereby one side or the other begins to alter, however slightly, its position. He detects a crack in one side. It appears that a consensus is possible. The meeting continues until the leader is fairly confident that a harmonious decision can be achieved. Then and only then does he call for a vote. Or, by that time, the formality of voting according to Robert's Rules may not be necessary. The final decision is simply understood by all.

But what happens when the leader cannot achieve a consensus, when even a small minority refuses to budge? A common approach to this predicament is that no decision is made even though a majority would clearly approve the measure. Action is postponed. But what takes place between meetings is vitally important to understand the decision-making process in Japanese society. The leader will meet with various individuals during the ensuing period in an attempt to strike some compromise face-to-face, one-to-one, behind the scene. A persuasive leader will use his unique powers to bring a dissenter around to the majority opinion. Working back and forth between the various factions, he usually obtains some compromise, however slight. At the next meeting the motion, or a revision thereof, is presented. Although everyone is well aware of the outcome, a reasonable amount of time must nevertheless be spent in discussion. Finally it is accepted unanimously. Harmony has been preserved, a sign of effective leadership.

The wisest of all Japanese leaders, however, be it in the corporate office, on the shop floor, or in the political party, are those who carefully reverse the process described above. Rather than seeking for a compromise after the conflicting issues are exposed at a group meeting, the most effective Japanese leaders build a consensus beforehand by meeting interminably with many individuals in the group to forge a proposal that reflects the concerns of all members. Once this leader feels he has a consensus, he presents it as a formal proposal or suggestion to his group. Even then long discussions are held although the conclusion, for all practical purposes, has already been decided before the meeting where its approval is a mere formality. The result is not just group approval but, most noteworthy, group responsibility for successful implementation. It's all part of the dynamics of the Japanese group taken for granted by most, the subtleties that future leaders must learn. Their initial training takes place in the school kumi.

The point of this discussion is that many a corporate decision is made in a similar manner. It is time consuming, to be sure. And it may appear as a terribly inefficient use of management's time. But it is simply the way of getting things done in Japan. One high-level manager in this writer's weekly seminar with businessmen said that he makes a careful and time-consuming effort to solicit the opinions of all his staff individually before coming to a decision to raise their "consciousness of participation." Asked why this was so important to him, he replied that it gave his people a sense of satisfaction, important for the morale of the office, and motivated everyone to make every effort to implement the policy successfully. He could then count on their full support even though some were initially critical of the proposal. This, to the Japanese, is the essence of participatory democracy as they apply their old traditional ideas of group harmony to the modern jargon of Western democracy, and even Western-style corporations.

Again, this attitude was reflected during an earlier period in Japanese history. In the seventh century, the ancient leaders of Japan clearly recognized the importance of harmony to the welfare of the nation. To many Japanese businessmen today, the precepts of Prince Shotoku Taishi, mentioned previously, are as relevant to their firm's well-being in the 1980s as they were to the well-being of Japan in the 600s. Again we quote from his Constitution:

> Harmony is to be valued, and an avoidance of wanton opposition to be honored. All men are influenced by partisanship, and there are few who are intelligent. Hence there are some who disobey their lords and fathers, or who maintain feuds with the neighboring villages. But when those high above are harmonious and those below friendly, and there is concord in the discussion of business, right views of things gain acceptance. Then what is there which cannot be accomplished?[2]

Leadership in Japanese society, then, be it private or public, takes on a different characteristic than in the United States. Americans judge leaders in charismatic terms. The leaders must stand out from the rest through a demonstration of forceful actions. They must be in command, in control. In other words, they must be in the forefront, the limelight. Simply put, they must lead.

Japanese leaders, in fact, do not usually stand out much from the others. They seldom display charisma. They reach the top not by standing out from among the others through forceful action, but by being able to unite others behind them through persuasion, not command. There are exceptions, of course, notably former Prime Minister Tanaka Kakuei, who performed like a one-man show. Not surprisingly, when he was convicted of accepting a bribe over the infamous Lockheed airplane case, there was clearly widespread satisfaction that the protruding nail finally got knocked down. Tanaka never showed the proper humility, an essential ingredient of a Japanese leader.

The kumi teacher in school is searching for leadership among her charges, to be sure, but that teacher also has the primary responsibility to shape the han and kumi into a harmonious group with desirable goals. The teacher obviously doesn't always succeed. Inevitably some children want to show off, to attract attention. A few don't get along well in the kumi. But the remarkable characteristic of Japanese schools is evidenced in the high degree of loyalty to the kumi and in the general acceptance of its influence over the child's personal attitudes. What is truly impressive, whether one evaluates it positively or negatively, is that the average Japanese child adapts to the kumi process by learning to live harmoniously within the group through a commitment of his loyalty to it.

Peer group influence, a prominent feature among youth in all societies, assumes to a great extent the form of the influence of the han and kumi in Japanese schools. It can exert a beneficial influence. It can have a negative influence as well. The least idealistic aspect of the Japanese kumi to some critics both foreign and Japanese concerns the potential of the kumi for stifling individuality and personal creativity. Although creativity and individuality are not easily measured, innumerable observations indicate that there is substance in this concern.

At the lower grades the children are clearly less inhibited, typical of schools in all countries. But, especially as the Japanese child progresses through the school, spontaneity, original ideas, and innovative thinking fade away. Japanese children generally learn to "sway with the breeze" in order to maintain group harmony. The herd instinct at the expense of individuality is an underlying motive in this society.

It must be remembered, though, that peer groups in Western societies also exert a powerful influence on most children's upbringing. In Japan, peer group influence is in part incorporated into the classroom in the form of the kumi, with the child thus coming more directly under teacher influence than is commonly seen in U.S. schools. From this perspective the school's influence on youth peer groups in Japan leads to generally more constructive goals of the group than in U.S. society where youth form highly independent peer group attitudes. The Japanese have problems of juvenile delinquency and school discipline, causing great concern, but they do not approach the level of those problems in the United States.

As mentioned previously, han activities take many tangible forms such as classroom work assignments (for example, a teacher may assign a science experiment to be conducted by each han) or projects in social studies to be carried out by the hans. The famous *happyo-kai*, when each han presents a project report in front of the class, is characteristic of Japanese schools. It inevitably stirs considerable interest and excitement. It also unites the han as they all stand before the class identifying them individually as members of that particular group, further solidifying a sense of loyalty.

In the preparation of the han report, the group works cooperatively as a team by drawing their desks together in school or by visiting the library to search out material from various sources. This type of han activity in the elementary schools also spills over from the classroom. After school the han may meet at some member's home to work out the plan for the report. This is especially noticeable the day or two before the class report is scheduled. And, although there may be considerable casual play when a han meets at a private home after school, there is invariably a certain seriousness of purpose that eventually consumes the group and promotes a fairly cooperative effort to get the job done on time. All of these han activities intensify group attitudes by the individual member.

A variety of other opportunities in the Japanese school fuse the han and kumi into a loyal harmonious group. Even the school lunch is organized in such a way as to solidify the han and kumi relationships. Very few Japanese public schools maintain cafeterias for mass gatherings of the students for lunch. This observer has yet to encounter one. Instead the students remain in their classroom and eat the prepared meal as a kumi. Consequently even during the midday break, the kumi remains together often with the teacher as a secluded group for this school activity that is as social, perhaps more so, as it is nutritional. The menu, in fact, is not appetizing to the Western palate.

This practice is in sharp contrast to the typical U.S. school where the students leave their homerooms to take lunch en masse in a large central cafeteria. Cafeteria employees usually handle the preparation and serve the meal as students file through the serving line. They are also responsible for cleaning up afterward. Teachers often eat together in a special section of the cafeteria separate from the students or, perhaps, in a nearby room. In turn, teachers serve on "cafeteria duty" patrolling the area trying to keep things under control. Cafeteria duty is one of the more hapless demands of the teaching profession despised by a good many teachers as demeaning, not to mention frustrating.

In Japanese schools, the food is also centrally prepared by a hired staff. However, the serving, and often the transporting of the meal to the kumi classroom, is ordinarily conducted on a rotating basis by the han system. Each han within the kumi, bedecked in aprons and masks, takes responsibility in turn for carrying the food from the central kitchen or from a dumb waiter on the upper floors, organizing the serving line in front of the room, and dishing out the food to the kumi members as they pass through. Many a teacher goes through the line with the students and remains in the room with the kumi for lunch. Upon completion of the meal the responsible han coordinates the collection of the utensils and returns the pots, pans, and dishes to the central kitchen. That han's work duty may be completed for the day.

Meanwhile the other hans are given various work assignments during the day. The room must be tidied up for the afternoon lessons by a different han. The adjacent hallway floor will be scrubbed, often on hands and knees with hand mops by another han, a traditional practice many Japanese adults look back upon with some degree of nostalgia as an important part of their moral training in school. And still another may be assigned the task of cleaning the hallway steps or the perennially smelly toilets, a memorable feature of most schools, since fulltime janitorial staff is in short supply in Japanese schools. The periodic *osoji*, the big cleanup, incorporates all hans in a schoolwide effort to keep the premises as tidy as possible. Japanese students are thus given heavy responsibilities for keeping their school clean, often through the small-group system.

Field trips also incorporate the han. Because most schools arrange many school excursions during the course of a child's education, including overnight, or longer, trips at the sixth and ninth grades, their conduct is of importance to this issue. Children are often assigned to seats on the bus or train by hans enabling the members to chat with each other during the ride. It's also common sense because it simplifies the teacher's task of checking to see whether all students of a kumi are present before the bus moves. The teachers simply check with the han-chos. Even this small act identifies the individual with the han.

At the destination of the field trip the hans are employed extensively. With large classes, and all but tiny rural schools have kumi consisting of 40-plus students, movements through temples, shrines, museums, or nature hikes are frequently and conveniently carried out by the han system, or with particularly large groups, by kumi. The arrangement is not only orderly and essential with such large numbers, it also has the added effect of further strengthening the bonds of group solidarity and loyalty to the han and kumi.

Other components of the Japanese school reinforce the teacher in the development of kumi and han loyalty. The role and organizational structure of the Parent-Teacher Association (PTA) is another case in point. Although imported from America, the PTA in Japan plays a unique role. The PTA is normally structured at the local school level according to each kumi. Parents, overwhelmingly mothers, and a very high percentage at that, attend the scheduled daytime PTA meetings usually according to kumi for the first hour in the kumi classroom. A general meeting in the gymnasium follows.

The session in the kumi classroom takes several forms. The meeting can be a get-together with the kumi teacher for a broad discussion of current issues, current assignments, student displays, and other school concerns. The students are dismissed early for this meeting. If some parents have a complaint to air, this is the opportunity to do so. For example, if there is a general feeling that the kumi teacher is not academically demanding enough, mothers will register their concern at this time. This has happened on a rare occasion over the years at our local PTA meetings, much to the embarrassment of the teacher who was, in a sense, being scolded by some mothers for not pressing the students harder. Usually, though, parents take this opportunity to indicate their cooperation and solidarity with the teacher's efforts.

Another popular session before the general PTA meeting incorporates the so-called *jugyo sankan*, class observation. All parents are strongly encouraged to observe a regular lesson taught by the kumi teacher scheduled immediately before the general PTA meeting. Mothers, and a sprinkling of fathers, dutifully sign the roster at the kumi door and then stand at the rear of the classroom during the lesson carefully watching the conduct of their children. The parents react according to student responses, laughing at cute remarks, nodding approval at the clever ones.

In either form the presence of parents in the kumi classroom several times each year corroborates a child's loyalty to the kumi. The child witnesses the presence of his mother along with his teacher in his classroom. He relates his mother, and his father on occasions when the PTA meetings are held on Saturdays and, although infrequently, on Sundays to accommodate the many fathers who work Saturday mornings, with his teacher and his classroom. Afterward, the parent and child have a certain common knowledge of kumi activities for discussing school-related topics at home. In particular, the parent has had classroom experiences that form the basis for parental-teacher collaboration of the kumi. The kumi's sphere of influence extends into the home itself.

Other pertinent practices somewhat peculiar to the Japanese school at the basic levels are the home visits by the teacher, *katei homon*, an annual event, and the teacher-parent interview, *kojin mensetsu*, scheduled several times a year. At the beginning of each year, the child brings home a schedule of afternoon time slots during the following week. Each parent is requested to fill in the times when the teacher can come to the home for a 15-minute visit with the parent. All kumi teachers in the school then arrange the various available time slots into the following week of afternoon home visits when the children have only morning sessions.

The teacher, frequently on bicycle even in the major cities, arrives according to the prearranged schedule at the child's home. The stated purpose is not for an extended session. Rather, it is intended to enable the teacher to obtain a general perspective of the child's home environment. The teacher theoretically is in a better position to understand the child's personality and behavioral patterns at school by having met with each parent in the home setting.

A comical incident occurred during the teacher's home visit to a Japanese neighbor. Parents, even in this overwhelmingly middle-class society, are still eager to put their very best foot forward for the visiting teacher. Therefore the father in the family was persuaded by his wife to come home from the office at noon to help prepare the house for the visit scheduled for three o'clock. About two o'clock the father attired in old clothes with boots on and pants rolled up was hosing down the front sidewalk. The wife and daughter, with aprons on, were inside washing windows.

About that time a young woman came riding up on her bicycle and asked the father for directions to, of all places, his own house. It was to his astonishment and horror the visiting teacher whom he had never met. Somehow she had gotten her schedule confused. The wife was completely beside herself throughout the visit that, although only about ten minutes long, seemed endless. It was a prime example of "life's most embarrassing moments" for Japanese parents.

The home visit goes far beyond its stated objective. The child, who is often at home during the visit having been dismissed early from school, witnesses his kumi teacher entering his house and sitting in his livingroom talking with his parent. It represents another reinforcement of his relationship with his kumi. Now the teacher and child have a common basis in discussing home topics. The triangular web of relationships between parent, child, and teacher is woven more intricately.

The parent-teacher interview takes another form of reinforcement of home and kumi. According to a prearranged schedule, usually later in the afternoons, the mother again dutifully goes to the kumi for a 15-minute interview with the kumi teacher one or more times each year, near the end of a school term. She patiently waits in the hallway for her turn hoping that the previous mother will not go much beyond her allotted time, especially during winter when the hallways are very cold and one is wearing slippers, mandatory footwear inside all schools. The discussion at this meeting dwells primarily on the child's academic performance, on his art work displayed on the wall for reference, or on his social behavior if that has become a problem.

Again, the significance of this meeting extends far beyond the meeting itself. The parent is drawn ever so inclusively into the kumi by physically visiting the kumi, entering the classroom, sitting on a kumi chair next to the teacher's desk, or, if in the winter, near the stove, and discussing with the kumi teacher the activities of the child. Often the teacher will bring out the grade book and go over the child's test results with the parent. Once again, the parent has had another opportunity to reinforce the child's relationship to the kumi enabling discussions of common topics at home, be it the art displays in the classroom or the results of kumi tests. It's all part of constructing a strong sense of loyalty to the kumi not only by the child but by the parent as well.

At the junior and senior high school level, all students join in the extracurricular club activities, another important device of the Japanese school to mold loyalty. The clubs run the entire gamut from tennis and brass band to the English Play Club. The ostensible purpose of the club may be tennis or English. However the manner in which they are run reveals another instructive aspect not only of school club activities but also of the very nature of Japanese society itself.

The junior high tennis club, for example, draws its membership from all levels and from many different kumi within each grade level. It represents a broad mix. However, upon entering the club the student makes two fundamental commitments. First of all, he must commit himself fully to the activities of the club; that means attending the early morning sessions every day, six days a week, on many holidays and Sundays, and throughout much of the summer vacation, depending upon the club. It's often a full commitment.

Second, he must commit himself to respect the hierarchical structure of the club, the *sempai-kohai* relationships. Older students run the club. Underclassmen follow. Regardless of one's personal desires or complaints about the way the club is run, loyalty to the club takes precedence. To do otherwise, to quit the club, for instance, is an act of disloyalty. No one likes a quitter in Japan, especially fellow members of the group. In fact, one of the characteristics of this society is the difficulty the individual faces when he or she wants to quit the group. That attitude is reinforced at school.

Students learn that to join a school club means just that, "to unite with," according to Webster. The club activities emphasize not just playing the trumpet in the brass band but the unity of its members. In many cases, one gets the feeling that club unity is more important than, for example, tennis. The reputation of a club is not necessarily based on the performance of its members in the stated object of the club. Rather, it is closely related to the degree of loyalty the members commit to the club. To the Japanese, without a total commitment to the group be it at work, school, or play, there can be little chance for success. Commitment comes first.

Even the final act of the school, graduation time, considered in more detail later, is carried out based on the kumi structure. For example, in virtually every elementary and junior high school in the nation, graduating students proceed into the graduation ceremonies in kumi formation, each kumi being led in by the kumi teacher. They are introduced as a kumi with the kumi teacher reading the individual names of his or her students as each walks to the stage to receive the diploma. And they leave the ceremony by kumi to go outside for the final group picture, kumi by kumi. They have all entered the school in the kumi, and their last formal action is, appropriately, carried out within the kumi.

An example of the solidarity built up within the kumi was displayed when our oldest daughter was graduated from the local public junior high school. The last good-bye of the kumi was quite emotional and memorable to say the least. A few of her classmates from the local community had been together from the first grade of the elementary school, and a few others had been together from the first grade of the junior high school. Most of the 43 students in H-kumi, however, had been together in the same junior high school homeroom only during the final year. Nevertheless, when they returned to their classroom to pick up their belongings for the last time after a highly emotional graduation ceremony, where many a tear was shed by both graduates and parents, some student had written across the board in bold letters, "H-kumi will live forever!" All students signed their name on the board as the ultimate demonstration and commitment of their loyalty to the group.

Loyalty to the group with the aim of achieving group harmony, a distinctive feature of Japanese society, which this aggregate of school activities reflects and nurtures, and which is so effectively applied in the modern means of industrial production, derives from the long history of the Japanese people. The root of it, in part, lies in the geographical circumstances of Japan over which the historical Japanese themselves have had no control, but rather have had to learn to adapt to. This is one of the reasons why it is difficult to fully adopt Japanese practices and techniques in the United States where the geographical, as well as the historical and cultural, basis of the society is so different from that of Japan.

Not only is it difficult to apply Japanese work customs to other countries trying to improve their productivity based on the Japanese model; it is even painful for children of Japanese businessmen to return to Japanese schools after studying for several years in other lands, especially the United States. With the rapid expansion of Japanese interests abroad, notably but certainly not exclusively in the United States, the problem has been magnified into a minicrisis with over 50,000 Japanese of school age now living abroad. According to the Ministry of Education, over 6,000 elementary, 2,000 junior high, and 1,000 senior high school students return to Japan each year to reenter Japanese schools.

The problem of the reentry of the *kikokushijo*, the returning-to-the-homeland student, involves several critical factors, all of which can be of dramatic proportions to a teenager. It is one of the major reasons many Japanese businessmen, some estimate half or more, leave their families in Japan when assigned overseas. The reentry problem relates to language, mathematics, and not surprisingly, fitting back into the Japanese group. The first two can be overcome with hard work and much study. The latter is not so easy.

For a young Japanese child to leave his homeland at age eight or ten to accompany the business family for a five- or six-year stay in New York or Los Angeles, even though the family will speak Japanese in the home and observe Japanese customs as much as possible while abroad, the lack of experience in a regular Japanese kumi during this tender school age may take many years to overcome after returning. The child who leaves the kumi for a protracted period may never fully adjust to group patterns and forever feel just out of the mainstream of Japanese culture, that is, nakama hazure, outside the group. Kikokushijo, the returning student, has the implication of being somewhat different from the "real Japanese."

In order to cope with this growing problem, the Japanese government has appointed a number of regular schools as special centers to enroll these special Japanese students. Although additional instruction in the written language and mathematics is provided in order to bring them up to a standard sufficient to follow the regular course of study, there is no course to teach them how to adjust to the kumi. And this can be a far more difficult adjustment for them to make than the course work. Students can't learn the intricacies of group behavior, Japanese style, from books, and they're not tested on it in the examination. It is the process of readjusting to "being Japanese" that this society takes for granted arising out of the long history of this nation.

The problem of the kikokushijo returning from overseas is compounded by the *tenkosei*, the student transferring from one school to another within Japan itself. With the rapid development of Japanese industry, more and more company employees are being transferred from their home base to posts around the country. Accordingly the accompanying children of school age face being transferred from their home kumi to another kumi in the school of the new community. The adjustment to the new kumi, predictably, can be such a trying experience that it is estimated that about half of all married employees with school age children leave their families at the home city when transferred to a new post. Students studying for entrance examinations are seldom transferred from their home kumi.

Tenkosei implies nakama hazure, a student coming in from outside the group. Students refer to the transfer student as a tenkosei for many months after he has arrived in the new school. Sometimes the old kumi children continue to think of the transfer student as a tenkosei throughout the year or until new kumi are formed at the beginning of the following school year. During that period the tenkosei, in a good many instances, is not considered as a full member of the kumi and is treated accordingly by the others. They're just a bit different, still somewhat of an outsider. Finally, the student who transferred into the school from another community even six or eight months previously becomes a full-fledged member of his group. He or she is now inside the group at last.

Certain unique cirumstances of Japan must not be overlooked in the evolution of this kumi mentality undergirding the society and its industrial sector. They are relevant to the formation of a sense of loyalty to the group, be it the han and kumi in the school or the small shop circle in the factory. As described before, this is a small island nation with a population of over 100 million, most of whom are crowded into a tiny strip along the east coast. That is group living. From antiquity the people on these islands found it necessary to band tightly together in the few small livable areas for sheer survival against the rugged mountainous landscape, the frequent earthquakes, the destructive typhoons, the inevitable landslides, the perennial floodings, and the heavy snows. Self-preservation is instinctive. Without local grassroots cooperative efforts, the society could not have endured. And because the various groups of the Asian mainland immigrants to these islands gradually coalesced into a physically homogeneous stock with a relatively common language and a common heritage resulting in common characteristics and even gestures, group formation traits grew naturally out of the native environment. They became indigenous in Japan as individualism in American society was an outgrowth of the American frontier experiences in the vastness and openness of North America.

Later, during the great feudal era of the Middle Ages, group loyalty became institutionalized in Japan under the immense influence of Confucian doctrine. The samurai warrior tradition of loyalty to the lord underwent fine tuning during that long period of chivalry. The samurai code, *bushido*, glorified unswerving allegiance to one's lord as well as an honor-bound covenant of loyalty to one's clan. Some would argue that this medieval bushido code of conduct, with its feudalistic connotations, remains alive in Japan today in the form of employer-employee relationships.

When Japanese teachers endeavor to mold their kumi and the smaller hans into a harmonious group, there is this long history of a fairly high degree of social unity and physical and psychological homogeneity behind it steeped in the geo-cultural roots of the nation. Group formation, group loyalty comes almost intuitively to the Japanese. It also reflects the sheer realities of this delicately balanced, densely populated island nation, as well as the common sense of the historical Japanese, who adapted their society to the practical necessities of the land.

To many non-Japanese, the tradition of group loyalty in this society smacks of conformity. The concept of the "Japanese mind" connotes a nation of think-alikes. From this interpretation it would appear that the Japanese worker is a captive of his company easily manipulated by his superiors, who themselves think alike. From this point of view, the whole population of think-alikes results in the image widespread in the United States of Japan Incorporated, a disdainful perspective of a society diametrically opposed to the highly diverse society of America.

There is some element of truth in this analysis, but probing beneath the surface, one finds the realities are far different than they readily appear. Take politics, for example. In the United States the Republican and Deomcratic parties, from any standpoint the only political parties worthy of the name, are theoretically in opposition. Great fanfare is given to their party conventions and to the differences between their respective platforms.

Seen from a distance there appear to be small differences in their fundamental positions on essentials such as the form of government for the country, foreign policy, defense policy, and even to a certain extent, domestic policies. Certainly the Democrats would support more social spending than the Republicans, but they would manifestly not alter the form of government, for example, into socialism, to achieve it. A change of political parties at the central levels in the United States results in minor structural changes. From this perspective, Americans are essentially conformists politically.

In Japan, there are real opposition parties, notably the Socialists and an active Communist party along with several other centrist parties. The Socialist and Communist parties present platforms that, should they gain power, would result in basic structural changes of the government, industry, and society. From this point of view, the Japanese are far more disparate, and some would even say more sophisticated, in their political attitudes than the Americans.

Where Japanese and Americans differ, though, is in the attitudes toward the group with which they are associated. The Japanese are taught throughout their school days to place their loyalties with their group, be it the classroom kumi, the tennis club, or the brass band. The activities and purposes of all three are different, and their activities and programs have little in common. But the attitudes of all members to their respective groups are similarly based on loyalty.

The significant factor about Japanese society is that virtually all groups, regardless of their goals, expect and receive the loyalty of their members. Hence it would be unthinkable for a member of the Conservative party to vote for legislation proposed by an opposition party. That is, cross-voting in the Japanese Parliament is a rare event. It's all block, or group, voting. A representative can oppose the measure in party meetings but would rarely venture to vote against it in the final count. In other words, the Japanese people support a broad perspective of political parties with far more diversity than that between the Republican and Democratic parties in America. But within each party in Japan one finds great similarity in group loyalty, different from the American political party where, for example, some Democrats from the South vote as often for Republican legislation as they do for Democratic proposals, a circumstance beyond comprehension to the Japanese politician.

The ruling Conservative party, the Jiminto, carries this one step further – to absurdity some would say. The party is wracked with what is called factionalism in the West, but it is really a form of groupism within the larger umbrella group, similar to the small hans within the kumi at school. Each faction or group within the party maintains a powerful sense of loyalty to that group and its leader, running into sharp conflict with members of another faction equally committed to their group and its leader. However, when party legislation is finalized, all factions within the party ultimately rally round the party platform. The kumi ultimately prevails.

The business world operates in a similar manner. Employees of each automobile company spontaneously assume a relatively similar attitude of loyalty to their company, for example, rarely resigning to take a better position with a competing company. Even if they became dissatisfied with their employment opportunities, seldom would a Japanese worker or administrator destroy or steal company property in retaliation or take his skills to a rival firm. In fact, it is extremely difficult for a newcomer, other than a recruit right out of school, to fit into the established group in another company.

Therefore, to talk in terms of Japan Incorporated, as a nation of lemmings where the people think alike, seems anachronistic because there are enormous competition and opposition in virtually every sphere of endeavor. However, what distinguishes the Japanese in industry, government, labor, and even the underworld from most other societies is the common factor of loyalty to the group, no matter the group. And that commonness is perpetuated in the Japanese school, which has a common purpose of developing a sense of loyalty to the kumi from the first grade.

This national ethic of loyalty to the group in Japan has been adapted successfully and naturally to the modern means of industrial production. A Japanese worker has experienced many years of group training in his various kumi, be it the classroom kumi, the han, or the various extracurricular clubs, all which function like a kumi. He has learned that he, as an individual, benefits by committing himself, sometimes sacrificially, to the furtherance of his kumi, his group. His practical sense of utility has taught him that his kumi benefits as well.

The Japanese transfers intact this deep-rooted sense of loyalty to the kumi to the workplace. His seat is simply transferred from one place to another. When a Japanese is graduated from school and enters the company, the ultimate sekigae, the changing of the seats, takes place. His commitment to his group, though, is unaltered. Loyalty transcends location. If anything the sense of loyalty becomes more deeply ingrained through employment with only one company until retirement and is rewarded with salary increases and promotions based primarily on seniority, a tradition essentially still in place.

Is it any wonder, then, that Japanese workers and managers seldom quit one company for another? Is it not understandable that unions are company-related rather than craft- or industry-related? Is it not natural that company strikes are, in comparison to strikes in the United States, infrequent in Japan? The Japanese worker experiences a powerful sense of security and loyalty to his kumi, his company. And to participate in acts of disloyalty, a strike, for example, runs counter to the Japanese mentality of kumi-loyalty and his practical common sense. Single company employment conforms to this pattern of relationships.

In contrast, many workers in the United States have a sense of work insecurity and look upon their unions as protectors. The union defends the employee's job security, his rights, his benefits. In other words, the union protects the worker from his own company, which is viewed as the enemy in the eyes of a fair number of American workers. They feel no compunction in "downing tools" when the union beckons, as the statistics in Table 2.1 reveal. The repercussions from this type of adversarial relationships within the company in the absence of mutual confidence are predictable.

Not so in the Japanese firm. On the strength of an unwritten moral code between the worker and his company, it is the company, not the union, which protects the employee by virtually assuring him employment until retirement. The Japanese worker has little obligation to his union as his protector because the company, his kumi, serves as his guardian. Obviously from this perspective, attitudes of the Japanese worker toward his company assume a different dimension from those of the U.S. worker.

This difference, in turn, reflects the unique attitude of the average Japanese manager and executive toward their employees. If management

TABLE 2.1
Days Lost in Labor Disputes, 1972-80
(1,000 workdays)

	USA	Japan
1972	27,066	5,147
1976	37,859	3,254
1980	32,288	1,001

Source: Labor Statistics (Katsuyo Rodo Tokei), Japan Productivity Center, 1983.

has a similar viewpoint about the company, which is, after all, their kumi as well, then their posture toward the work force is somewhat different from that of many of their U.S. counterparts. Examples abound. That many departmental or divisional managers, even some corporate directors, place their desks not in separate offices but amidst the cluttered desks of the staff indicates their attitude toward, and even dependency on, those under them, their kumi, as it were. Separate, independent offices in many companies are used for small meetings rather than for the department head's private office.

Another good example of loyalty concerns the custom of single employment until retirement. When bad times befall the Western firm, rationalization procedures follow the almost instinctive response of reducing the number of employees. In other words, a certain percentage, oftentimes running into the thousands, of the work force is summarily laid off either temporarily or permanently. The plant closures by U.S. steel companies resulting in the laying off of thousands of employees is a good example. It can be and often is a ruthless procedure, traditionally practiced not only in steel but also in the automobile industry. It is justified in terms of the highly competitive nature of the market place, both domestically and internationally. No wonder the Western auto or steel worker intuitively turns to his union for protection from his employer. Inevitably U.S. unions will increasingly demand job security.

Not so in Japan, particularly in large corporations such as the giants in the automobile and steel industries where job security is not at stake. Even though these Japanese firms are deeply involved in the highly competitive domestic and international market place, the approach to rationalization at home takes on a different form. Rather than dismissing part of the work force and thereby undermining the loyalty of the workers to their kumi, a variety of measures to cope with excess employees is carried out. Often, executive salaries are first reduced. Next, the firm may transfer excess workers from headquarters to its various sales offices to help strengthen sales during a slack time. Or a major paper manufacturing firm may transfer much of the work force of a bankrupt subsidiary to various mills where, it should be noted, they are not needed. The additional employees are assigned a variety of odd jobs to keep them busy during what is hoped to be a temporary lull in business activity. In some extreme instances, major firms pressure a supplier to take on their excess employees in return for continued business in a desperate move to take care of their people.

Many Japanese companies, though, carry excess employees even during slack times, a burden of enormous financial consequence, not to mention the gross inefficiencies in personnel management. This is particularly true in the service industries. However, to do otherwise would undermine the loyalty of the worker and impair the harmony of the kumi, the company. The worker expects his kumi, that is, his company, to protect him until retirement by carrying him on the payroll right up to, if worse comes to worst, bankruptcy. Most executives instinctively accept this as their sense of obligation, their sense of loyalty to their workers, regardless of the consequences.

A good example of the Japanese approach to excess employees came about during the severe depression of the paper-pulp industry in the late 1970s and early 1980s. The major companies were attempting to rationalize their operations as demand for paper products was sharply curtailed while costs, especially for oil, which this industry consumes in enormous amounts, continued to climb. The official responsible for personnel management of one of the major firms, a member of this writer's weekly seminar for businessmen, when asked why he didn't lay off the many excess employees responded simply that, "We have no system for laying off our workers." That method, so frequently employed by U.S. companies, was simply out of the question to the Japanese management.

Because of the widespread attitude of company loyalty, both on the part of the workers and management, mergers or take-overs among different or competing firms changing the face of corporate America, are rare in Japan. There are take-overs, but they occur almost always between friendly, related firms or among subsidiaries of a major firm. The problems of uniting two separate work forces and two different managements, that is, two different kumi, into one are beyond comprehension to most Japanese businessmen.

One final example, among many others, of the tangible effects on work practices resulting from the inordinate sense of loyalty concerns the widespread custom of zangyo, overtime work. Statistics are difficult to obtain in order to determine the extent of zangyo. Nevertheless, an average white-collar male administrative staffer from the lowest level up, in most industries, remains in his office from one to two hours, or even longer, after the official closing time. This is not an occasional event during sales campaigns or budget-making periods, but it occurs every weekday in addition to the regular Saturday morning session. Although according to a recent European report the average Japanese worker has the longest workweek among all non-Communist nations at 39.6 hours, compared with 35.8 hours for his U.S. counterpart, a 50 to 60 hour workweek is common among male office employees in Japanese companies.[3] Only the nonadministrative class receive compensation for extra hours.

What keeps the Japanese tied to their desks for such long hours? Are they so busy, or inefficient, that they can't complete their work by five o'clock? Are they so dedicated to the company that they volunteer to remain at the office in order to promote the general welfare of the firm? Do they enjoy their work so much that they cannot stop on time?

There is, depending on the company, an element of some or all of these factors underlying zangyo. However, the sense of loyalty to the kumi, the office staff, and to the company also plays a critical role. The evaluation of an employee's worth to the company is based on his commitment to it, and overtime work is an important expression of one's sincerity and loyalty. The white-collar administrative staffer may wish to return home early to be with his wife and family or to drive golf balls at the nearby practice range. However, to break ranks and depart before the others, whether work duties allow it or not, runs counter to his consciousness of loyalty and his sense of shame. He simply cannot walk out of the office before his colleagues. At considerable personal sacrifice to himself, and especially to his family, the confirmation of sincerity, his loyalty, is demonstrated by remaining with his kumi until all are ready to leave no matter the hour. Loyalty to the kumi must be reconciled with personal desires.

An example close to home demonstrates the Japanese mentality behind this attitude toward the group. During the student unrest and turmoil of the late 1960s and early 1970s on our campus, when the Japanese student movement erupted in concert with student movements in the United States and Europe, one of our activist senior students was arrested for throwing Molotov cocktails in a student raid on the train station in Shinjuku, the huge commuting hub in Tokyo. It was, as he explained it, a tactic meant to embarrass the government dominated by big business that exploits the workers, a typical Marxist interpretation of Japanese society. He was jailed for six months when he refused to show remorse, remaining silent, and loyal to his group, in front of the judge.

Upon his release this exconvict returned from prison to successfully complete a final term for graduation. He then was employed by a small printing firm. Several months later in a casual meeting, he described how difficult it was to adjust to the transition from university life with its leisurely schedule of one or two classes a day to the extended workday at the office running to 6:30 each night, plus Saturday mornings. When asked why he didn't leave the office at 5:00 when the company officially closes and the office girls depart for home, this young man who had devoted much of his university days scheming to overthrow the capitalist system, in complete sincerity replied, "But, Sensei, I couldn't leave the office before the others."

To claim that these attitudes permeate every worker and employer in Japan is beyond credulity. What makes Japan so highly competitive is that those who deviate very far from the loyalty norm form a small minority. This deep sense of loyalty to the company characterizes "the tie that binds" the typical blue- and white-collar Japanese employee to the company. It has been one of the major factors underlying the economic miracle of postwar Japan. The school kumi has played out its role most effectively in the process.

3

THE LITERATE WORKER
Kokugo: The National Language

Literate: a person who can read and write; an educated person.

– Webster

According to Webster's definition, the Japanese are a literate people. By any international standard, Japan can be characterized as an educated nation whose work force is one of the most literate and well-educated bodies of workers in the world today. Some would judge it number one. Few nations, if any, have attained the mass literacy standards that Japan has. Few nations, if any, have virtually eliminated illiteracy from its shores as this nation has.

These are strong observations. Nevertheless they're self-evident to anyone familiar with Japan. No one can deny that every employer in Japan, down to the smallest and most rural level, can hire new employees with the conviction that virtually all can, at the minimum, read the newspaper and, moreover, are capable of reading with understanding fairly complex instructions on the care and operation of a new machine. This is truly a most enviable state of affairs as Japanese industry heads into the twenty-first century of high technology. Is it so in the United States?

Japan has achieved total literacy in the kokugo, literally the national (koku) language (go). In the daily school schedule, the subject listed for teaching language is not called Japanese (*nihongo*), but rather kokugo, the national language. This contrasts with U.S. school schedules where the class for teaching English is never listed as "the national language."

The differentiation is not only symbolic but substantial. The Japanese are one of the most homogeneous peoples in the world not only in physical appearances but also in language. There are no large foreign-born or foreign-oriented groups of people living in Japan, such as the Hispanics in the United States who number into the millions, a great many of whom are struggling with the national language of the United States. The litany of smaller minorities within that country, such as the Chinese, Japanese, Vietnamese, Cuban, Korean, Haitian, and Filipino, seems endless. Nearly 20 million Americans speak a language other than English at home. Accordingly some groups in the United States have made a strong case for bilingual curricula in U.S. schools to accommodate these minorities, a controversial issue still unresolved.

In Japan the vernacular or mother tongue of all Japanese is the national language. Even the overwhelming number of Korean-Japanese, the only substantial group of over a half-million within this country that could be considered somewhat foreign oriented, have been assimilated languagewise into Japanese societies. The vast majority of them use the kokugo indistinguishably from the Japanese themselves. Most of their children attend the regular public schools. They pose an insignificant language problem for this country.

When the first grade teacher form Hokkaido to Kyushu begins the initial kokugo lesson, that teacher can assume that every child with rare exception speaks the national language in a manner that can be described as native. This is in sharp contrast to the United States where many first grade children, running into the hundreds of thousands, cannot speak English nativelike when they begin to learn how to read and write it. Indeed, during a visit by this writer to a high school in the greater Los Angeles area, the history teacher explained that 85 to 90 percent of the junior class students could not comprehend with even a fair degree of understanding the U.S. history text. Hence reading assignments could not be made. Outside the classrooms of this school almost all students converse only in Spanish. One could not help wondering if this school was situated in the United States.

In contrast the linguistic homogeneity of the Japanese people, and thus the Japanese worker, gives the Japanese company an advantage over competitors in the United States that have significant numbers of employees who are not functionally literate in English because of their foreign-oriented home environment. Again one cannot help wondering how an American plant manager copes with the graduates of a local high school who are far more familiar with a foreign language than with English. A situation similar to that simply does not occur in Japan.

But the ramifications of a kokugo in Japan and in the United States extend far beyond the issue of linguistic minorities and immigrant children learning the national language. Rather, they relate to the differences in effectiveness of teaching reading and writing of the national language to Japanese children and of teaching English to the average, and particularly below average, child in U.S. schools. In order to better understand the differences and their influence on industrial competitiveness, we must begin by looking into the first grade kokugo, or reading class, in Japan.

Every Japanese child in the public schools throughout the land begins the study of the kokugo on the same day and with textbooks that are quite similar. In other words, they all essentially begin together. This is not only by design but by decree. The Ministry of Education not only fixes the opening school day, it enforces a textbook approval system carefully monitoring the contents of each manuscript submitted for approval. The result is that all first grade textbooks are similar in content and difficulty although they are not identical.

With such a centralized system of educational control over textbook content, a certain degree of similarity in teaching methods is inevitable. The average teacher is naturally influenced by, and a good many dependent upon, the teacher's guide accompanying each textbook. That guide is also carefully scrutinized by the Ministry of Education for approval so that it too conforms to a national standard of reading and writing. Literacy, from the first grade, is thus an affair of state in Japan.

A national standard for teaching the kokugo is of great import. All children regardless of their native ability, their personal needs and interests, or their family background begin together the long and arduous study of Japanese, the kokugo. Individual differences are given little consideration. Every child is expected to keep up with the basic standard set by the Ministry. That standard is demanding right from the beginning, increasing rapidly in complexity as the child moves through the school, as can be seen by the three samples taken from our children's reading texts in the first, fifth, and ninth grades of the local public school (Figures 3.1-3.6).

At the end of compulsory schooling upon completion of the junior high school, virtually every Japanese child, except certain handicapped children, has achieved functional literacy in the kokugo, that is, the ability to read and write sufficiently to carry out responsibilities at home and

よみましょう

にじ

にじが　でました。

のはらの　いけの

上に　みえました。

FIGURE 3.1 The Rainbow (First Grade)

いけに　つきました。

にじは、　もっと

とおくに　みえました。

みんなは、　また

はしって　いきました。

FIGURE 3.2 The Rainbow (First Grade)

念した。

しかし、健康は、日に日におとろえていった。一九三四年五月のある朝、夫人は、つかれたからだをおして研究所へ出かけていったが、午後になると、寒気がして熱が出てきた。

「きょうは、これで帰らせてもらいますよ。」

研究室を出て、庭を横切ろうとした夫人は、ばらの花に目を留めた。立ち止まって、しばらくの間しみじみとながめていたが、ふと、しおれかかった木があるのに気づいて、所員に声をかけた。

「ジョルジュ、お願い。水をやってね。」

それが、キュリー夫人の、研究所での最後のことばになった。

アルプスの高山にある病院で、夫人は、手厚い治りょうと看護を受けたが、一九三四年七月四日、苦難と栄光に満ちたその生がいを終えた。六十六才であった。

（作 新川 和江）

おして

治りょう
看護。
苦難。

FIGURE 3.3 Madame Curie (Fifth Grade)

長い戦争が終わり、平和がやってきた時、キュリー夫人を何よりも喜ばせる大きな
ニュースが伝えられた。祖国ポーランドが、百五十年ぶりで、りっぱに独立したので
ある。だき合って喜び合いたい父や夫が、すでにこの世にいないことはさびしかった
が、キュリー夫人は、久しぶりに雲が晴れたような気持ちで、また研究に精を出した。

生活は、いぜんとして質素であった。設備の整った研究室と、研究に打ちこむ静か
な時間がじゅうぶんにあれば、キュリー夫人はそれで満足であった。ラジウムの権利
を自分のものにすれば、たちまち大金持ちになれるのに、残念がる人もいたが、

「ラジウムは元素です。だれも、それをひとりじめしてはならないのです。」

キュリー夫人は、そう答えて、静かにほほえむだけだった。

キュリー夫人に面会を求めてアメリカからやってきた、ある雑誌記者は、キュリー夫
人が、研究用のラジウムも私有していない話を聞いて感動し、とんで帰ると、さっそ
く「キュリー夫人にラジウムを一グラムおくる運動」を起こした。たちまちのうちに、
十万ドルの金が集まった。

晩年のキュリー夫人は、白内障という目の病気で視力が弱っているにもかかわらず、
自分のそれまでやってきた研究を書き残すために、『放射能』という本を書くことに専

●
久しぶり
いぜんとし

権利

雑誌記者
私有

視力

FIGURE 3.4 Madame Curie (Fifth Grade)

輪をつるし、鉄の刺叉を手にして立っている。そして一匹の「猹」をめがけて、ヤッとばかり突く。すると「猹」は、ひらりと身をかわして、彼のまたをくぐって逃げてしまう。

この少年が閏土である。彼と知りあったとき、わたしもまだ十歳そこそこだった。もう三十年近い昔のことである。そのころは、父もまだ生きていたし、家の暮らしむきも楽で、わたしは坊ちゃんでいられた。ちょうどその年は、わが家が大祭の当番にあたっていた。この祭りの当番というのが、三十何年めにただ一回順番が回ってくるとかで、ごくたいせつな行事だった。正月に、祖先の像を祭るのである。さまざまの供物をささげ、祭器もよく吟味するし、参詣の人も多かったので、祭器を取られぬように番をする必要があった。わたしの家には「忙月」が一人いるだけである。（わたしの郷里では、雇い人は三種類ある。年間通してきまった家で働くのが「長年」、日決めで働くのが「短工」、自分でも耕作するかたわら、年末や節季や年貢集めのときなどに、きまった家へ来て働くのが「忙月」とよばれた）一人では手が足りぬので、彼は自分の息子の閏土に祭器の番をさせたいが、とわたしの父に申し出た。

父はそれを許した。わたしもうれしかった。というのは、かねて閏土という名は耳にしていたし、同じ年ごろなこと、また閏月の生まれで、五行の土が欠けているので父親が閏土と名づけたことも承知していたから。彼は

15　　　　10　　　　5

FIGURE 3.5　Living History (Ninth Grade)

ぼうなんて思やしない。番をするのは、あなぐまや、
はりねずみや、猹さ。月のある晩に、いいかい、ガリガ
リって音がしたら、猹がすいかをかじってるんだ。そう
したら手に刺又を持って、忍び寄って……」

そのときわたしはその「猹」というのがどんなものか、
見当もつかなかった──今でも見当はつかない──が、
ただなんとなく、小犬のような、そして獰猛な動物だと
いう感じがした。

「かみつかない?」

「刺又があるじゃないか。忍び寄って、猹を見つけたら
突くのさ。あん畜生、りこうだから、こっちへ走ってく
るよ。そうしてまたをくぐって逃げてしまうよ。なにし
ろ毛が油みたいに滑っこくて……」

こんなにたくさん珍しいことがあろうなど、それまで
わたしは思ってもみなかった。海には、そのような五色
の貝がらがあるものなのか。すいかには、こんな危険な
経歴があるものなのか。わたしはすいかといえば、果物

屋に売っているものとばかり思っていた。
「おいらとこの砂地では、高潮の時分になると『跳ね魚』
がいっぱい跳ねるよ。みんなかえるみたいな足が二本
あって……」

ああ、閏土の心は神秘の宝庫で、わたしの遊び仲間と
は大違いだ。こんなことはわたしの友だちは何も知って
はいない。閏土が海辺にいるとき、彼らはわたしと同様、
高いへいに囲まれた中庭から四角な空をながめているだ
けなのだ。

惜しくも正月は過ぎて、閏土は家へ帰らねばならな
かった。別れがつらくて、わたしは声をあげて泣いた。
閏土も台所のすみに隠れて、いやがって泣いていたが、
とうとう父親に連れてゆかれた。そのあと、彼は父親に
ことづけて、貝がらを一包みと、美しい鳥の羽を何本か
届けてくれた。わたしも一二度何か贈り物をしたが、
それきり顔を合わす機会はなかった。

今、母の口から彼の名が出たので、このこどものころ

惜

15　　10　　5　　10

FIGURE 3.6　Living History (Ninth Grade)

59

work. In comparison, it is estimated that "about 13% of all 17-year-olds in the U. S. can be considered functionally illiterate. Functional illiteracy among minority youth may run as high as 40 percent."[1]

The eradication of illiteracy is easily described but immensely difficult to achieve, particularly in Japan because the written language is a highly intricate system. It is, in fact, an adaptation that took place hundreds of years ago when the culture of continental China had such a profound influence on Japanese society. In the process the monosyllabic Chinese language using the ideographic script was adapted to the polysyllabic language spoken by the Japanese. The result is one of the most complex forms of a written script devised by man.

Many foreign observers believe that it requires considerably more time and effort to attain functional literacy in the Japanese language than it does to achieve an identical standard in English. And yet, at the end of the junior high school, the Japanese have achieved virtually total literacy, and a great deal more. This cannot be said of students in the United States. Many of the foreign-oriented minorities, and significant numbers of the so-called indigenous or native-speaking population, leave school with inadequate language skills. They add up to a horrendous figure of "some 23,000,000 American adults who are functionally illiterate by the simplest tests of everyday reading and comprehension."[2] This definition usually refers to the inability to read job applications, driver's license examinations, and newspaper want ads, all critical for an independent existence in today's society, let alone for a fulfilling life. According to a U.S. Library of Congress report, the number of illiterates in America is not shrinking, but growing – rising to 2.3 million each year including school dropouts and immigrants.[3]

The Japanese would not tolerate such a situation. Indeed, they have gone far beyond the rudiments of functional literacy for all. Since 94 percent of all teenagers now continue to the high school level,[4] practically all youth are plunged into the most incredibly difficult and fairly advanced stages of the Japanese language. By the time they are graduated, and about 98 percent of high school students complete their studies, they have achieved a mass literacy standard in the most complex form of a kokugo that would simply be considered beyond comprehension in the United States, and in most other countries in the world as well. Unless one has experienced the written forms of Japanese in a daily newspaper, it is impossible to convey adequately the magnitude of the literacy accomplishments of this society.

How do the Japanese maintain this standard? Painfully. Exhaustingly. And yet rather naturally. Over the many years of Japanese history, far too intricate to consider at length, a positive attitude toward the written language has been carefully nurtured not only among the upper classes of Japan; the spill-over into the lower levels of the society was well underway by the time a national school system was inaugurated over a century ago. Ironically the literary tradition in Japan was greatly stimulated by events that transpired during the feudal period of the samurai or warrior fame.

During the Tokugawa Era (1600s to the mid-1800s) the feudal regimes adopted a unique policy aimed at developing the martial and literary arts. Fundamental to the life of the samurai was the systematic pursuit of reading and writing skills. Hence literacy among the privileged classes was widespread, for females as well as for males, when Japan entered the modern era in the mid-nineteenth century. Literacy, however, was not restricted to the upper classes. It had already attained an impressive level among the working classes as the new era dawned in Japan. Its practical value gained appreciation by the townspeople who, without decree or compulsion, increasingly undertook voluntarily to have their children educated. By the time the first national school system was inaugurated in 1872, Japan had already achieved a mass literacy standard few nations, including the most advanced, could equal.

Based on this broad foundation, the Ministry of Education has been setting nationwide standards of reading and writing ever since, which have gained not only grassroots support but also grassroots expectations. This society and government simply take for granted that every child must, repeat, must learn to read and write the kokugo. The resources of the nation are, in a sense, employed in the effort. This attitude toward reading and writing has by now become a national ethic giving the Japanese people a great sentiment of national unity and pride in their language accomplishments. In other words there is an ongoing pervasive, nationwide campaign for total literacy. For all practical purposes, the goal was achieved years ago.

Even though the goal has been attained, the Japanese never relent. The intensification continues. There is always a new generation that must undergo the process. But with total adult literacy, the influence of the famous, and at times infamous, *kyoiku mama*, the educationally minded mother, the pressure on the child to learn to read and write is enormous not only at school, but particularly at home. This factor is of incalculable importance to the economic resurgence of Japan and to its future growth.

Japanese youth, on the whole, cope with the pressures fairly well under the circumstances. It's applied even handedly. The entire school is involved in the process of reading and writing. The teachers take it very seriously. The PTA stresses it. The parents expect it. The older brothers and sisters reinforce it. The Ministry of Education decrees it. Industry depends on it. There is, if you like, a perpetual and self-propelling national campaign for literacy in Japan, although no one but a foreign observer would describe it in that manner. To the Japanese it seems natural. The child, without realizing it, is plunged into this campaign. It is, as it were, difficult for the Japanese child not to learn to read and write the kokugo, a condition unimaginable in the United States.

But there is obviously a great deal more involved. For example, even though the written form of the Japanese language is highly complex, it lends itself especially at the initial stages to a certain degree of systemization. The Ministry of Education has carefully organized the written symbols in as far as possible from the simple to the complex. They are all plotted on a long, long chart, from one to 1850 for the first through ninth grades, and divided precisely according to grade level so that each language teacher, parent, and child knows exactly which characters must be learned each year.

All first grade children under the highly standardized curriculum are initially introduced to the very simple characters such as up 上 and down 下. Each week a few more are added with varying degrees of complexity for a total of 76 during grade one. The process gets underway naturally as every child slowly but inexorably becomes engulfed in the long and tedious process of learning the kokugo.

However, even before Japanese children enter the first grade and begin studying the several thousand characters and the various pronunciations of each necessary to read a daily newspaper, they have already achieved a remarkable level of reading ability with the so-called *kana*. This special set of 48 simplified phonetic symbols is used to represent the 72 fundamental syllables of the Japanese language. For example, Mitaka, the name of our community, is initially learned in school as み た か . Whenever one writes み, it is always mi; た is always ta; and か is always ka. Each kana sound remains constant no matter the order of usage.

Once a Japanese child learns the several dozen simplified kana symbols, he can then read and write every word in his vocabulary, which is, of course, extensive. As he progresses through the system, the kana symbols gradually diminish in use and are replaced by the more intricate Chinese characters so that, for example, once the child learns Mitaka in character form (三 鷹), he no longer uses みたか (Mi ta ka) in kana form. The simplified writing forms are dropped as the complex forms are gradually introduced although kana symbols remain in the adult language forms to diversify verb endings and in other restricted usages as well.

The use of kana at the initial stages of reading and writing the Japanese language gives the language teacher an enormous advantage over his U.S. counterpart. According to one study, most Japanese children acquire the ability to read the kana for the Japanese syllables before entering elementary school.[5] They have either learned the simple figures at home or in the proliferating preschool kindergartens. In other words, most Japanese children can read and write their entire speaking vocabulary in kana form before they enter first grade. In essence, the Japanese first grade teacher begins with a class already well along in reading skills, a condition restricted to a minority of children even in the better schools of the United States.

The first grade textbooks under Ministry of Education approval naturally all begin with stories in kana, as shown previously, with most children already reading them. The simple character for up, 上 or *ue*, then replaces う (u) and え (e), the kana, the transitional form of writing. The adult forms of the language are thus gradually introduced. The process of mass literacy is underway. Nothing will impede its progress.

In contrast, children in the United States learning to read their kokugo in script form based on the alphabetical code are confronted from the very beginning of their schooling with adult word forms. After all, the English word for house, the sound known to every six-year-old child brought up in an English-speaking home, is written in the same form used by adults. A Japanese child, on the other hand, learns house first in the simplified kana, which he already knows by first grade, as いえ (*ie*). Later, as he matures, he will learn the adult written form as 家 (ie). The transition is gradual.

Some scholars argue that the use of these characters or ideographs in themselves give the child learning them an advantage over the child learning to read languages such as English written with the alphabet. Dr. Makita Kiyoshi, the leading researcher on reading problems in Japan and a distinguished psychiatrist, believes that because many characters have hieroglyphic or pictographic origins, they in general convey the meaning they represent. In other words, the character at a glimpse conveys the meaning it represents to the cerebral cortex without any sort of decoding or spelling out process that is necessary with the alphabetical languages.[6]

Aside from the technical aspects of the language far too complex to consider in this context, it is necessary to consider the teaching methods because they are of critical importance in achieving what is accepted as the total literacy of Japan, an achievement few other nations have attained. Teaching methods in the kokugo in the overwhelming number of classrooms in Japan cannot be described as creative, innovative, or imaginative. However, surprisingly, they can be characterized as motivating.

The major success of the Japanese teacher lies in his ability to stimulate children to want to learn to read and write. This is one of the key aspects of Japanese education, which few other nations have been able to accomplish to a similar degree, the ability of the school and the society to motivate the majority of children to want to succeed, to want to learn to read, to want to advance, to want to improve. It is the motivation of aspirations, considered in Chapter 5.

How does the classroom teacher accomplish this mass literacy standard? By sheer diligence, patience, and perseverance. First of all, language teaching in Japan is a continual process of memorization, repetition, drilling, and testing. Memorize, repeat, drill, and test. The higher a student goes in the school, the more the student, every student, memorizes, repeats, drills, and takes tests. There are no secrets in teaching methods in Japan. They are the traditional methods.

To a foreign observer, the kokugo class, especially at the upper school levels, can be deadly dull. That has been the case in the majority of our class visits to dozens and dozens of junior and senior high schools. The typical secondary school teacher, for example, rather faithfully follows the teacher's guide by painfully poring over the lesson sentence by sentence, dissecting it for meaning, analyzing nuances, and repeating the meanings of new characters. A student is called upon to stand and read a passage. He then promptly sits down. Seldom is a discussion conducted. Seldom do the students ask questions. No abstract speculations here. No creative writing assignments in the American sense are given whereby a student's imagination is set loose on paper. Copious notes are taken verbatim. And so the process of mass literacy goes on day in and day out, five and a half days each week, 230 days a year, for 12 rather demanding years.

Even during the first grade, the extensive use of commercially prepared tests is routine. Most teachers employ those accompanying the textbook. Our children's first grade test files, preserved for future reference, bulge with dozens and dozens of reading test papers administered and painstakingly corrected by the teacher. Even though a report to the U.S. National Commission on Excellence in Education claimed that "American school children are the most tested in the world and the least examined,"[7] the author has vastly overstated the case. It sounds clever and was meant to register a point. But children in a number of other countries, notably Japan, are tested far more and examined far more than U.S. children.

The examination grades calculated on a scale of 100 are often posted on the wall for all to see, and to compare. The test scores are also carefully recorded in the teacher's notebook of test results not only to determine the report card grade but to have available to show the parent during the teacher-parent interview. The time and effort required by every language teacher to grade the multitude of tests and compile the results is an extremely heavy burden. Few teachers, nevertheless, would dispute their necessity.

Every child takes the same test together because the class in most instances is handled as one large unit of 40 or more students. Japanese elementary teachers rarely divide their class into reading groups according to ability, a common practice in the United States. Accordingly group teaching methods, such as choral reading in which the entire class reads a passage in unison, are a common practice. Oftentimes the teacher has the whole class read the entire lesson aloud simultaneously. It can be cacophonic. Nevertheless the effect is to involve all students in the total class effort, a mutually supportive approach. This contrasts with many classrooms in the United States where students within the same classroom are divided into groups according to ability, each group working separately with textbooks graded to the level of the group. In Japan the entire reading class works with the same basic text in an effort by the teacher to teach all students at the same pace, a remarkable effort with remarkable results.

Mention must be made of the school's efforts to incorporate the home in the process of learning to read and write. Each week or so the teacher sends home a class letter or announcement for parents. Comments on the progress of the class are included along with the exact pages of the lessons in the kokugo, as well as the other subjects, for the following week. The parents are strongly urged to work with their children at home on the lessons under study at school. Advice by the teacher to the parent concerning precisely how the parent can help at home is included. A good many mothers in this middle-class society, you can be certain, are cooperating.

In this entire process, however, of the greatest significance is the teacher's attitude, which underlies the teaching methods, regardless of the lack of creativity or innovativeness. Seriousness of purpose is perhaps the best way to express that attitude. No matter the sex, the personal problems, the teaching methods, or the area of the country, the Japanese language teachers uniformly exude a sense of seriousness to their students in teaching reading and writing. This is not a casual matter. This is deadly serious business. The teacher's attitude constantly impresses upon the students from the first grade that a major goal in life is to conquer this complex written form of the kokugo. Most children accept the challenge.

Not only is the attitude of the kokugo teacher important; so are his qualifications. There is a vast pool, a surplus, of qualified Japanese language teachers available. After all, the entire student body has undergone a rigorous language course during the 12 years of preuniversity schooling. From this source, a supply of university graduates is always available for the kokugo classrooms of Japan. The language classroom in the United States, in contrast, is apparently staffed by large numbers of unqualified teachers. A report sent to the president cited that "half of all the newly employed English teachers are not qualified to teach their subject."[8] Newsweek reported on a controversial test designed for teachers in the Houston, Texas, area in which 44 percent of the teachers failed the reading test.[9] That simply would not happen in Japan.

Again, no one, most of all the Japanese themselves, would claim total success in the kokugo from the point of view of their own expectations. Far from it. Some Japanese, particularly the better educated among the prewar generation, criticize the schools for reducing the number of characters to be learned in school from the incredible number the well educated of the past mastered. There is no complacency here. And yet, in comparing the literacy standards of this society with those of other nations, and especially of the United States, the performance of the Japanese on a mass level is most impressive. But in reading and writing, the Japanese tend not to compare their standards with ours. Rather they have their own traditional internal literacy standards, and they are, from any international perspective, remarkably high. They are part of the fabric of a national literary ethic.

Every Japanese language teacher can rely on one additional indispensable aid, a crutch, if you will, to instill into his students the seriousness of purpose in learning to read and write. That motivation derives from the constant threat of the end-of-term examination, the famous *kimatsu tesuto*, the high school entrance examination, or the ultimate test, the university entrance examination. Few school systems in the world are so dominated nationwide by an examination mania as are the Japanese schools. Few school systems are so pervasively influenced from top to bottom with examination preparation.

There is ample justification, though, for the Japanese student to be engrossed with the university entrance examinations. The better the university, the more likely is employment with the better company; note, not the better paying company but a more prestigious company; beginning salaries are comparable. Because the so-called lifetime employment system prevails and greatly restricts the possibility of transferring from one company to another, one kumi to another, due to job dissatisfaction, it is critical that the young Japanese candidate make the right choice of work from the beginning. Once in the firm it's too late. The better university thus reduces the risk or rather enhances the chances of successfully making the most important career decision of one's life. That decision is directly related to the results of the entrance examination.

At the heart of every examination is the kokugo test. No one can aspire to passing the high school or university entrance examination without a high level of attainment in the written forms of the Japanese language. The fact that over 35 percent of the cohort, or age group, has achieved that standard to enter the university testifies to the magnitude of success this nation has achieved in its literacy standards.[10]

Add to the 35 percent of the relevant age group who have attained a literacy standard in the kokugo sufficient to pass the university entrance examination the additional 20 percent or so who worked very hard to prepare for the exam but failed and you have over half the student population reaching nearly a university standard in the national language. From any international comparison, this is an outstanding achievement in mass literacy.

It goes much deeper, though. Because the regular language curriculum in the public schools is heavily influenced by requirements of the university entrance examination, and this is especially so at the high school level reached by about 95 percent of all students, virtually the entire student population is, in a sense, undergoing a literacy program six days a week designed to prepare every child to enter the university. How absurd! No other nation has set that kind of a literacy goal for its public schools.

Can the Japanese do it? No, of course not. All high school students are certainly not capable of university-level study. However, what the Japanese have achieved in the process is an extremely high literacy standard, perhaps the highest in the world, of virtually all of its students. Even those students who didn't take the university examination and went straight to work upon high school graduation have achieved an impressively high standard of reading and writing. Consequently the mass of ordinary Japanese factory workers can be characterized as educated, as any employer will testify. Is it so in America?

The Japanese blue-collar worker who runs the lathes, the drill presses, the fork lifts, and the increasingly advanced instruments has in fact gone through a reading and writing program in the kokugo heavily influenced by the university entrance examination. And even though he may not have achieved the level his high school teacher felt sufficient to recommend him to take the university entrance examination, he has achieved a considerably higher literacy standard than his counterpart in the United States who has not entered the university. Man to man, woman to woman, the shop floor worker, even the garbage collector, of Japan is one of the most literate, if not the most literate worker, in the world today.

Inevitably, in any national school system so dominated by the university entrance examination, with its emphasis on reading and writing, along with mathematics and English, there are certain distortions. And the Japanese school system is encountering them with increasing frequency in its unrelenting campaign to raise the mass literacy and numerary standards to unprecedented levels. The fallout effect is evidenced by the increasing incidents of classroom unruliness, an indictment of the Japanese school to which critics refer with justification.

During the early 1980s, the Japanese public read with increasing frequency in the national dailies about cases of violent acts conducted by a disgruntled student or a small group of them in various secondary schools, usually near final examination time at year's end. The act took the form of the destruction of school property, an attack on a teacher, or incidents against fellow students. In many of these cases the perpetrators were those students who received low grades, usually in the kokugo and/or mathematics. The student who is falling behind the relentless pace of the classroom can become disorderly, drop out, or continue in school and be graduated with lower grades.

Caution is necessary to appreciate the Japanese scene concerning the reporting of school disturbances. When an act of school violence occurs, or a teenage suicide takes place anywhere in the nation, the story may be carried in the major national newspapers and even reported on nationwide television. When other scattered incidents of school violence or, increasingly, so-called bullying are given national publicity, the public becomes alarmed. The schools come under heavy criticism. School discipline is obviously weakening. The schools are deteriorating.

But even with school indiscipline, the Japanese situation is unique. The level of schooling most affected by the problem is not the high school, but the junior high school. And much of that is attributed to the pervasive influence the high school entrance examination exerts on the junior high school curricula. With compulsory education ending at the junior high school level, every student in the land faces the academic demands of the high school entrance examination.

For example, one junior high school in Tokyo became the focus of attention of the entire nation for about six weeks during a recent academic year. The cause célèbre involved an incident in which a teacher in retaliation attacked a student who had been harassing this particular teacher for some time. The injury to the student apparently was not serious. Nevertheless conditions at that school were investigated from every possible angle by the news media and government officials. To many Japanese who followed it closely on nationwide TV and in the popular press, that school became symbolic of deteriorating school conditions.

Even though conditions at the school were certainly bad in the context of Japanese education, in comparison to conditions in similar inner schools of many American cities, they would be viewed in an entirely different light. If the Washington *Post* reported major incidents of classroom violence from throughout the country, space for news and advertisements would be sharply reduced or, perhaps, eliminated. Even the Los Angeles *Times* could not fully report school violence within California. The California State Department of Education reported that "two dozen California school teachers were assaulted everyday, usually by their students," and that "each day an average of 215 California youngsters were attacked while on public school grounds."[11] An episode of serious school violence in a high school in Louisville, Kentucky, would certainly not reach the front pages of the New York *Times*. Nor is it likely that the case of a teacher attacking a student in a Houston secondary school in retaliation for abuse would be covered nationally on the 6:30 nightly TV news. In Japan, both could easily be reported in the national press and on television. Such is the nature of that society. It also reflects the public's deep interest and concern for education.

Even though the incidents of school violence, bullying, and, to a lesser extent, school vandalism at the secondary level have become an annual national issue near final examination time, the number and severity of them compared with conditions in the United States remain relatively small. For example, a government report for the president of the United States, entitled "Chaos in the Classroom: Enemy of Education," stated that the cost of school vandalism in the United States each year exceeds spending for textbooks. Fortunately for the Japanese, they do not come near that dismal record. Nevertheless, as with literacy standards, the Japanese wisely tend not to compare their educational problems with those of other nations. Rather, they have set their own internal standards for comparison. From this perspective, the problem of school discipline has come to the fore in part because the Japanese are not accustomed to encountering such problems in the school, even in schools in a massive metropolis like Tokyo or Osaka.

Another factor underlies the increasing number of incidents of school violence in Japanese secondary schools. In the past, teenagers less inclined toward academic study, many coming from lower income households, quit school at age 14 or 15 to enter fulltime employment. The secondary school historically catered to those who were seeking university entrance and who viewed the secondary schools as a means of preparation for the university. This clientele had a distinct purpose in continuing in secondary schools to age 18; those who were not so inclined dropped out. The Japanese secondary schools simply did not have potentially disruptive students in the past.

During the late 1970s, the trend toward secondary education to 18 for all became pronounced so that today more than 90 percent of the student population completes high school, probably the highest percentage in the world. The result is that the Japanese secondary school, with its major emphasis on academic preparation for university entrance, must deal with older and larger teenagers who are less academically oriented and who in the past dropped out at the age of 14 or 15 to enter the factory. It is inevitable that school indiscipline would increase under these circumstances.

Even though school discipline has become a problem for the Japanese, it is far less of a problem than in U.S. schools. Moreover, if you consider that only 75 percent of U.S. secondary students complete high school, and less than 60 percent in New York City,[12] for example, which means that quite frankly many of the potential teenage troublemakers in U.S. society leave the school well before graduation thereby easing the discipline burden of the school, the situation in Japan has a different perspective. Can one imagine how much more serious school discipline in America, already one of its most serious problems, would be if the 25 percent who drop out remained in school? If U.S. secondary school principals had to deal with nearly 95 percent of all teenagers remaining in school until graduation, as in Japan, the magnitude of school violence could potentially be too great to comprehend.

The result is that nearly all Japanese teenagers remain in school for 12 years and are exposed to the more advanced levels of reading and writing the kokugo, the Japanese language. The demands for language proficiency are very great so that even the less academically oriented student must undergo the rigorous curricula set by the Ministry of Education for the nation at large. The result even with these students is a fairly literate graduate ready for work. In contrast, the 25 percent of U.S. teenagers who drop out before graduation feed the huge pool of 23 million functionally illiterate adults and are, in the main, not ready for meaningful employment. Chronically unemployed, they are a burden to the economy.

Even though many potentially disruptive students quit the U.S. high school long before graduation, Americans have almost come to expect student violence in many of our big city schools. And Americans rarely attribute the school violence, which takes on endemic proportions in some of our inner city schools, to the rigorous academic demands of the classroom. In other words, what the Japanese consider a major problem of school violence, the Americans, in fact, would be relieved to contend with. The Japanese have yet to encounter the really grave problems of student indiscipline, a result of the widespread use of drugs, alcoholism, or immoral behavior, the United States is struggling with. Even so, a national effort is underway in this country to curtail school violence before it gets out of hand.

But to return more directly to the issue of the Japanese language itself, other related factors contribute to the success of Japanese industry. For example, there is an extraordinary degree of hand dexterity required in writing the characters. To illustrate, all of the thousands of children who live in our city of Mitaka must learn to write 三 鷹 (Mitaka) as part of their address. And every local first grade child except the handicapped will learn first to recognize it. It must be committed to memory, along with 76 characters required as a minimum by the Ministry's curriculum for all first graders. The number of required characters increases to nearly 2,000 by the end of junior high school.

The taka (鷹) of Mitaka, which literally means hawk, three (三) hawks in this case, consists of 24 strokes. Every stroke must be in its proper place, or the character just isn't taka. There is also a specified order in writing the 24 strokes. The child must repeat this order over and over again until it is correct. And these 24 strokes must not only be written in the proper order but the entire character must fit within a rather small block by the third grade. The exercise notebook consists of row after row of blocks for each character (Figure 3.7).

In order to write each character with its varied number of strokes and stroke order ranging from one to 24 or more, each one in the same size box and with a certain degree of balance, a very high standard of manual dexterity is required by every Japanese child. Writing Japanese is akin to an art. Each character is viewed, in fact, as a work of art. Each child literally becomes a practicing artist.

The written form of the Japanese language is taught not just as a means of communication but as an art form. Every elementary school student as part of the regular curriculum learns to write his language not just with a pencil but with a brush in a class called *shuji*, or calligraphy. Every child through junior high school must take regular classes in shuji, that is, drawing the characters with an artist's brush. Fundamental to learning the written Japanese language, then, is the practice of literally drawing it as an artist would a picture.

In our own community of Mitaka, the city schools, in fact, hold an annual exhibition of children's writing (shuji). Each teacher at each grade level conducts a lesson in which a writing specimen with just one or two characters is written. The teacher then selects the best "pictures" to be submitted to the city officials for display in the city hall. It's quite an honor for a first grade child to have his writing specimen on display at the city hall.

Every elementary school in Japan will also have displayed somewhere in the kumi's room, or in the hallway outside each room, an exhibition including every child's writing specimen, a fairly good-sized brush work of a character such as "light" (光) in the fourth grade or

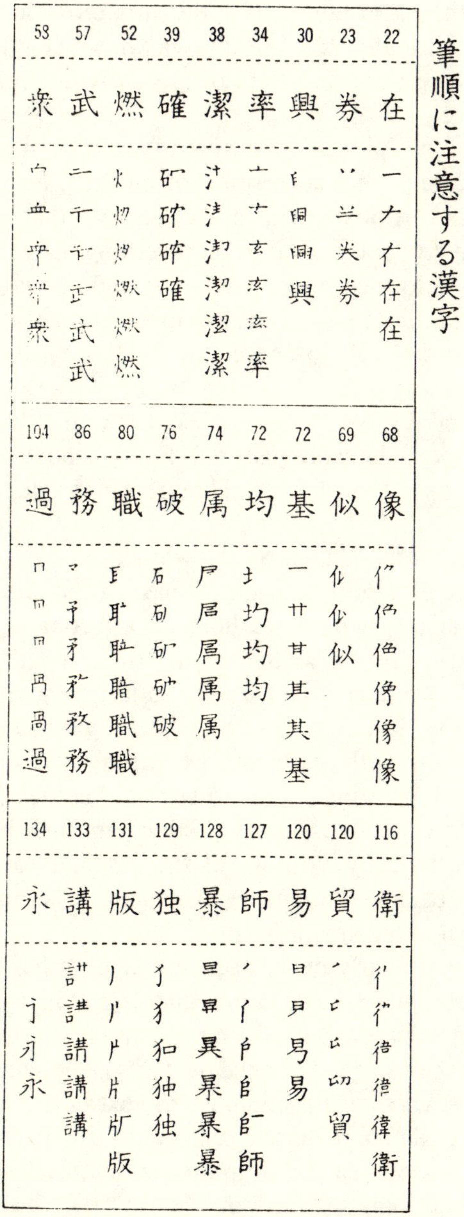

筆順に注意する漢字

53	57	52	39	38	34	30	23	22
衆	武	燃	確	潔	率	興	券	在

104	86	80	76	74	72	72	69	68
過	務	職	破	属	均	基	似	像

134	133	131	129	128	127	120	120	116
永	講	版	独	暴	師	易	貿	衛

FIGURE 3.7 Third Grade

73

"snow" (雪) in the sixth grade. Close scrutiny may show a small mark at the bottom of certain strokes (大). This is to notify the student that he did not flatten out the brush sufficiently as he tailed off or withdrew the brush from the paper completing the stroke. A circle (大) around another stroke indicates the withdrawal has been made properly, indicative of the scrupulous attention given to learning to write the Japanese language.

The quality of the "picture" of a word in every kumi exhibition ranges from highly artistic with a keen sense of balance, form, and shape, to eratic and disproportionate. However, the fact that every child has participated in an art contest, as it were, involving the written form of his language instills into the child a unique attitude toward his language. Many Japanese children gain a feeling of deep respect for the written word, an attitude difficult to appreciate by those who write with the alphabet.

Figures 3.8 and 3.9 are two examples of a writing lesson taken from the walls of our local elementary school. Every school will display each child's writing in such a manner. The teacher graded these samples accordingly.

In what home in the United States would you have hanging on the livingroom wall a picture beautifully framed of the one word "respect" (尊敬)? In what city would we hold an art contest for children in which every entry was the written word "light" (光)? In what school newspaper would we devote half a page to large drawings of the word "sky" (空)? In what U.S. city would people pay, sometimes dearly, to enter an exhibition gallery to admire highly valued works of art exquisitely framed featuring one word such as "peace" (平和)? In what community would you witness many children enrolling in private classes to learn how to artistically write words such as "harmony" (和)? Such is the artistic approach to the Japanese language. It is fundamental to the ongoing campaign of literacy in Japan.

This means that nearly every Japanese worker has experienced 12 years of, as it were, manual arts in the schools, not in a shop class but in the daily language classes. Both the female and male students have thus achieved an advanced stage of manual dexterity. And within this category are those workers who never accomplish the extremely high demands of balance or shape of the more intricate characters. But the fact that virtually every adult can write even the simple *kanji* character for an everyday word such as "shopping" (買物) or "house" (家) or "test" (試験), each stroke in the proper order in a tiny space means that essentially all

Japanese workers have accomplished a fairly high degree of precision in the manipulative skills.

These are the supple hands that craft the fine cameras, the robots, and the VTRs flooding the world's markets. These are the hands manipulating the computers and the precision machine tools producing lasers, optical fibers, and even grand pianos in increasing numbers. And these are the hands designing the shiny motorcycles and video games as well. They have all, to a man and woman, been carefully and painstakingly trained to use their hands adroitly, some better than others, of course. This skill is fundamental in the process of producing the most literate, and certainly some of the most skillful, workers in the world.

This precisionlike systematic approach to teaching not just the kokugo, but all other subjects, is characteristic of the Japanese school. It is the minute attention to detail, to order, to shape, to balance that every Japanese worker has undergone as a student during everyday of the long school day, the long school week, and the long school year. The influence of the Japanese language lessons obviously extends far beyond the classroom achievements in teaching reading and writing.

Other elements within the society that strengthen and reinforce the school's efforts at maintaining total literacy are worthy of mention. For example, several of the national daily newspapers publish a daily *Elementary School Newspaper* and a weekly *Junior High School Newspaper*. These editions are delivered to the home, not the school, every morning along with the regular daily paper throughout the land on a regular subscription basis. These newspapers are highly professional publications using the full facilities of the parent company. The articles are carefully prepared to meet the interests of the school level concerned. A typical feature article of the day will cover a special event in a particular school somewhere in the nation. Several front page articles are geared for the higher elementary school grades. Several are designed for first graders.

The equivalent situation would have the New York *Times* publishing a daily edition for elementary school students to be distributed throughout the United States delivered to the doorstep through subscription. The main features would cover school events in towns in Georgia, Oregon, Texas, and other states covered by their local reporters. And each day certain articles would be written for first and second graders. In addition to an eight-page weekend edition for elementary school students, the *Times* would publish a slick 12-page junior high edition for nationwide distribution. Its competitor, the *Wall Street Journal*, would do the same.

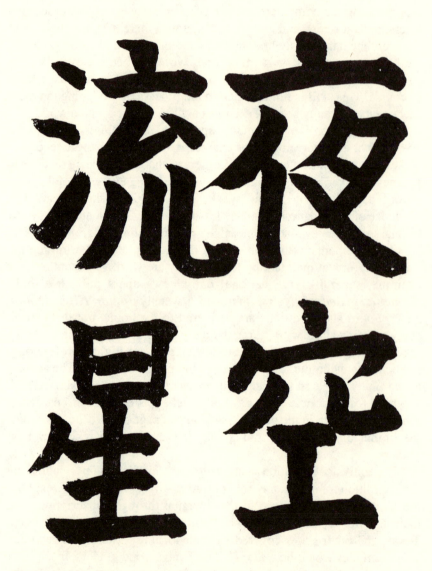

FIGURE 3.8 Falling Star (Sixth Grade Calligraphy, Well Done)

FIGURE 3.9 Falling Star (Sixth Grade Calligraphy, Average)

The literacy achievements of Japan from top to bottom, within the school and out, are clearly one of the most impressive accomplishments of this society. Another way of appreciating the success of the literacy program in Japan is to consider the degree of reading disabilities, often referred to as dyslexia in U.S. studies. Dyslexia has become a major topic of research among U.S. scholars and teachers in the postwar era as they attempt to determine the causes of the high number of reading disabilities among children in the United States.

The classic work with Japanese children has been conducted by Dr. Makita Kiyoshi, mentioned previously, from the Department of Neuropsychiatry, Tokai University School of Medicine. His research results have been presented at international forums for the past 20 years. One of the earlier reports, "The Rarity of Reading Disability in Japanese Children" carried in the *American Journal of Orthopsychiatry*, set the tone for all of his subsequent work.

Dr. Makita sums up his research results accordingly.

> While dyslexia, reading disability, reading difficulty, reading retardation, or whatever you prefer to call it comprises a formidable portion of child psychiatric practice in the Western countries, its incidence in Japan is so rare that specialists in Japan do not get referrals in the daily practice of child psychiatry.

In fact, none had been brought to his attention since he started his children's psychiatric service at the university hospital a decade previously. This was "quite an astounding difference" from his experience in the United States.

In a study to determine the degree of reading disability among Japanese children, Dr. Makita surveyed teachers on the number of their pupils who had difficulties in learning to read the kokugo. Out of approximately 10,000 children covered in the project, only 0.98 percent had reading difficulties of varying degrees. Dr. Makita concluded that "This is an extremely small incidence when compared to that reported in the foremost Western countries."[13] He was, of course, particularly referring to the United States.

Dr. Makita's research has come under heavy criticism over the years by U.S. reading experts who cast doubt on the rarity of reading disabilities among Japanese children. These specialists have become so accustomed to reading disabilities in their schools that it seems inconceivable that Japanese schools could not be afflicted with the same malady. This writer, unknowingly at the time, confirmed Dr. Makita's conclusions in an article entitled "Why Noriko Can Read: Some Hints for Johnny," published in an American professional journal.[14] The paper dealt with how Noriko Susan, the author's daughter who, along with all of her classmates in the neighborhood elementary school, competently learned to read and write Japanese. The thesis was roundly criticized in a rebuttal piece by U.S. reading specialists.

A visit to any standard elementary school in Japan, in comparison with a similar school in the United States in which all children from the neighborhood attend common classes, will confirm Dr. Makita's research conclusions. The rapidity with which virtually every child in the class reads from the Japanese textbook stands in contrast to the substantial number of children in the typical U.S. classroom who stumble over words, losing the sense of the passage in the process. In the American hometown of this writer, the reading specialist confirmed that 25 percent of all elementary children are considered remedial, that is, their reading level is two or more years below the standard. This community of 15,000 thus finds it necessary to employ with federal assistance a total of four remedial reading teachers for the system, a rather common ratio. Obviously one of the major academic problems of the average elementary school teacher in many public schools in the United States concerns reading disabilities. As a former public school teacher in the United States, this writer can attest to that problem.

The Japanese public school has been able to achieve virtual total literacy of its graduates, a claim few other nations, if any, can make. To the U.S. teacher, such a condition borders on the unreal. In consequence Japanese companies ranging across the board from computers to bicycles have a built-in advantage with their highly literate work force drilled in the basics of reading, writing, and mathematics. This advantage in the flexibility of the literate worker can only become pronounced as industrial production becomes more directed toward high technology, as tertiary industries replace smokestack industries, and as the white-collar worker displaces the blue-collar worker in our technologically oriented societies. The literacy standards of Japan's schools are fundamental to the competitiveness of Japan's industry. Is it not so in the United States as well?

4

THE COMPETENT WORKER
Sugaku: Mathematics

Competent: able; having sufficient power, skill, or resources to accomplish an object.

– Webster

The emergence of Japan in the postwar era as a super economic power can be attributed to a very great extent to the competency of the domestic work force right down to the shop floor level. In "having sufficient power, skill, or resources to accomplish an object," that is, of manufacturing a product that competes most successfully on international markets, the very basis for Japan's survival, the Japanese worker is demonstrably outstanding in the world today. The justification for that description is, of course, at the global market place itself.

As modern industrial societies become increasingly complex and sophisticated technologically, the necessity of mathematics becomes more and more prominent. The very foundation of the new era in high technology is imbedded firmly in mathematics. Thus the level of mathematical standards of every nation involved in the international competition to develop more advanced products such as the fifth generation computer becomes of enormous consequence. It is precisely in mathematics that the average Japanese worker as well as the engineer is so well prepared in school and so competent in the factory.

Second only to kokugo (Japanese), then, comes the importance of sugaku (mathematics) in the Japanese school curriculum. The results are similar. The Japanese school maintains one of the highest, if not the highest, mass standard of mathematics in the world today. Again, as in reading and writing standards, one cannot fully comprehend the magnitude of the mathematical achievements of this nation unless observed firsthand.

Curiously, there has developed in this country what could be described as a powerful "mathematics lobby." This is not an organized association of mathematics teachers that lobbies for mathematics legislation in the usual political sense. That isn't necessary. Rather, it represents the enormous influence that mathematics exerts in the school curriculum, in the examinations, on educational radio and TV, and in Japanese society in general.

It is simply taken for granted in this country that every child must attain at the very minimum "functional mathematics," that is, the ability to perform mathematical calculations in order to accomplish requirements successfully at home or work. Most go far beyond that. The parent expects the school to accomplish this goal. The teacher sets out resolutely to attain it. And the government, in effect, as in reading and writing, decrees it with its nationwide curriculum.

The Ministry of Education in approving textbooks for the public schools has very carefully systematized the teaching of mathematics into a step-by-step procedure. Each step is carefully laid out and elaborated in great detail in the teacher's guide accompanying the textbooks. Although there are some variations among the textbooks, they are all basically organized in the same step-by-step procedure from the simple to the complex, in exactly the same manner as the Japanese language texts. The consequences are similar.

As in the language classes, most teachers follow rather closely the mathematics teaching guide accompanying the textbook. This certainly does not mean that each third grade kumi in a given school is exactly on the same page or problem as the others, all following along in lock step formation. Far from it. If you walk down the hall from kumi to kumi, grade to grade, you find teachers at each level handling the lesson somewhat differently. However, if you have in hand a copy of the teacher's guide available only from the publisher, you will soon become aware that virtually all teachers at each grade level are covering the same unit, and most are using the sample problems as well as the methods of calculation included in the guide. In addition many math teachers will employ the unit tests provided by the textbook publishing company.

The result is that essentially every child in the nation is exposed to a very similar approach to learning basic mathematical functions. Every child is carefully and painstakingly led through the same precise step-by-step procedure in learning to divide with a two-digit divisor, for example, or to multiply by a fraction. The teacher's guides, which the Ministry of Education considers as a national guideline and therefore expects the classroom teacher to follow, are themselves carefully prepared so that the teacher can readily follow each step in the teaching process, for example, for calculating the area of a rectangle.

One of the most important factors concerning the heavy use of, or in some cases dependency upon, the teacher's guide in the Japanese classroom is that even in the hands of poor teachers, most students still learn the basics. This is an extremely critical point because, quite frankly, many math teachers here and throughout the world, even those who are competent in mathematics, are not stimulating teachers. The majority are not examples of what we would characterize as good teachers in the sense of being able to present an interesting and challenging 40-minute lesson in mathematics day in and day out. Nevertheless, in spite of any given Japanese teacher's mediocre teaching ability (and the Japanese have no dearth of them), he or she can still be effective presenting basic mathematical processes and understandings by following the carefully structured teacher's guide, with constant drilling reinforced with frequent testing.

Many critics, particularly in the U.S. educational world, frown upon teacher dependency on teacher's guides on the grounds that the creativity, imagination, and innovativeness of the classroom teacher are sacrificed through the slavish use of the teacher's guide, which itself is often a dreary document. The U.S. elementary teacher covering the basic mathematical functions is expected, to some degree, to use the teacher's edition of the textbook as reference. But to be dependent upon them by carefully following their directions with sample problems and precise step-by-step methods of calculation smacks of instruction rather than teaching.

Who can argue with that? A great deal of what happens in a Japanese mathematics class can be classified as instruction rather than teaching; instruction means giving directions whereas teaching implies the development of the thinking process, to put it crudely. Take, for example, the multiplication table, which most Japanese children learn by the end of the second grade, and usually the slower learners have it no later than the third grade. The Japanese children learn it rhythmically in rote-manner. They repeat it over and over again as a chant until everyone gets it.

Our eldest child, when she was in the local second grade, chanted the multiplication table at school, on the way to and from school, and at home until she had it completely memorized. At that stage, the teacher placed a star behind her name on the list posted on the wall for all to see. By the end of the year the roster was completed. Even today, when she takes a university course in mathematics in English, her mother tongue, she invariably works out problems involving multiplication using the Japanese chant. She had, perhaps through "instruction," learned the basics, but they have never been forgotten.

Whether it's instruction or teaching, and of course it's some combination of the two, one gains the impression that every mathematics teacher in Japan confidently believes that he or she forms an integral part of the mathematics lobby, whose predominant purpose in life is to maintain the high standards of the subject. Because of the unique role mathematics has come to occupy in the scheme of education in Japan, the mathematics teacher commands a degree of respect that few other teachers enjoy. The typical math teacher is determined to preserve that prestigious status to which the subject has long been accustomed.

A certain attitude, an aura if you will, surrounds the Japanese mathematics class that most students come to understand and accept. Admittedly the Japanese themselves would not describe it that way. But to this foreign observer, a former U.S. public school teacher, the special role of mathematics stands out conspicuously in the scheme of education in this country. It means that the vast majority of Japanese students are willing to bear laboriously with seemingly infinite patience the interminable repetition, drill, and testing that mathematics teaching in Japanese schools entails. The mathematics classes especially at the junior and senior high schools are, from U.S. perspective, deadly repetitious but also, significantly, deadly serious. One cannot help marveling that classroom indiscipline isn't far greater in many of the math classes.

The initial attitudes toward mathematics in every country are formed in the elementary school. And it is at this level where the Japanese teacher excels in instilling a positive attitude toward, or at least a healthy respect for, mathematics. The first factor of critical importance about elementary school mathematics in Japan is that the teacher, entrusted with all subjects at this level and with over 40 students per kumi, is competent in basic mathematics regardless of his or her skills in the art of teaching. After all, every elementary school teacher went through the regular school curriculum completing a very rigorous course in mathematics in the process. Consequently, every public school elementary teacher with very few exceptions is proficient in elementary school mathematics, and a great deal more. According to many reports, this is apparently not the case in the United States.

Another important factor concerns the role of male teachers in Japanese schools. In particular men teachers have traditionally played a major role in elementary education in this country both as teachers and administrators. It was only about 1970 that women teachers first outnumbered men at the elementary school level. Even today 44 percent of all elementary teachers are male. Female elementary school principals and head teachers are few. Of a total of 23,693 principals, only 509 (2 percent) are women; of 24,413 head teachers, 888 (3.5 percent) positions are held by women. At the junior high school level, 67 percent of all teachers are male. Out of 9,920 schools, 19 are administered by women.[1]

The many male teachers and administrators provide a special impetus to mathematics teaching in the school. It is taken for granted that men teachers are not only competent in mathematics but that they also enjoy teaching the subject. Most male elementary teachers respond accordingly by treating mathematics as a special subject that requires particular attention and deserves favored treatment. As they get out the textbook to begin the lesson, they exude a certain positive attitude which students cannot fail to notice. The male principal confirms this positive attitude at every opportunity. The mathematics lobby is at work right from the elementary school level onward.

In the United States, we are told, there exists a severe shortage of teachers qualified to teach mathematics at every grade level. This is particularly so among males. One of the major reasons for this condition, which is growing more acute with each academic year, concerns the sharp differences in salaries for mathematics majors entering industry and for those entering teaching. In some areas to attract mathematics majors, industry pays starting salaries nearly double that of teaching. It actually becomes a hardship for the male mathematics graduate throughout America to choose the meager compensation of a teaching career.

The consequences are predictable. With U.S. industry attracting the bulk of the mathematics graduates, the schools too often pick up the leftovers. Or, the local school must turn to the unqualified teacher to fill the mathematics classroom. It's estimated that half of all newly employed mathematics teachers in the United States are not qualified to teach the subject.[2] The charge is also made that a good many elementary teachers, although no one really knows the extent, are not qualified to teach mathematics.

In a report to the National Institute of Education, the situation concerning mathematics teachers in the United States was summed up succinctly:

> Even as the country is facing a need for citizens with ever more sophisticated mathematics skills, there is a growing shortage of qualified mathematics teachers. Colleges are turning out fewer and fewer graduates certified to teach mathematics, and those already in the classroom are leaving in record numbers for positions in business and industry.[3]

The situation in Japan is diametrically opposite. There is no shortage of qualified mathematics teachers in the classrooms at any level. In fact the universities are graduating increasing numbers of mathematics majors each year. Nor does Japanese industry steer the new mathematics teachers away from the classroom by dangling attractive salaries before them. Beginning teachers' salaries remain competitive with industry. For example, in a recent year, new mathematics teachers in Tokyo entered the classroom at an initial salary of 177 thousand yen ($737) a month, factoring in the annual bonuses. At the same time, Hitachi, one of the leading firms in the electronics industry, paid a beginning monthly salary of 183 thousand yen ($762) including bonuses to its newly graduated engineers.[4] Although starting salaries have been raised annually, the rate of increase has been modest in both categories.

These initial salaries, both industry and teaching, should be evaluated from an overall perspective of the local economy. Even though a beginning teacher's salary is as attractive as that of an electrical engineer, neither income will go very far particularly in the great cities of Japan. For example, in order for either the math teacher or the engineer to own a small ordinary private house on a small parcel of land within the Tokyo area, he will have to finance an investment equal to about a quarter of a million dollars. And yet the schools produce math majors in increasing numbers to fill both the needs of the classroom and the factory.

Not only is teaching competitive with private industry in beginning salaries; it is rare for experienced male mathematics teachers to leave the teaching profession in order to enter industrial engineering or some other technical position within the industrial world. The tradition of remaining with one employer until retirement includes teaching as well as private industry. It would also be quite difficult for a middle-aged math teacher, regardless of his experience and level of mastery, to leave teaching and try to fit into a commercial firm. An older "outsider" joining the company, a different kumi, would have an arduous feat to carry out. Few classroom teachers at any age would attempt it. Consequently the Japanese school finds itself in a competitive position vis-à-vis private industry for recruiting the mathematics graduate and in retaining experienced classroom math teachers. From all reports, this condition is contrary to the U.S. scene.

This should in no way imply that the average female elementary teacher is incompetent or deficient in mathematics, incapable of effectively teaching the subject at this level. Women teachers are quite competent and effective, all the more so because of the officially approved teacher's manual, as described above, which carefully prescribes each lesson step-by-step with examples for drills, and because of the widespread use of unit examinations commercially prepared by the textbook publisher. The implication here is that the typical female elementary school teacher does not pay quite the same attention to mathematics as does her male counterpart, although she must treat the subject with great attention. Consequently, there is a remarkably high mass standard of mathematics in Japanese schools regardless of the gender of the teacher.

As in language teaching, there are no secrets underlying the standards of mathematics in Japanese schools. Through a self-propelling momentum built up through the ages, a positive attitude toward the subject of mathematics and the willingness on the part of the teachers and students alike to devote many, many hours to the drills and tests underlie the achievements. It is a rather drudging process requiring a great deal of patience and perseverance. And supporting the process at home stands literally an army of parents who encourage the child to exert every effort to study mathematics in order to pass the examination. The mathematics lobby is at work in the home as well as in the school.

However, several unique practices employed in all Japanese schools in the mathematics classroom are worth noting. The first is the practice, beginning in grade one, of working out problems without resort to paper and pencil, that is, in your head. The constant drilling of addition, subtraction, multiplication, and division of problems mentally, without writing them down, is a set requirement in mathematics. For example, every child is taught to learn mathematics by mentally calculating drills such as the following taken from a standard second and third grade textbook (Figures 4.1 and 4.2). Obviously the bright students find these problems fairly easy, but for the slower student, such abstract thought processes are quite demanding. How many U.S. third graders can readily calculate in their head 830 minus 320? Perhaps the more appropriate question is how many of them are ever required to calculate such a problem in their arithmetic classes?

Another standard procedure reinforcing the ability to visualize mathematical concepts is the use of the abacus, introduced in public schools at the third grade level. (Figures 4.3 and 4.4). Children are required to buy one and practice its use. They can even practice on it at home every evening at six o'clock when a nationwide radio program is broadcast in which young people manipulate the abacus to the well-known voice of a narrator who reads out long numbers in a religiouslike chant for grade school students. The ancient abacus, a method of adding and subtracting by visually displaying the process of computation with beads, sharpens the child's sense of mental calculation. Indeed, many Japanese adults and students, when an abacus or a calculator is not available, mentally add and subtract long numbers by actually manipulating their fingers as if they were using an abacus. Although the Japanese dominate the international market for modern automatic calculators, they have all been taught how to calculate on one of the simplest devices designed by man.

The results of this concerted effort are naturally not uniform. Although the mass standards are among the highest, if not the highest, in the world today, some students inevitably do badly in the subject, and many of these acquire a certain degree of apprehension or even dislike toward mathematics. But what cannot be disputed is that even those within this group, which in comparison to its U.S. counterpart is remarkably small, have attained a minimum standard in basic mathematical computation enabling them to accomplish successfully essential work requirements in the Japanese labor force. Even these workers are not a drag on the productivity of a company, or the society for that matter. And even many, if not most, of them have a certain degree of respect for and appreciation of mathematics.

Again, as with the kokugo, the sugaku teacher in a Japanese school always has at his or her side the great motivating influence of the examinations, ultimately the university entrance examination. Mathematics is one of its major pillars. Critics of Japanese education cast

けいざんれんしゅう・2

あんざんで しましょう。

❶ 70＋6　23＋4　3＋25　2＋54

39＋1　67＋3　6＋84　8＋92

19＋7　43＋9　85＋8　77＋6

6＋45　7＋56　9＋32　2＋69

❷ 69－9　25－3　47－5　58－4

30－6　80－7　70－5　100－2

21－5　33－9　52－4　45－7

93－4　54－6　73－8　82－5

❸ 7＋7＋7　　　6＋8－9

20－3＋6　　　23－7－8

FIGURE 4.1 Second Grade Calculation Exercises (Calculate in your head)

89

計算れんしゅう•2

❶ あん算でしましょう。

13+52	51+24	78−43	96−45
26+64	37+48	90−36	74−56
57+25	46+39	62−27	84−28
35+65	83+17	100−47	100−81
240+430	380+540	830−320	940−370

FIGURE 4.2 Third Grade Calculation Exercises (Calculate in your head)

doubt on the ability of teachers to achieve such high mathematical standards without the threat of the entrance examination hovering ever so closely over the class. This is, to be sure, a vital factor. The examination is ever present, and its requirements exert a pervasive influence down to the elementary school level.

So great are the demands in mathematics for high school and university examination preparation that many elementary, junior, and senior high school students go beyond the requirements of the school by enrolling in the ubiquitous *yobiko* and *juku*, which deserve our attention. The yobiko, the amorphous system of commercially operated, profit-making preparatory schools, and the juku, local private classes, attract hundreds of thousands of youth eager to improve their chances of passing the entrance examinations either to the high school or university. The proliferation of this profitable industry has become one of the most bewildering developments in postwar Japanese education. It represents an added, although indeterminable, dimension to the already demanding school curriculum. Mathematics, along with Japanese, is one of the basic attractions of this extracurricular system.

たし算とひき算

①　そろばんのたし算やひき算では，左のけたから右へじゅんに計算します。

621＋357 の計算

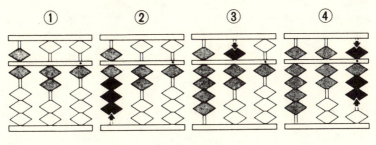

①　②　③　④

❶　652＋237　　591＋405　　732＋216

　　120＋826　　311＋672　　631＋356

978－357 の計算

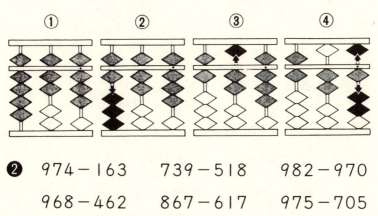

①　②　③　④

❷　974－163　　739－518　　982－970

　　968－462　　867－617　　975－705

FIGURE 4.3 Third Grade Textbook

たまをおくには，ひとさしゆびとおやゆびをつか
います。

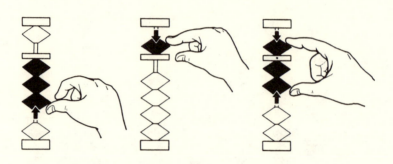

たまをはらうには，ひとさしゆびをつかいます。

7をはらうとき
は，(1)一だまを2
こはらってから，
(2)五だまをはら
います。

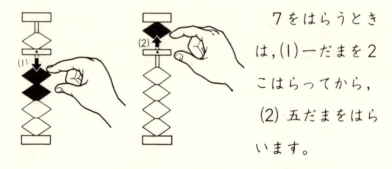

★　そろばんをつかうときは，どんなことに気をつ
　　ければよいか，しらべてみましょう。

❷　つぎの数をそろばんにおきましょう。
　　また，はらいましょう。
　　315　　268　　940　　73.6　　50.9

FIGURE 4.4 Third Grade Textbook

Yobiko are privately run schools. Many of them are recognized by the government under the category of miscellaneous schools. They come in various sizes and shapes. Some enroll elementary, junior, and senior high school students who are enrolled during the daytime and Saturday morning in the regular school. The program for these students features a heavy load of courses every evening with afternoon classes on Saturday and all day on Sunday. Some of these students are attending classes seven days a week.

The yobiko, in addition to the above, schedule a full daytime course for recent high school graduates, the famous *ronin*, literally masterless warriors, who have failed the university entrance or, having passed the examination for a lower level school, have decided to try to enter a top-rated school the following year. This group devotes most of its time preparing for next year's examination. Several yobiko are mammoth institutions, the largest enrolling 35,000 students with branches all over the country. They require entrance examinations, with several of those for the top courses reputedly rivaling the entrance examinations to some of the major universities. They have acquired national reputations and, consequently, can charge fees similar to those of private universities.

The variety of courses, as well as the extracurricular activities, offered by the larger yobiko operations defies analysis. They run the gamut from the elementary school level to the university level, one of the few institutions in the world offering such a broad spectrum of courses all in the same buildings. They also sponsor the entire range of clubs. Because of their high course offerings, they are able to specialize to such a degree that a separate curriculum is specified just for those who want to enter Tokyo University schools of science, or Tokyo University schools of humanities, or "first-rate national universities" (science), or "first-rate private universities" (nonscience). Some use English catch phrases such as "High-Class Course" to attract the eager applicant. The aspiring university student chooses his course and sits for the entrance examination specifically designed for that course.

The one common characteristic of them all is their singular purpose: intense examination preparation. Classes are often large, sometimes running into many hundreds of eager students gathered together in cavernous classrooms. All are engrossed in the practice of test taking by listening to many lectures and working through limitless numbers of work sheets. They are also subjected, willingly, to a constant barrage of mock tests.

The yobiko have recently achieved increased notoriety, and thereby attractiveness, to many eager students through their uses of computers. The administrators of the larger schools have compiled vast amounts of computerized test data enabling them to apply the results of their tests in the most effective manner. By giving their own examinations to anyone who pays the fee and by comparing the results with the actual test results from their graduates on university exams from previous years, they can fairly accurately predict the enrollee's chances of passing an entrance examination to any given high school or university. This itself spurs the students to further study as they watch their relative positions rise or fall on the test charts posted to show their progress toward the score that should predict success. It can be a merciless, as well as effective, process in response to the demands of Japanese youth who are intent on passing an entrance examination in which mathematics plays a major role. The following timetable of a ronin preparing for the university entrance examination is taken from a yobiko schedule showing the rigorous schedule these young Japanese follow each week. It represents an extremely heavy load of 34 classes a week.

Juku are in a class by themselves. Reminiscent of the dame schools of a bygone era in the United States and England, the numberless juku are privately run neighborhood classes that do not require government approval or recognition. There are, in fact, thousands of them in the Tokyo area alone. They are run by former teachers or by regular teachers setting up shop in the evenings in their homes. A typical neighborhood juku for elementary children offers a special mathematics course for fifth and sixth graders on Wednesdays and Fridays from 4:00 to 6:00. On Tuesdays and Thursdays a special course in kokugo, Japanese, will be offered to the same children. An evening course for junior high students from 6:00 to 7:30 in mathematics I and from 7:30 to 9:00 in mathematics II may also be offered. There may be a Saturday afternoon schedule as well in mathematics and Japanese, in addition to English, for junior and senior high school students. Some juku run classes on Sunday. And some have special kindergarten courses for children whose parents hope to have them enrolled in private elementary schools upon examination.

Again, there is no magical methodology in a juku class. Far from it. In contrast to the large classes, 40 to 50 in the public schools and hundreds in some yobiko classrooms, neighborhood juku often divide their enrollees into smaller groups of about ten. The teacher begins by administering tests to determine each child's ability. What then transpires is a wearisome process in which each child often independently works

Yobiko Sample Weekly Schedule
(Fulltime Student)
"First-Class University Preparatory Course" (Social Science)

Day	Time					
	1:20-2:10	2:10-3:00	3:10-4:00	4:10-5:00	5:20-6:10	6:20-7:10
Monday	English	Japanese Classics	English	Mathematics	Mathematics (Elective)	Mathematics (Elective)
Tuesday	Japanese History	Japanese History	English	Modern Japanese	Geography	Geography
Wednesday	English	Japanese History	English	Modern Japanese		
Thursday	English	Japanese Classics	English	Mathematics	Politics-Economics	Politics-Economics
Friday	World History	World History	English	Chinese Classics	Chemistry	Chemistry
Saturday	World History	Japanese Classics	Mathematics	Mathematics (Elective)	Physics	Physics

through pages and pages of drills usually taken from a commercial publication. The teacher simply goes around to each child commenting, explaining, and correcting mistakes. The drills are supplemented by some general board work.

There are few disciplinary problems at the yobiko and juku. It's all in earnest. After all, each child's family of its own accord pays a monthly fee to enroll. And it comes high especially in the famous yobiko. Attendance is purely on a voluntary basis. Yobiko teachers, many regular school teachers earning high fees on their "research day" off from regular chool duties, or university faculty supplementing their regular salaries, enjoy teaching at a yobiko because of the intenseness of the student and the absence of extra burdensome duties that accompany regular teaching. There is a commonness of purpose among the students and teachers in a yobiko and juku that is difficult to fully appreciate without experiencing it. Both are seriously engrossed in the overriding concern: examination preparation.

The yobiko and juku, however, do not cater simply to the brightest children preparing for the better high schools and universities. The basic clientele is drawn from the large pool of average students eager to get into the best schools. In addition, there are also yobiko and juku students who are falling behind the rigorous mathematical requirements of the regular public school and who enter yobiko, and especially juku, not to reach beyond the regular school standard as many students do but rather to catch up. The yobiko and juku, therefore, provide the public school teachers added assistance in their efforts to raise the standards of their students.

The consequences of this unique system is that hundreds of thousands of Japanese youth, particularly those in the one or two years before the junior high, senior high, or university entrance examination as well as the thousands of ronin, are sacrificing much of their leisure time to enroll in this vast web of private, profit-making schools and classes. For example, it is estimated that 60 to 70 percent of all junior high students attend private afterschool classes at least two to three times a week for two hours each time; the majority are enrolled in mathematics classes. Some teenage, and even younger students, are literally in school seven days a week, all seeking to enhance their school grades and their chances of passing the entrance examinations to the next school. Obviously this also further raises their mathematical ability above the minimum standards set in the regular public school. In other words the regular Japanese public school mathematics teachers have an important assistant, the yobiko and the juku, in their efforts to maintain high mathematics standards.

The teacher has, among others, yet another aid called the *homutesuto*, the Home Test, which typifies the vast array of available commercial workbooks. Every publisher of Japanese textbooks, carefully chosen by the Ministry of Education to enter this rather lucrative business, publishes a series of Home Tests. These are commercially produced manuals based on the officially approved textbook published by the same company. A variety of other workbooks, such as *Ten Minutes*, a drill book with a series of ten-minute drills for practice at home, offered by various publishers, are also widely available.

The Home Test workbooks are so designed that the student can work on one lesson each night at home corresponding to a lesson in the text, with the exact number of the page to which it conforms in the student's school textbook. The Home Test workbook begins a unit with material similar to that in the unit in the official textbook. However, the last few problems of the unit become just a bit more difficult than the textbook material in order to stretch the student's work beyond his classroom assignment.

The Home Test workbooks are just that, tests for home use. They are not usually required for use in the classroom, even though they are published by the official publisher of the officially designated mathematics textbook. They are available only at bookstores and must be purchased by the individual student and parent privately. However, depending on the school and the teacher, there are various inducements to the parent. Sometimes the availability of such supplementary materials is casually mentioned in the weekly or bimonthly letter from homeroom teachers to each parent. Although it is impossible to determine how widespread the use of these Home Tests and other similar publications are, an indication may be gained from their ready availability in the bookstores and from the high quality of the publications themselves. The Home Test manuals indicate that many children are working on mathematics problems at home each evening, not just on school assignments but also from the voluntary use of the Home Test and the workbooks related to the juku or yobiko classes. It contrasts sharply with U.S. students of whom two-thirds spend less than one hour a night on homework.[5]

The weekly or bimonthly duplicated letter from the teacher to each parent, a standard practice in Japanese elementary schools, is often employed by the teacher to involve parents in tutoring the child at home in mathematics. By noting the exact pages from the textbook to be covered during the following week, the concerned parent can check on the child's home study. The mother can refer to the text itself because every parent knows exactly where the teacher is working in the math class at school.

Some teachers go beyond this information. With the introduction of a new unit in school, the concerned teacher explains to the parent in the letter the purpose of the lesson. In addition, the parent is given an explanation, with examples, of how the exact mathematical computation in the lesson is being introduced. The purpose is to induce the parent to reinforce the classroom teaching at home by using the same methods of calculation being used at school. In Japan it can be taken for granted that a good many parents are doing just that.

Another influence on the student involves the use of national educational radio and television for the teaching of mathematics during daytime and evening broadcasting. For example, every night on nationwide telecasting, the national educational channel carries one or more mathematics courses. This is in addition to the regularly scheduled school broadcasts during the daytime designed for direct classroom use. The extent of the radio audience in mathematics is difficult to judge, but there are a number of mathematics courses taught over the national educational broadcasting station. The society surrounding the child gives mathematics very special treatment.

Another factor contributing to the impressive levels of mathematics achievement in Japanese schools relates to the standards of the kokugo, the national language. Because the literary standards of the masses of Japanese children are impressively high, the mathematics teacher can capitalize on this in the mathematics classes. From the first grade, word problems and written explanations can be used effectively. Japanese elementary school mathematics textbooks from the first grade on are characterized by many sections with fairly detailed word problems accompanying the equations, building the understanding of the numerical symbols. In the United States, with major reading problems in the school, word problems must be delayed until reading skills are mastered.

Another influence, admittedly difficult to ascertain, concerns the similarity in the abstractness of the written Japanese language and mathematics. The ideographs used to express the written language represent an idea. The single character __ always represents at an instant the concept house. The number 2/3 at an instant always represents two parts of a whole. In the daily lessons in language teaching, every child is drilled in the process of visualizing a mathematicslike symbol representing a concept. When he turns to the mathematics lesson, it is merely an extension of his language lesson in visualizing a single symbol that represents a single concept. In other words, Japanese children appear to be more comfortable with mathematical symbols, because of their similarity-to their language symbols, than do American children who use the alphabetical letters with their varying and, at times, illogical combinations representing a concept.

With this massive program, both official and otherwise in what can be described as an ongoing national campaign to promote mathematics, the school curriculum can be designed in a way unimaginable in the United States. One way of appreciating this is to present a series of pages of mathematical problems for each grade level from standard textbooks used in the local compulsory elementary and junior high schools (Figures 4.5 to 4.18). These schools can be called typical of schools throughout Japan because they all follow a standard curriculum. Every Japanese child throughout the land is being drilled and tested daily on these kinds of problems from the first to the ninth grade.

Upon leafing through this progression of mathematics lessons from the first grade of the Japanese elementary school to the last year of the junior high school, keeping in mind that many of the private schools are more advanced than the public school, it becomes understandable why comparative studies involving U.S. and Japanese students in mathematics achievement produce consistent results. For example, a well-publicized study conducted by the Dallas *Times Herald* in 1983 was centered on a test developed especially for that newspaper by four prominent U.S. educators, including a Nobel Prize-winning scientist. Although the test was designed to compare the educational achievement levels of Dallas 12 year olds with those of seven other countries in several subjects, the results in mathematics were most conspicuous.

According to the final report, "American children are among the worst students of mathematics in the industrialized world. . . . The Japanese pupils did twice as well as the American youngsters and significantly out-scored pupils from all the other countries. The United States finished last." The gap between the two was significant. The average score for the Japanese 12-year-old students was 50.2 percent, in sharp contrast with the children from Dallas whose average score was 25.3 percent. But of great importance were the reactions of local school officials to the content of the examination in mathematics. "Very little on the test was included in the curriculum," according to the principal of one of the Dallas schools involved in the program. Japanese officials who took part in the study explained that the mathematics needed to answer all but three

◾ 1ねんの おさらい

1 69の 十のくらいの すうじは
なんでしょうか。

また, 80の 一のくらいの す
うじは なんでしょうか。

2 どちらが おおきいでしょうか。
(68, 86) (70, 39) (80, 57)

3 こたえが 9に なる かあど
は どれと どれでしょうか。

7+2	9−4	10−1	5+4

4 ぜんぶで なんえんでしょうか。

FIGURE 4.5 First Grade

100

1. What is the number in the ten's place in 69?
   What is the number in the one's place in 80?

2. Of the following, which number is the largest?

3. Which cards make 9?

4. How much do these coins add up to? (Each is a five-yen coin.)

❶ つぎの (あ), (い), (う)の ずを くみたて

　ると, 下の どの はこが できますか。

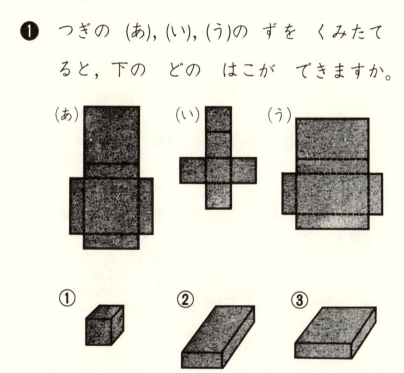

FIGURE 4.6 Second Grade

By folding each figure (あ), (い), and (う), which shape will they make at the bottom?

けいさん (2)

こうじょうで はた
らいて いる 人は
438人です。そのうち,
女の 人は 75人で
す。男の 人は なん人ですか。

★ しきを かいて, けいさんの しかたを
かんがえましょう。

	百	十	一
438	●●●●	●●●	●●●●● ●●●
438－75	●●●○	●●●●● ●●●●● ●●●	●●●●● ●●●
363	●●●	●●●●● ●	●●●

$$438 - 75 = 363 \qquad こたえ \quad 363人$$

FIGURE 4.7 Second Grade

There are 438 people working in a factory. Among them 75 are women. How many men are working there?

*We can work out this problem according to the following equation:

102

❹ 長さが15cmのテープ3本を, 下の図のように

つなぎめをどこも2cmにしてはりあわせると,

ぜんたいの長さは何cmになりますか。

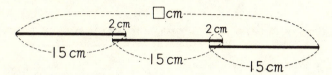

FIGURE 4.8 Third Grade

4. Using three pieces of tape each 15 cm long, if we fasten them
together as shown, how long will the tape become?

② 1mのテープを同じ長さに3つにおって, その

2つぶんの長さを切りとりました。切りとった長さ

は何mといえばよいでしょうか。

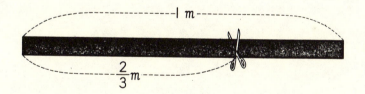

$\frac{1}{3}$mの2つぶんを, $\frac{2}{3}$mと書き, 「三分の二メー

トル」と読みます。

FIGURE 4.9 Third Grade

2. If we have a piece of tape one meter long divided into three sections
as shown, and cut off two of the sections, what do we call the part
with two sections?

Two sections each 1/3 of a meter become 2/3 of a meter.

❶ 色をぬった長さは何 m ですか。

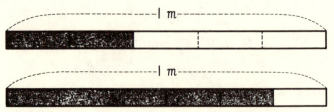

❷ 右の図の入れものに
はいっている水のか
さはそれぞれ何 ℓ で
すか。

❸ $\frac{1}{3}$ℓ の 3 つぶんは何 ℓ ですか。また，$\frac{1}{5}$ m の 5
つぶんは何 m ですか。

FIGURE 4.9 (Continued)

1. How much of a meter is the shaded part?

2. How much of a liter is the shaded part?

❷ つぎの三角形をかきましょう。また，ⓐ，ⓘ，
ⓤの角を大きいじゅんにいいましょう。

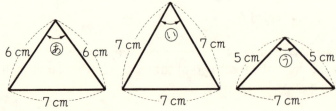

FIGURE 4.10 Third Grade

❸ 右の図のように，長方形の
紙を２つにかさねており，
点線のところで切ってひろ
げましょう。どんな形がで
きるでしょうか。

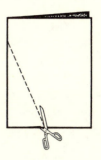

FIGURE 4.10 (Continued)

2. Of the three angles (あ), (い), and (う), place them in order of their size from smallest to the largest.

3. If we fold a rectangular paper into two, and cut along the dotted line as shown, when we unfold the part cut off what shape will it form?

(れんしゅう・1)

❶ 　１辺が１ｍの立方体のはこを，
右の図のようにつみました。
①はこは何こありますか。
②全体の体積はどれだけでしょう
か。

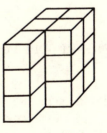

FIGURE 4.11 Fourth Grade

❷ 下の図のような立方体や直方体の体積は 何 cm³
ですか。

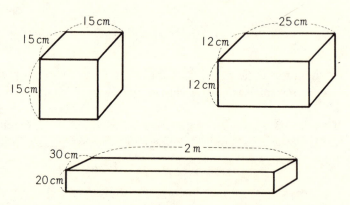

❸ 下の図のような形の体積をもとめましょう。

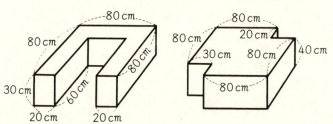

FIGURE 4.12 Fourth Grade

1. In the picture, each side of each block is 1 meter.
   1) How many blocks are there?
   2) What is the volume of the entire figure?

2. How many cm³ is the volume of each figure?

3. Figure the volume of each.

❻ 右の図のような形の土地

があります。色をぬった

部分の面積は何 m² ですか。

また，何 a ですか。

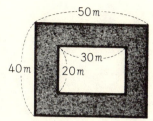

❼ 100本のえんぴつを，1人に1ダースずつ分け

たら，16本あまりました。何人に分けたので

すか。

FIGURE 4.13 Fourth Grade

6. What is the area in square meters of the shaded area?

7. We have one hundred pencils and give each person one dozen pencils. How many persons are there if we have 16 left over?

1 右の図の平行四辺形の面積

を計算するには，どの辺を底

辺にすればよいでしょうか。

また，この平行四辺形の面

積は何 cm² でしょうか。

2 上底が 20cm, 下底が 36cm で，高さが 25cm の台形の

面積は何 cm² でしょうか。

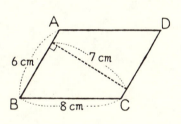

FIGURE 4.14 Fifth Grade

1. Calculate the area of the parallelogram.

2. If the upper length of a parallelogram is 20 cm, the lower length 36 cm, and the height is 25 cm, what is the area in cm²?

3　下の図のような三角形の面積はそれぞれ何㎡でしょうか。

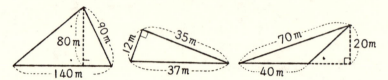

4　右の図の四角形では，対角線が垂直になっています。

　この四角形の面積は何 cm² でしょうか。

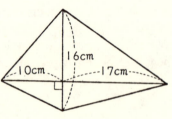

5　右の図のような形をした土地があります。

　この土地の面積は何㎡でしょうか。

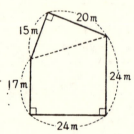

FIGURE 4.14 (Continued)

3. Calculate the area of the triangles.

4. Calculate the area.

5. What is the area of a piece of land shaped like this?

三角形の拡大図, 縮図のかきかた

■ 方眼を使わないでも,
右の三角形の $\frac{1}{2}$ の縮図を
かくことができます。

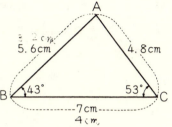

★ どんなかきかたがあるか, いろいろ考えてみましょう。

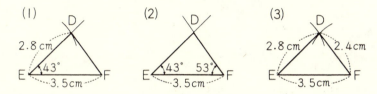

(1)　　　　　　(2)　　　　　　(3)

★ 上の図は, 3とおりの三角形の縮図のかきかたを示した
ものです。それぞれのかきかたを説明しましょう。

★ 上の3とおりのかきかたで, 三角形ABCの $\frac{1}{2}$ の縮図をか
きましょう。また, できた縮図について, かくときに使わ
なかった辺の長さや角の大きさを調べ, 正しい縮図になっ
ていることを確かめましょう。

1　右の三角形GHJの1.5倍の拡
大図を, 3とおりのかきかたで
かきましょう。

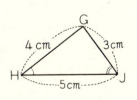

FIGURE 4.15 Sixth Grade

109

65. ∠XOY と点Aがある。OX についてAの対称点をB, OY について Aの対称点をCとする。∠XOY＝45° のとき，∠BOC の大きさは，いくらか。

下のおのおのの図について調べよ。

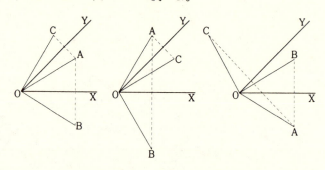

66. 次のような四角形 ABCD をかけ。（長さの単位は cm とする）

(1) AB＝5, BC＝6, CD＝3, AC＝5, BD＝7

(2) AB＝5, AC＝5, AD＝3, ∠BAC＝70°, ∠CAD＝30°

(3) BC＝6, AC＝6, BD＝6, ∠B＝70°, ∠C＝80°

67. AB＝4 cm, BC＝3 cm の長方形 ABCD が，図のように直線 *l* 上をころがるとき，点Aはどんな線をかくか。

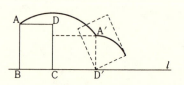

68. 立方体を1つの平面で切るとき，切り口の形が，次のようになる場合があるか。

　　正三角形，正六角形

69. 右のような立方体の面にそって，頂点Aから頂点Gまでいく最短の道は，どのような線か。

　　また，その道はいくつあるか。

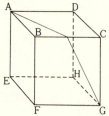

FIGURE 4.16 Junior High School First Year

6.　図形と証明

48. 右の直方体の3辺 AB, AD, AE 上に, それぞれ, 3点P, Q, R を とり, AP＝AQ＝AR となるよう にすると, △PQR の形は, どん な形になるか。

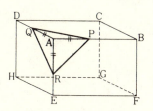

49. 右の図のように, 同じ中心をもつ 大小2円で, 中心角の等しいおう ぎ形 OAB, OCD をつくる。

このとき, AC＝BD であること を証明せよ。

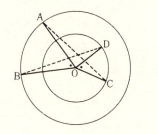

50. 右の図のように, 正方形 ABCD の 頂点Dに, 正方形 EFGH の中心 が重なっている。

このとき, 次のことを証明せよ。

(1)　AF＝CG

(2)　2つの正方形の重なっている 部分 PFQD の面積は, 正方形 EFGH の面積の $\frac{1}{4}$ である.

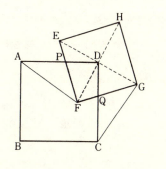

51. △ABC の ∠A の二等分線が BC と交わる点をDとする。 Dから AC に平行な直線をひき, AB と交わる点をEとし, E から BC に平行な直線をひき, AC と交わる点をFとする。 このとき, AE＝CF となることを証明せよ。

FIGURE 4.17 Junior High School Second Year

111

図形の計量

160. 台形 ABCD で，∠A＝∠B＝90°，

AB＝12 cm，AD＝5 cm，BC＝9 cm

とし，対角線の交点をEとする。

⑴　AC, AE, BD, BE の長さを求

めよ．

⑵　△ABE, △BCE, △CDE,

△DAE の面積を求めよ.

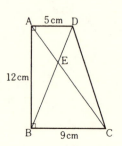

161. △ABC の辺 BC 上の点を D とし，

直線 AD 上の1点をPとするとき，

△ABP：△ACP＝BD：CD

を証明せよ。

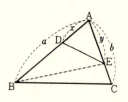

162. △ABC で，中線 BE, CF の交点をGとするとき，△BCG と四

角形 AFGE の面積は等しいことを証明せよ.

163. 右の図で，AB＝a，AC＝b，

AD＝x，AE＝y とする。

⑴　$\dfrac{\triangle ADE}{\triangle ABE}$, $\dfrac{\triangle ABE}{\triangle ABC}$ を，a, b,

x, y を使って表せ．

⑵　$\dfrac{\triangle ADE}{\triangle ABC}=\dfrac{xy}{ab}$ を証明せよ．

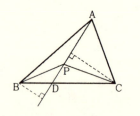

164. △ABC の各辺を3等分する点を，

右の図のように，P, Q；R, S；U,

V とするとき，△PRU の面積は，

△ABC のどれだけにあたるか。

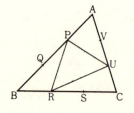

FIGURE 4.18 Junior High School Third Year

of the questions is covered in the regular public elementary school curriculum.[6]

In a much broader international study of 13 year olds in mathematics conducted by the International Educational Achievement Assessment Association (IEA), headquartered in Stockholm, the results had a familiar ring. In this mammoth research project involving about 8,000 students in several hundred schools in each of 21 countries, the mathematics test included sections on algebra and geometry. In a repeat performance of a test given 16 years ago by the same organization, Japanese junior high students came out on top once again in this worldwide study, according to initial reports.[7] Obviously the Japanese school had prepared the students well in mathematics. Related to the scores in mathematics, Japanese primary and junior high school students also scored the highest marks in the science section of the tests in the previous examinations. In the most recent test, although the international comparisons are not yet available, Japanese elementary students scored about the same as they did previously while the junior high students increased their average by 3.7 percent.[8]

After all students pass through nine years of the public school mathematics curriculum, many supplemented with yobiko and juku courses, they are finally ready to take the senior high school entrance examination given by each prefecture. Elementary and junior high schools are administrative units of the local community because compulsory education extends through the junior high school for a total of nine grades. Because the high school is noncompulsory, an entrance examination is required even though nearly 95 percent of all students enter the senior high school.

The high school is administered by the prefectural body. Therefore each of the 45 prefectural units plus Tokyo construct their own individual high school entrance examinations. There are certain differences among them. However, they are all based on the standardized junior high school curriculum and are consequently fairly similar in content and level of difficulty.

The five subject areas being tested to enter the high school in every prefecture include Japanese, mathematics, science, social studies, and English. The following three questions were taken from the six mathematics problems included in a recent entrance examination for Tokyo public senior high schools. Every third-year student, 14 to 15 years old, in the public junior high schools undergoes a mathematics course aimed primarily at preparing for an examination with questions like the following (Figure 4.19). Many of the brightest students will find the questions relatively easy and will choose the more demanding private high schools in order to prepare more strenuously for the better universities.

With the end of the ninth grade of the junior high school, that is of compulsory education in Japan, the resemblance with the U.S. educational system ends because nearly 95 percent of all Japanese students continue through the high school. In the United States only 75 percent of the age group is graduated from high school. In mathematics, however, there is little resemblance between the two schools almost from the very beginning of first grade. For example, in a nationwide test conducted by the National Assessment of Educational Progress (NAEP), an organization administered by the Education Commission of the States, 32 percent of the third grade children tested could not calculate correctly the problem 64 minus 27, which involved borrowing with two-digit numbers.[9] Even these poor results were interpreted positively as indicating an upswing in the mathematical standards of U.S. schools because only 30 percent solved the problem correctly when the test was given several years earlier.

In the Japanese third grade, children are expected to be able to calculate problems such as 940 minus 370, which involves borrowing with three-digit numbers. However, the Japanese child is drilled on the calculation of such a problem by working it out mentally rather than with paper and pencil. This is a much more demanding exercise than subtracting 27 from 64 with paper and pencil.

The huge gaps between our two schools, however, appear in the mathematics classroom in the upper grades. Again, using the NAEP report,[10] the following two problems were given to 46,000 13- and 17-year-old students across the land, statistically representative of about 9 million samples, with results that many concerned Americans have come to expect.

> You will not have enough time to work out this problem with a pencil. Therefore estimate the product of this multiplication problem by choosing the correct answer.
>
> Problem: 3.04 x 5.3
>
> Answer: a 1.6
>   b 16
>   c 160
>   d 1600

数　学

1　次の各問に答えよ。

〔問1〕　$2 \times (-3)^2 + 5 \times (-4)$　を計算せよ。

〔問2〕　$6x - 7y - 4(x - y)$　を計算せよ。

〔問3〕　不等式　$2x - 3 < 5(x - 6)$　を解け。

〔問4〕　二次方程式　$(x + 4)^2 = 9$　を解け。

〔問5〕　大，小二つのさいころを同時に投げるとき，両方とも奇数の目の出る確率を求めよ。

〔問6〕　右の正四面体O-ABCにおいて，点Mは辺OBの中点，点Nは辺OCの中点である。

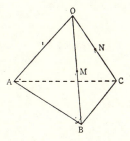

次の①，②に答えよ。

①　辺OAの中点をPとする。この正四面体を3点P，M，Nを通る平面で切ると，4点O，P，M，Nを頂点とする立体O-PMNができる。

正四面体 O-ABC の体積は立体 O-PMN の体積の何倍か。

②　正四面体O-ABCの1辺の長さを12cmとする。2点M，Nを通る平面が辺OAと垂直に交わる点をQとするとき，線分OQの長さは何センチメートルか。

2　ある運送会社では，A工場で生産された同一規格の製品を，次の〔　〕の中に示すきまりに従って倉庫に運んでいる。

> ・　運ぶ製品の個数は，1回の運送につき，大型トラック1台当たりちょうど30個，小型トラック1台当たりちょうど20個とする。
> ・　運送料金は，1回の運送につき，大型トラック1台当たり4万円，小型トラック1台当たり3万円とする。

次の各問に答えよ。

〔問1〕　大型トラックa台と小型トラック5台とを同時に使って1回で運ぶことのできる製品の個数は全部で何個か。aを用いた式で表せ。

〔問2〕　大型トラックと小型トラック合わせて20台を同時に使って1回で運んだ製品の個数が550個であった。このとき使った大型トラック，小型トラックの台数はそれぞれ何台か。

FIGURE 4.19 Tokyo Metropolitan Public High School Entrance
Examination

115

〔問 3〕 大型トラックと小型トラック合わせて何台かを 1 回だけ同時に使って製品を運ぶのに，その運送料金の合計がちょうど 50 万円になるようにしたい。この金額で運ぶことのできる製品の個数は，そのとき使う大型トラック，小型トラックの台数によって異なってくる。50 万円で運ぶことのできる製品の個数は，最も多い場合 何個か。

[3] 右の図で，点Oは原点，点Qの座標は
(0，4)で，曲線 l は
$$y = \frac{1}{2}x^2 \quad (x \geqq 0)$$
を表している。

点Pは曲線 l 上を動くものとする。

線分OQを 1 辺とし，線分OPを対角線にもつ平行四辺形PQORをつくるとき，次の各問に答えよ。

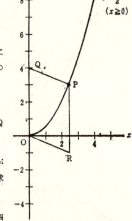

〔問 1〕 点Pの x 座標が 2 のときの直線PQの式を求めよ。

〔問 2〕 平行四辺形PQORの対角線QRが x 軸と平行になるときの点Pの座標を求めよ。

〔問 3〕 点Pが曲線 l 上を動くとき，平行四辺形PQORの二つの対角線OP，QRについて正しく述べたものが，次のア〜オのうちに二つある。それらを選んで，その記号を書け。

　ア　二つの対角線OP，QRは互いに垂直に交わることがある。

　イ　二つの対角線OP，QRの交点の座標が(2，3)になることがある。

　ウ　二つの対角線OP，QRの交点の y 座標が負の値になることがある。

　エ　二つの対角線OP，QRの交点が動いてできる図形は直線である。

　オ　二つの対角線OP，QRの長さが等しくなることがある。

〔問 3〕 上の座標平面上の点(0，3)を定点Aとする。x 軸上にある・印の点のうちの一つの点をPとし，線分APを 1 辺とする正方形APQRを，3 辺PQ，QR，RAが線分APの長さに等しく，頂点Q，頂点Rが・印の点の上にあるようにつくる。次の①，②に答えよ。

　①　点Pの座標を(p，0)とするとき，正方形APQRの頂点Qの座標を求めよ。

　②　正方形APQRの面積が 90cm² であるとき，正方形APQRの周上にある・印の点は全部で何個か。

FIGURE 4.19 Tokyo Metropolitan Public High School Entrance Examination (Continued)

116

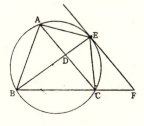

5 右の図で，三角形ＡＢＣは円に内接し
ている。

　∠ＡＢＣの二等分線が辺ＡＣ，弧ＡＣと
交わる点をそれぞれＤ，Ｅとする。このと
き，三角形ＥＡＣは二等辺三角形になる。

　また，点Ｆは点Ｅにおける接線と辺ＢＣ
を延ばした直線との交点である。

　次の各問に答えよ。

〔問 1〕 ∠ＤＢＣ＝35° のとき，∠ＡＥＣの大きさは何度か。

〔問 2〕 ＣＥ＝10cm， ＣＦ＝8cm のとき，線分ＡＢの長さは何センチメートル
か。

〔問 3〕 三角形ＡＢＣが鋭角三角形で，∠ＥＣＦが直角であるとき，線分ＡＣと線
分ＢＥとの関係について正しく述べたものを，次のア～エのうちから選び，そ
の記号を書け。

　ア　線分ＡＣと線分ＢＥとは，長さが等しく，垂直に交わる。

　イ　線分ＡＣと線分ＢＥとは，長さが異なり，垂直に交わる。

　ウ　線分ＡＣと線分ＢＥとは，長さが等しく，垂直には交わらない。

　エ　線分ＡＣと線分ＢＥとは，長さが異なり，垂直には交わらない。

FIGURE 4.19 Tokyo Metropolitan Public High School Entrance
Examination (Continued)

1. In the following figure of a pyramid, O is the apex, M is the midpoint
    between O and B, and N is the midpoint between O and C. All of the
    edges are the same length.

    Question:
    If P represents the midpoint between O and A, the volume of the
    small pyramid OPMN would be what fraction of the original pyramid
    OABC?

3. In the following graph, Q has the coordinates x=0 and y=4. The
    curve 1 represents y=1/2x2 (X≥0). Any point P on the curve makes a
    rhomboid QPRO.

    Question:
    If P is located at x=2, what is the equation for the line OP?

5. In the triangle ABC and circle ABC, the line BE disects the triangle at D and meets the circle at E. The line BC is extended until it meets a line parallel with AC.

Question:
If the angle DBC equals 35 degrees, what is the angle AEC? If CE is 10 cm, and CF is 8 cm, how long is AB?

Only 21 percent of 13 year olds could answer that problem correctly. But what is most revealing was the percentage of correct answers by 17-year-old students, those who will, one year later, either enter some form of higher education, go directly to work in one of our factories producing increasingly complex products in competition with Japanese products, or enter the ranks of the unemployed. In fact, only 37 percent of the junior class students chose the right answer.

The second problem:

An army bus holds 36 soldiers. If 1,128 soldiers are being bused to their training site, how many buses are needed?

This problem was answered correctly by 7 percent of the 13-year-old students and by 18 percent of those aged 17. If the reader turns back to review the test questions for the entrance examination to Tokyo public high schools, which greatly influence the mathematics teaching of the final year of the junior high school for students aged 14 to 15, you can readily see the magnitude of the differences of the mathematical standards between U.S. and Japanese schools. And we are comparing 17-year-old U.S. youth on simple elementary problems with 14- to 15-year-old Japanese youth on highly complex problems.

The level of mathematical standards in the schools of Japan and its importance to Japanese industry cannot be underestimated. The significant feature of the Japanese school is not that it is producing a mathematics elite, which it is. In fact, recent statistics even indicate that that elite may be expanding. The University Entrance Examination Center reported that for the third year in a row, the number of applicants to national colleges and university departments of natural science has increased, while that to the social sciences has decreased. Recently science applicants have been increasing by up to 8,000 over the previous year. Of the total number applying for national universities, one-third were in a science-related area.[11] In sharp contrast, U.S. students have rejected a college preparatory curricula in the high school in large numbers. The proportion of students taking a general course of studies, that is, less demanding than the academic course for college preparatory, increased from 14 percent to 42 percent from the mid-1960s to the 1980s.[12]

But the United States also turns out its share of mathematicians of the highest order, a math elite. U.S. achievements in space have been accomplished through the creative application of the most advanced uses of mathematics. The spectacular feat of placing an earthly being outside a space craft untethered represented surely the highest order of imaginative mathematics by Americans. The Japanese, in spite of their mathematical standards, lag considerably behind the United States in space developments.

However, the Japanese school produces, in addition to an elite of advanced mathematicians like the American elite, a "mass elite in mathematics," unlike the American masses. This mass elite is represented by the blue-collar worker from the female employee in the textile mill to the male operator of the forklift who are all fairly well grounded in basic mathematics. When the inevitable time comes that they must undergo retraining for a higher level of work required in Japan's rapidly evolving technological society, which presupposes a basic knowledge of mathematics for more specialized training, they should be able to make the transition smoothly. Can we say this with confidence about the blue-collar work force in the United States?

Of the highest order of significance is this Japanese blue-collar father, and especially the mother, who encourage, nay prod, their children to study mathematics at home and school. It is the working class, the vast majority considering themselves as middle-class according to many nationwide surveys, that endorses and sustains the inordinately high mathematics standards of the Japanese classroom. Fine products incorporating advanced technology from the factories of Japan are a reflection of this positive attitude toward mathematics that pervades Japanese society.

5

THE DILIGENT WORKER
Gambare!: Persevere!

> Perseverance: continue steadily in doing something hard;
> sticking to a purpose or an aim; never giving up what one
> has set out to do.
>
> – Webster

A super economic power the size of the U.S. state of Montana, endowed with few natural resources supporting a population half that of the United States, is truly an enigma. Yet, as we have seen, that description befits Japan. At the risk of oversimplification, one could ultimately attribute Japan's substantial economic and industrial achievements to a very great extent to the diligence and perseverance of its people. How else can one account for the Japanese gross national product attaining a level only below that of the United States and possibly of the Soviet Union, two economic superpowers blessed with vast mineral resources and massive land areas. There are even some responsible analysts who predict that Japan will overtake the United States as number one in gross national product during the twenty-first century.

The very notion that Japan could potentially become the most productive nation in the world as measured by GNP appears inconceivable not only to many Westerners but to the Japanese as well. After all, only two score or more years ago this tiny land lay emaciated

121

from a war it could not possibly win. Rising from its self-inflicted holocaust, Japan now finds itself among the upper reaches of the world economic order. Surely the perseverance of the Japanese people has been an essential ingredient in the dramatic struggle from the catastrophe of Hiroshima to the forest of high-rise office buildings in Shinjuka, Tokyo. But to achieve number one industrial status in the world is an illusion of grandeur few Japanese hold.

One of the major motivating spirits that has buoyed this society through adversity in its tenacious pursuit of postwar national regeneration can best be illustrated by the exclamation, "Gambare!" "Persevere!" "Endure!" "Don't give up!" Throughout the lifetime of the Japanese they are surrounded, encouraged, and motivated by the spirit of gambare. It begins in the home. The school takes it up from the first day the child enters the classroom. It continues through graduation. The company then thrives on it. It engulfs every facet of society. It is employed in work, study, and even at play and leisure. Gambare is integral to being Japanese.

To survive, the Japanese people have always had to gambare – persevere, endure – because life has never been, and is certainly not now, easy nor comfortable for most Japanese. Many have sacrificed terribly over the years for this nation to transform itself first in the 1800s from a feudal to an industrialized society, and later in the 1900s from total economic collapse into an industrial giant. Many are sacrificing today for Japan to maintain its new position among the great economic powers of the world.

Entering the international arena of industrial competition with two strikes against them, a large population living in a minuscule useable land area with sparse mineral resources, the Japanese have had an enormous burden, a challenge if you will, placed upon them. The overall geographical limitations have unfortunately not been altered by economic success. No, indeed. For this nation to remain in the upper ranks in the competition for international markets, the Japanese must forever persevere.

The role of gambare should be recognized as grassroots in the Japanese social structure. For example, the Ministry of Education does not stipulate in its directives or manuals that teachers should continually encourage their students to persevere. It isn't necessary. It doesn't have to be enforced from the top. In fact, it derives from the very foundation of the society.

Gambare is the basic rallying cry for every group in Japanese society from the housewives' associations to the political parties to the underworld to the factory shop floor circle to the very classroom itself. It has the same meaning to all: whatever activity you are engaged in, do your best to the very end. But it extends beyond that. It holds the implication that everyone in the group is in the same rocking boat. All must persevere together in order to survive, to succeed. It implies the work-together-or-sink-together concept, a realistic perspective of this land.

Gambare is also a major component in developing a strong sense of competition, especially group competition. Regardless of the group's purposes or the ages of the participants, the goals must be pursued through a collective effort. And that corporate effort is marshaled by the constant reminder to gambare, not just by the leader of the group but by the individual members themselves. The grassroots nature of gambare in itself represents a significant element of the Japanese challenge.

The seriousness of purpose, the commitment to gambare, characterizes Japanese society to its very roots. Another way of describing it is that the ordinary Japanese assumes a deep sense of conscientiousness in carrying out his duties in the form of his responsibility to his group. He is forever encouraged by his leader or, in the case of students, his teacher, as well as by his fellow workers or students, to gambare. This serves as a constant reminder that every member of the group or the kumi rides in the same narrow ship perpetually sailing alongside a precipice. All must gambare together to avoid catastrophe, to avoid going over the edge.

This mutual sense of responsibility, a sense of duty to the group, characterizes the Japanese work force. This reciprocal feeling that nearly everyone in the group, in the office, or in the factory department is gambaring inspires the individual to give of himself to accomplish the collective goals. He is not alone. He is part of a group effort. And when he witnesses his fellow worker letting up a bit or experiencing some difficulty, he calls out with determination: "Gambare!" Keep at it! He not only reinforces his compatriot's will to persevere, he strengthens his own commitment to the effort.

Although this may appear as an unsophisticated effort by employees indoctrinated by their superiors to work harder, the actual situation indicates otherwise. Gambare inundates the highest corporate offices and governmental agencies. The presidents of corporations and ministers of government bureaus apply gambare in the same manner as workers on the shop floor. All must persevere together or the goal is unattainable. Thus the vast majority of white-collar workers from the president on down commit themselves to the corporate gambare effort. The executive conveys to his subordinates a sense of conviction commensurate with his position that they can rely on him to make the maximum effort for the success of the company.

And so it goes. The heads of divisions gather their department chiefs together for the daily briefings, sometimes at an early morning meeting. The proceedings are imbued with the spirit of gambare to begin the day's work. The commitment is there. Don't give up! The department heads transmit that commitment in their departmental meetings. In other words the sense of gambare infuses the white-collar employees of a company, a majority of which will most likely be graduates of universities. This is a sophisticated, highly literate group of people deeply involved in the process of gambare.

Many blue-collar workers begin their day much the same way as the white-collar employee by attending a brief meeting. It, too, ends in the spirit of gambare. In the more activist companies workers may sing the company song or chant the company motto as they prepare for work. But this practice is apparently dying out. It isn't really necessary, but it implies a commitment of effort. The blue-collar workers can take it for granted that the office staff is also gambaring. That, in itself, represents a motivating factor up and down the corporate line.

Another ingredient involved in gambare is the conviction that to succeed one must make personal sacrifices. Gambare incorporates the sacrificial effort of endurance to compete effectively. One of the most admired traits of an individual in Japan is personal sacrifice. It signifies that person has gambared, that is, paid a price for his success. The compulsory course in ethics in the school curriculum is based on the study of individuals, some from the West like Helen Keller, who have persevered through adversity to achieve their goals. These are the types of individuals to be emulated by the Japanese.

This attitude extends to the very foundation of the society. For example, the humblest workers washing dishes in a restaurant, or the city garbage collectors, maintain a sense of gambare few workers in similar menial jobs in the United States exhibit. They, too, exhort their fellow workers to gambare when the going gets tough or when the weather turns bitterly cold. There comes even to these unskilled workers a sense of responsibility and duty to their fellow workers who are also gambaring, that is, enduring to get the job done. The esprit de corps, the spirit of gambare, among the work force at all levels is an impressive aspect of this society few nations can match.

The Japanese take a considerable sense of pride in completing a job successfully. If one has persevered, sacrificed, endured, the fruits of the efforts are especially gratifying. There is in a very real sense an immense satisfaction in accomplishing a task that can only be appreciated if a sacrificial effort is involved. A sense of responsibility and a sense of pride in the outcome are characteristic of the Japanese people in every endeavor – be it the gangsters in the notorious criminal syndicates, the engineers in the renowned electronics industry, the assembly line workers in the automobile plants, or our garbage collectors for the city of Mitaka.

Gambare in no way implies that the method used by the Japanese to accomplish a job is the most efficient or prudent way to get the job done. That simply is not the case in many instances. The effort may be admirable but the approach time consuming and inefficient. As in all industrial societies, inefficiency is a serious problem in every sector of Japanese industry. Inefficiency in the corporate offices is particularly notorious where, ironically in the nation that comes close to world supremacy in the manufacture of modern office equipment, office automation has been slow in coming. But inefficiency in Japanese industry at any level is usually not attributable to complacency, lethargy, or plain loafing on the job.

Inefficiency in Japanese society can result from the inordinate amount of time it takes to reach a consensus of the group before action can be taken or from the suppression of individual initiative by the group when it could have resulted in increased efficiency. The group can exert a powerful sanction over an individualistic member in its excessive forms. But the critical point is that even here, the typical worker is committed to gambare in increasing his efficiency. The company thrives on this commitment.

Where does the Japanese worker acquire a keen sense of gambare? It begins literally at birth in the home. Parents use it frequently during child rearing to induce the child to learn to walk, to eat with chopsticks, to ride a bike, to learn the kana in order to read children's stories. The child also encounters it on television and radio at any time of the day or night. He hears both his parents use it with each other and with their friends. By the time the child begins school, he is fairly well versed in the spirit of gambare.

With entry into school the child begins the formal introduction into groups and organized competitive activities. Gambare takes on added importance and will influence his school life until graduation. In school, gambare is used with study assignments, examinations, sports, and even play. It is used as a disciplinary device when the child does poorly in an examination. It is even used when one succeeds. Whether one is at the top or the bottom, one must always gambare.

The school, then, is one of the primary instruments within this society for instilling and perpetuating the spirit of perseverance into the masses of Japanese young people. Study, examinations, repetition, memorization, the kendo club – it's all quite serious business. One must sacrifice in order to succeed on the examinations. One must devote many hours of sheer drudgery to learn mathematical equations, to memorize the new ideographs of the language, or to repeat over and over again the meaning in Japanese of the English vocabulary lists required of all Japanese junior high school students.

Few observers would characterize the typical Japanese lesson in school as very stimulating. There are creative teachers, to be sure, but they are rare noticeably so at the upper levels of the system. One could make a similar conclusion about the teaching corps in most countries. But based on many years of observing classrooms throughout the world, one inescapable conclusion can be drawn. Although the average U.S. classroom teacher is not particularly stimulating, in common with his or her counterpart in other countries, there is, nevertheless, considerably more creative teaching in the public schools of the United States than one encounters in Japan. For example, very few questions are asked by the Japanese students in a standard junior high school class in mathematics, kokugo, science, or any other subject. That is not the case in the average U.S. classroom.

Yet the Japanese school is impressively capable of instilling into the average student the underlying spirit of gambare, the seriousness of purpose, the desire to succeed on the examination regardless of the effort required. And that examination threat itself is an important crutch that the teacher always has at beck and call. But gambare is not simply a matter of examination preparation or memorizing mathematical principles or the multiplication tables. It penetrates every school activity extending far beyond examination preparation.

It is at the elementary school level, the formative stages of attitudinal development, that the Japanese educational system is most effective in instilling the spirit of gambare, the attitude of perseverance, diligence, and conscientiousness. The majority, the vast majority, of Japanese teachers, themselves all products of the system, carry with them into the classroom the attitude of gambare. As a matter of course they take their responsibilities quite seriously. Naturally they want their charges to memorize the material included in the teacher's manual as stipulated by the Ministry of Education because a teacher's worth is usually judged in terms of the rate of success the students achieve on examinations.

But one of the teacher's major responsibilities, which is not stipulated in the manuals, is to instill the spirit of gambare into the students. Whenever there is a task to perform, an activity to participate in, a test to prepare for, the child is encouraged by the teacher to gambare. In essence, the teacher is conveying to the seven-year-old child that even though the repetition of the multiplication tables may be boring, the child must persevere because it is necessary for every child to learn them. A measure of sacrifice is essential. Every child is sacrificing with homework assignments. Every child in the basketball club at the junior high is sacrificing by reporting to school every morning at 7:00 for practice six days a week plus holidays. The brass band members are sacrificing in the same manner when they have to show up for preschool rehearsals every morning, six days a week plus summer holidays. They are all learning the meaning and significance of gambare.

But is it really necessary for the junior high brass band to practice every morning – even during summer vacations? If you want to "stick to a purpose or an aim," you do, according to Webster's definition of perseverance. Is it really necessary for all 10- and 11-year-old children to struggle with complex geometric patterns for examination questions precious few will ever encounter in real life situations? If the aim is pure mathematics, it's doubtful because the average student will forget the memorized equations after the examination. However, if the aim is instilling the concept of "continue steadily in doing something hard," according to Webster, then there may be justification for the demanding exercise.

This factor should not be lost in any consideration of the Japanese school in contemporary society. Most Japanese, including the teachers themselves, realize that much of the highly complex mathematical study all students struggle with to pass the entrance examinations to the high school has little if any relevance to the future of the vast majority of students. After all, how many Japanese during the course of their adult lives will ever have to figure out "If P is located at x=2, what is the equation for the line OP?" taken from the problem included on the Tokyo high school entrance examination. A few will, of course. Clearly most will not.

But to the traditional Japanese way of thinking, as interpreted by this foreigner treading on sensitive cultural territory, there is far more to the Japanese school than learning subject matter for examination preparation. That may even be the superficial. Fundamental to becoming a mature Japanese is the concept of spirit. We from the West have traditionally associated this as part of Japanese morals or ethics. During the American Occupation of Japan, our officials promptly banned the previously required course in morals. We interpreted it as an integral instrument in promoting emperor worship and ultranationalistic attitudes, both viewed as antidemocratic to be purged from the new democratic schools for Japan.

There was some justification for that action. But it neglected a critical aspect of morals education to the Japanese, which seems to be closely related to the traditional spirit of gambare – persevere, endure. In the prewar days gambare was related to survival, pure and simple. During the wartime, of course, the spirit of gambare was put through its ultimate test for sheer survival. And, as history tells us, the Japanese persevered through both periods.

Older Japanese look back to both eras with a certain feeling of nostalgia. There is something sentimental about the period in their lives when they and the nation itself underwent the ultimate test everyday for individual and social survival during the prewar depression and the devastation of the war ending with the atomic bombings. The terrible postwar depression and food shortages also fit into this pattern of testing the Japanese individual power and the corporate power of the nation to gambare for sheer survival.

Something is missing in contemporary Japanese society as a supereconomic power. The test, the challenge, of gambare for physical survival is gone. The nation has become affluent. This is a middle-class society. Life can be very difficult in this terribly overcrowded land, but few Japanese are confronting the daily test of physical survival. Endurance, yes. Survival, no.

The Japanese need to be tested, to be challenged, in order to nourish their innate quest for spiritual growth, not, to be sure, in the religious sense of the Christian seeking spiritual growth. Rather, it is in the Japanese sense of the need to test the strength of one's perseverance and endurance to overcome adversity, a trial of one's endurance, both individually and corporately as a nation. That, crudely interpreted by a non-Japanese, is the essence of gambare, of being Japanese.

In a discussion of the problems of contemporary Japanese education, several senior citizens recalled their prewar school days claiming that their schools gave them a spiritual foundation. In trying to explain how the prewar school actually accomplished this, they gave the example of their physical education classes when students had to give their all, to exert themselves completely, in order to win the marathon race or swimming meet. It seems that what they were trying to express was the need to test the spirit of gambare – endurance. It is the nostalgic feeling of surviving the test of gambare that remains so strong in this society. It makes a Japanese a true Japanese; the sense of satisfaction in experiencing the test – the test of gambare – and persevering through it.

Perhaps one's imagination can get carried afar in this interpretation. But witnessing the intenseness of examination preparation on the part of this generation leads to the conclusion that the traditional attitude of gambare is still at work within most of the Japanese youth of today. That much of what this generation must learn to enter the high school will be of little use to them later is irrelevant. That they are being challenged, that their power of gambare is being tested once again, is an underlying motive in their desire to succeed. The cycle of Japanese history is being repeated with this generation, although in a vastly different form than in the past.

Examination preparation, the backbone of the school system, from this perspective goes far beyond the mathematics or English class with its rote memory of abstract equations and emphasis on detailed rules of grammar. That is the superficial aspect of the Japanese school that tends to distract us from the fundamental. Rather, examination preparation epitomizes the daily tests of perseverance and endurance, fulfilling not only a mathematical function but a spiritual need of the Japanese. The entrance tests to the high school and university have, to this observer, replaced the physical tests of survival of a bygone era as a challenge to one's depth of gambare, of endurance. Their importance to this society and its industrial competitiveness extends well beyond the classroom.

The ultimate question, though, comes to this. How do the Japanese elementary teachers get children to accept as necessary the sacrificing of their free time for study? How do teachers instill into their charges that even voluntary club activities require sacrifices of spending early morning hours and even Saturday afternoons at school? How do the Japanese teachers get their students to accept the necessity of gambare in an affluent middle-class society?

It is extremely difficult to identify the derivation of gambare because of its broad cultural diffusion, but it is related to the stark realities of Japan as a nation. For example, all Japanese children learn from first grade that their ancestors made tremendous sacrifices in the face of overwhelming odds for sheer survival. The inevitable confrontation with nature, mentioned earlier in the form of volcanoes, destructive typhoons, massive flooding, heavy snows, terrifying earthquakes – they're all a fundamental part of domestic life. Children learn about the valiant efforts their forefathers made to bring this insecure and physically isolated land into the modern world. There were no oil fields, no gold rushes, no lush prairies, no vast colonial empires to spark the progress. It required human perseverance – the spirit of gambare.

One of the teachings every Japanese child learns in school, and outside the classroom as well, concerns the critical geographical limitations this nation faces. Teachers often refer to Japan as a small country, or, more particularly, as a narrow country. Some still call it a poor country out of habit. The children learn about Japan as an immensely overcrowded nation where the overwhelming number of the 121 million people are literally squeezed into a tiny area along the mid-eastern seacoast. They learn early that Japan's one natural resource, limited deposits of coal, is being depleted, and at the seemingly perennial cost of many lives of coal miners in major mine disasters.

All Japanese children also learn and experience firsthand that not much has changed from 1,000 years ago. The destructive typhoons arrive on schedule every year. The subsequent flooding takes its annual toll of many lives. The frequency of earthquakes provokes constant discussions about the impending "big one" like that of 1923 which demolished large areas of Tokyo killing thousands. When the school building begins to shake and the classroom windows rattle, the faces of the children reveal their deep fear of natural disasters in this land prone to such occurrences. That many children are sitting on earthquake cushions made by their mothers to hold over their heads during the real event cannot ease the anxiety felt with the first breath-taking sway of the building. In addition, the massive snowstorms cut transportation arteries in the mountainous areas of the country periodically throughout the winter, all extensively reported on nationwide television.

The fragility and the inconveniences of life in Japan surround every child. The overcrowding he experiences wherever he goes reminds him, and the school merely reinforces it, that the twentieth-century Japanese are as subject to the vagaries of nature as were their tenth-century ancestors. Earthquakes cannot yet be predicted. Typhoons cannot be circumvented. Huge loss of life through natural catastrophes cannot be avoided in an overpopulated country. Some would even say that contemporary Japanese society is more delicately poised on the verge of disaster than that of the ancestors because modern industrial nations like Japan survive on fossil fuels, most of which must be imported into these islands from all over the world. The lifeline of this nation remains tenuous at best. The Japanese child cannot escape that fact of life.

Children are taught in schools in multiple ways that Japan has been a poor nation primarily because of its natural limitations and that the Japanese people have always had to gambare in order to adjust to the harsh realities of this land. They are taught in their history classes that their ancestors early on had to gambare – to sacrifice – in order to survive, and that to modernize and industrialize, the Japanese people have had to run twice as fast as their Western industrial rivals. They learn, for example, about the United States as a rich nation blessed with abundant resources and talented people. They study the history of Japan traditionally learning from the West, especially about modern science and technology.

In other words, Japanese children develop a certain mental attitude of inferiority to Western nations and Western people. And yet they also gain great respect for their ancestors who, despite the enormity of their adverse conditions, persevered through much suffering to bring Japan into the modern world. Still there persists the general feeling, a legacy from the past, that Japan continues in an inferior position to the United States and the West, the lands of Ben Franklin, Lincoln, Shakespeare, Bach, and Einstein. Japanese children in school learn that for their race of people to keep up with the West, they have had to continue to persevere under trying difficulties. They are taught, not necessarily overtly, that gambare is as necessary for contemporary Japanese society as it was 1,000 years ago.

A simple example of this attitude in the contemporary school can be found in our son's second grade social studies textbook, as always approved by the Ministry of Education, used at the neighborhood elementary school. The course for the entire year concentrated on one topic: Work (*Iroiro na Shigoto*). Curiously enough, in a middle-class society where massive numbers of children live in cities, not one chapter was devoted to the white-collar office worker. Rather, each chapter

＊さかなやさんの 一日です。 はたらいている人のつもりになって、 しごとをするときの きもちを かんがえてみましょう。

FIGURE 5.1

FIGURE 5.2

きんじょの
人が、手つだいに
きて います。
あさ 早くから、
夕がた おそくま
で、はたらきます。

あしたは、
となりの うちの
田うえです。

子どもを あずかって います。

FIGURE 5.3

なわを　はって　います。なんの　ためでしょう。

田うえが
はじまりまし
た。
　どろ田の
なかで、こし
を　かがめな
がら、せっせ
と　なえを
うえます。

FIGURE 5.4

田に　水が　ないと，いねは　かれて　しまいます。

どてが　きれると　どう　なるのでしょう。

FIGURE 5.5

田うえが すんでから
も、 いろいろな しごと
が あります。
しんぱいな ことも
おこります。

どうぐや くすりを つかって,
なんども くさとりを します。

むしや びょうきを ふせぐ ために, くすりを まきます。

FIGURE 5.6

おとうさんたちは、とおい

山で、とまりがけで　しごと

を　します。

のこぎりの　音や、

木の　たおれる　音が、

ひびきます。

おとうさんたちは、

どんな　ことに、気を

つけて　はたらいて

いるのでしょう。

FIGURE 5.7

FIGURE 5.8

こわれた　つぶや、たね
の　ある　つぶを　とりの
ぞく　人も　います。
　かんに　つぶを　入れる
人や、かんに　ふたを
する　人なども　います。
　どの　人も、おなじ
ばしょに　立ったまま、
いそがしそうに　手を
うごかして　います。

かんに　つぶを　入れます。

ふたを　します。

はかりに　かけます。

FIGURE 5.9

この こうじょうでは、
まい日、ゆかを 水で
きれいに あらって
います。
また、こうじょうの
中で、しごとを する
ときに はく くつを、
きめて います。
なぜ、このような
ことを するのでしょう。

FIGURE 5.10

focused on work requiring hard manual labor where perseverance and endurance are essential to get the job done. The text begins with a day in the life of a fish monger and moves on to the rice farmer, the woodcutter, and the worker in a canning factory, among others. The following pages were taken from the heart of the textbook (Figures 5.1 – 5.10).

Gambare has by now become a cultural trait institutionalized by the school, and the child accepts it as a natural part of his life. Teachers do not instruct their students to study for the kimatsu tesuto, the term examination, in order for Japan to compete with the United States. That isn't necessary. It has simply become the normal function of the school and the teacher to employ gambare under any trying circumstance to motivate, to urge, and, of great importance, when necessary to shame. Shame, the fear of disgrace, is one of the great issues in Japanese culture and psychology. It is closely allied to the concept of gambare.

When a Japanese child lets down, does not give his all, his teacher challenges him to gambare, not just to persevere to accomplish a goal but to exert every effort toward keeping that child "running full speed" in any endeavor. If repeated efforts fail, then a sense of shame is brought to bear upon the laggard. The sense of shame relates not only to the fact that the child has failed to live up to his individual potential but also to the fact he has let his group down. To succeed, all must gambare together. Failure becomes more likely when one of the group does not heed the call to gambare.

Peer group pressure, as has been noted, is a powerful factor in every society. But it is especially potent in Japanese society where the fear of personal embarrassment among the young is pervasive. Perhaps the primary reason students seldom ask questions during class and dread to be called upon to stand and answer a teacher's question is the fear of making a mistake in front of their group. The resulting embarrassment and shame are agonizing to the typical Japanese teenager.

Teachers, as a last resort, play upon this acute sense of embarrassment and shame when a student does not persevere. He has let the goup down. Others are sacrificing. He must be ashamed of himself for not gambaring, sacrificing, while his peers are. He must then take responsibility and show remorse. The sense of shame for letting others down can be engulfing to Japanese youth, leading to the ultimate act of repentance, suicide, an act many Japanese can understand and empathize with as the demands of gambare simply overwhelm certain individuals.

The sense of gambare is engulfing in Japanese society in part because the home reinforces the school and vice versa in the effort to instill it in the child. The unique phrase kyoiku mama, educationally minded mothers, has come into everyday language in the postwar period as a result of this development. It is the phenomenon of many middle-class parents resorting to unusual means to motivate their offspring to gambare for examination preparation, in part to avoid the family embarrassment of failure. It falls on the mother to pursue this goal because many fathers come home late from work every evening and work Staturday mornings as well.

The kyoiku mama takes her responsibility very seriously. She must maintain a household atmosphere conducive for study, especially during the final year of schooling at each level before the next entrance examination. That means an area must be preserved within the tiny house or apartment where the child can devote hours to study, to memorization, to the practice of test taking with mock examinations, as well as preparing for the yobiko or juku classes in the evening and/or weekends. The family life style is often patterned around the study routine of the child as the kyoiku mama exerts every effort to exhort the child to gambare in the preparation for the examination.

The child at the final year of the elementary school who plans to enter a private secondary school or who is at the final year of the junior or senior high school thus comes under great pressure not only from the school but from the home as well in his examination preparation. In fact, the Japanese have coined a special name for the student at each of these upper levels known as jukensei, the examination student. When someone refers to a student as a jukensei, invariably others defer to him in every way possible in order not to interfere with his examination preparation. His friends, relatives, and teachers will shower encouragement on him. Gambare!

Consequently, at home and at school, gambare is a primary motivating influence on the average Japanese student to do his best in whatever endeavor he has set before him. The tennis club, the mathematics lesson, the lunchtime duty, the osoji, the afterschool yobiko, and the entrance examination are all pursued with a sense of gambare. And even the final school event, graduation, is saturated with gambare.

A graduation ceremony in a regular public school in Japan from the elementary level onwards is an event pregnant with reinforcements of gambare. Perhaps nowhere in the world are such elaborate elementary and junior high school graduation exercises conducted as those in Japan. Not only are they unforgettable, they are intended as the final effort of the school to implant its influence on each child as he goes on to the next school or to the company with the spirit of gambare.

The graduation ceremony of the nearby elementary school, from where our three children received their entire basic education, is fairly typical and represents one of the most formal events of a child's early life. Mothers come in their finest black kimonos and dresses; fathers, in their black suits. In this ceremonial attire we then unceremoniously put on well-worn school slippers, or our personal slippers if we remembered to bring them from home, at the entrance of the school carefully removing our shoes because no one enters the school building with street shoes on at any time. In fact, one of the more humorous scenes of the Japanese school to a foreigner is a drafty gymnasium full of adults in formal attire endeavoring to keep their feet warm in open-heeled slippers.

The seats are all prearranged in the gymnasium with the parents instructed to take the back seats by a designated time. At the appointed moment the sixth grade kumis, with all dressed in their best clothes, come marching into the gym one at a time led by their teacher as "Pomp and Circumstance" rings out over the loudspeakers. It is the last act of solidarity between students and their tannin no sensei, their teacher who had been with them for two years. It all, naturally, runs like clockwork precision because it has been well rehearsed for weeks.

The ceremony itself is one of extreme formality with students standing, sitting, and even bowing on command. The principal attired in formal tails and sometimes even white gloves reads a most serious and ceremonial speech replete with the spirit of gambare. Then follows a parade of short speeches by a representative from the local school board, the principal of the nearest junior high school where most students will enter, and perhaps the previous principal of the elementary school itself or the president of the PTA. The speakers often urge the students to gambare. Other local dignitaries formally attired are then introduced and duly recognized. This recognition is especially important to local political figures.

Following that the presentation of the graduation certificates is made with each student one-by-one parading to the stage as the teacher calls the graduate's name, bowing to the principal, receiving the diploma, turning and bowing stiffly to the audience, and hurriedly returning to his or her seat. With that completed the fifth graders, the only other students in attendance, then enter into a long and well-rehearsed choral chanting in which they invoke the call over and over again: "Never forget our school.

Never forget our school!" They finally challenge the graduating sixth graders to "Gambare! Gambare! Gambare!" The chant begins in a low tone rising in crescendo to the final gamba'e. It's a memorable moment of an impressive ceremony. It's repeated in a variety of forms at each level of schooling until the Japanese student finally becomes a Japanese worker.

Every Japanese worker, a product of the system, has thus undergone a common school experience enmeshed in the spirit of gambare. Some schools are more immersed than others. Nevertheless every, yes, every school in a multiplicity of ways encourages the students to gambare from the first year onward culminating with the graduation ceremony. Therefore, when the new employees arrive for the initial company orientation, representatives from the president on down urge them to launch into their working life by gambaring for the company. Nearly all have been well prepared for the tasks, the challenges, and the sacrifices that lie ahead.

This sense of gambare, which permeates the work force from the top echelon down to the lowest levels, provides one of the primary keys to the success of the Japanese company. The employer can expect the new employees graduating from the school not only to be literate in reading, writing, and arithmetic but to do their utmost for their company. The managers can expect the new recruits to persevere, to sacrifice if need be, for the general welfare of the company. Not all do, to be sure, but the vast majority respond accordingly. The Japanese company has been well served by the school.

The Japanese firm thus relies heavily on the Japanese school to produce a literate graduate who can fit in harmoniously with the company spirit. The morale of the employee is considered of great importance because perseverance is maintained through a mutual sense of sacrifice. And because every graduate has experienced a similar upbringing through a school system with a high degree of similarity bordering on a national effort to instill a sense of gambare, this school experience common to all enables the company to thrive on a work force with a common sense of perseverance.

It's a two-way effort, though. Management must gambare in return if it is to maintain the level of gambare of the new crop of employees. Management responds accordingly. Not only do the vast majority demonstrate their perseverance by remaining daily at the office from one to two or more hours after the younger staff and the blue-collar employees leave, they take short annual vacations. Managerial vacations average about five days a year. Many take even fewer days. Few take the two- or three-week vacations allotted to them.

It is the mutual sense of gambare throughout Japanese industry that strengthens the productivity of Japanese factories. It is reminiscent of the Protestant work ethic made famous by Max Weber's classic *The Protestant Ethic and the Spirit of Capitalism.* Written at the turn of the century, it analyzed the immense vitality of nineteenth-century Western capitalism as dependent upon hard working Protestant entrepreneurs who firmly believed that turning a profit was good in the sight of God. To the Christian, hard work was God's calling. Wasting time, loafing on the job, was the deadliest of sins.

If Weber were alive today, it seems doubtful that he would be inspired to write a similar book about Western societies such as the United States or England and the Protestant work ethic there. Instead, to locate the work ethic at work in the world today, one of his prime examples would undoubtedly be Japan, without the Protestantism. Ironically what Weber witnessed in the Christian West in the nineteenth century is well represented in the East in the twentieth-century non-Christian land of Japan.

This nation has achieved an attitude toward labor on the part of its work force worthy of being dubbed the "Protestant work ethic." And, as in the West of the last century, it underlies the success of Japanese industry of this century. Fundamental to that achievement has been the spirit of gambare – perseverance – carefully nourished throughout the upbringing of every Japanese worker during his many, many days at school. The work ethic is alive in Japan today, thanks, in part to the Japanese school.

We often encounter in our readings on Japan how this society has transformed itself into a modern nation from its feudal past in approximately 100 years. That time frame encompasses the period from the establishing of Japan's formal relations with the United States and other Western countries in the 1860s to the economic miracle of the 1960's-70s. The capital city of Tokyo, for example, exhibits all the trappings of a modern Western city with skyscrapers, gleaming hotels and department stores, rapid transit, traffic jams, and all the rest. On the face of it, Japan has undergone modernization.

This theme as played out in the modern stage, screen, TV, and other art forms depicts the painful process of old Japanese agrarian values undergoing a dramatic urbanizational transition. Old Japanese feudal patterns are being replaced with modern democratic ideas based on the Western model of the United States. From this perspective, where does gambare fit in? Is there a place for it in a modern society?

Again, what appears on the surface in Japanese society often masks a unique reality beneath. The travel books encourage the tourist to step off the glittering main streets of modern Tokyo on to the narrow side streets to return to the old Tokyo, the old Japan. Although that is still possible, even these physical remnants of the past are disappearing with modern towering structures replacing the old. There is, however, another way of looking at contemporary Japanese society and its industry that reflects on the theme of Japanese stability rather than change, on the persistence of the old rather than the emerging new. From this perspective, the concern focuses on how the old spiritual values have survived the modern era of industrialism instead of being replaced by so-called modern values, implying Western or American.

To this author, who has been living in Japan for over two decades, what is most impressive about this society is its underlying stability based on the old rather than the new. Certain enduring characteristics of the old Japan undergird the new Japan, with all its sparkle, speed, noise, and efficiency. That's superficial. The foundation of this modern industrial supereconomic power is the old traditional values of this very old society. And one of the essential ingredients of the base of the modern is the enduring spirit of gambare – persevere – from the past. One of the most fortunate aspects of modern Japan is that the spirit of gambare existed as a fundamental feature of being Japanese long before Western industrial influences reached these shores. The rapid and successful transition from the rural to the urban, the agrarian to the industrial, was dependent on the persistence of the old value system implied in the simple cry: Gambare!

The importance of the Japanese school in today's modern Japanese society is that it persists in perpetuating this old value system of gambare, which Westerners like to call the work ethic, with each new generation. It was reflected in the experience of the university student referred to previously. Even though the young fellow was smitten with Marxist patterns of Western political ideology, his first test in the real world of work brought him back to the enduring values of old Japan. "Sensei, I can't leave the office before the others," proved his sense of being Japanese. It was his honest way of reflecting gambare.

6

THE FUTURE WORKER
Dento: Tradition

Tradition: an inherited pattern of thought, action or social custom; cultural continuity in social attitudes and instructions.

— Webster

The dawn of high technology has emerged. The information society is upon us. Lasers, robotics, optical fibers, microelectronics, super computers, biotechnology. The world of tomorrow has been ushered in today. Conspicuous among the leaders in the competition to develop advanced technology stands, or rather races, Japan. Many of its firms are embarked on an all-out effort not necessarily to win the race, as if that were possible, but to compete among the leaders in the high technology stakes of the future.

As in all competitions the Japanese enter, with two strikes against them at the outset, their chances depend almost exclusively on the sagacity, the competency, the foresight, and the vitality of the people. However, the Japanese people are not, it is worth remembering, peculiarly endowed. They, too, must solve the intricacies of producing a laser beam just as firms in other countries must. The Japanese have no mystical wand to wave over the shop floor to produce miraculously microchips outperforming microchips made abroad. To be in the vanguard of the high technology era, the so-called electronic society, the Japanese are fully aware that they must work harder than their U.S. competitors.

149

With zeal unsurpassed, the Japanese are doing just that. They have unleashed their characteristic enthusiasm and keen sense of competition to the effort. With an element of impetuousness, the Japanese have accepted the challenge of high technology. The spirit of gambare, a cultural tradition that sustains the Japanese in any endeavor, may be of inestimable value to Japan in the global competition for advanced technology.

The Japanese have once again been confronted with a new challenge, the twenty-first century of high technology. In the modern history of Japanese industrialism, this represents the third great moment of historical consequence. The initial industrial challenge came during the late nineteenth century following the 300-year seclusion policy. Japan then moved successfully from agrarian feudalism to industrial modernism by adapting Western technology to traditional Japanese cultural traits. The challenge was met.

The second epochal challenge followed World War II. The massive destruction of Japanese industry during wartime provided the seemingly unfortunate circumstances for an industrial regeneration of unprecedented proportions. Once again, Japan was destined to look westward for a model. Impelled by historical precedent this society met the challenge by demonstrating a skillful capacity for adapting Western technological innovations to traditional Japanese cultural traits. Not only did Japan meet the challenge: it forged ahead sufficiently to provide a challenge of its own to the United States and other Western countries.

The emergence of the third great industrial challenge to the Japanese, high technology, marks the beginning of an unusual era. The conditions this time are markedly different from those in the past. Previously Japan found itself in a vastly inferior position to the United States and the West vis-à-vis technology. There was always a Western model, a teacher for the Japanese to learn from. Japan was traditionally the subservient student. She could dispatch her emissaries to the Western countries to glean whatever technology possible to adapt to traditional Japanese cultural and social elements. Remnants of that attitude persist today.

However, the third great industrial challenge to Japan emerges at a time in her history when she is technologically on a near-equal footing, depending upon the yardstick, with the United States and Western Europe. For the first time the Japanese, still running at a faster pace than the U.S. competitors, begin the race in what could perhaps be described as rough equivalency. The challenge now, in historical contrast, is not to catch up with the United States which previously provided the great inducement to this very proud race of people. Rather, the challenge for the end of this century and the next is to remain in the vanguard alongside the other leaders. And this challenge is as challenging to the Japanese as the previous ones were. The traditional spirit of gambare is being once again rejuvenated to meet the technological challenge of the twenty-first century.

But the will to win in and by itself is insufficient to produce winners. Spirit cannot compensate for lack of physical endurance. The Olympics, for example, are always stark reminders to the Japanese that no matter how zealously their athletes aspire for gold medals, the spirit of gambare is simply not sufficient to overcome the strength and endurance of Western athletes with their larger and more powerful physiques. In the annual Asian games, though, the Japanese contingent is usually near the top levels.

In the global race for high technology, the major combatants are primarily from the United States and Western Europe. Fortunately for the Japanese, size or physique is irrelevant in this electronic marathon. Brain power rather than muscle power will be the deciding factor. Even devoid of natural resources and a horrendous lack of space, the Japanese hold better odds in this competition than they do in international competitive sports where their smaller physical size inevitably undermines their skill and spirit.

The development of high technology has become the goal of all industrialized nations. Our concern here, then, is whether Japan can maintain its international competitiveness in advanced technology not just through the 1980s, which it has accomplished rather successfully so far, but into the year 2000 and beyond. For example, can Japanese companies continue to hold such an impressive share of the electronics market throughout the world as electronics assume the central role in high technology? In other words, can the highly competitive Japanese industry of today sustain its competitiveness into the twenty-first century?

As the Japanese pioneers of Western technology in the nineteenth century understood, the competitiveness of an industrial society depends to a large extent on the productivity of its schools. This assumption is even more applicable for the twenty-first century than it was for the nineteenth century. Our focus, then, is whether the Japanese school can be entrusted to produce a loyal, literate, competent, and diligent worker imbued with the spirit of gambare into the twenty-first century of high technology. And that is, perforce, an extremely difficult issue to be addressed.

It is essential to understand that the Japanese school of today, which, it has been argued, produces a loyal, literate, competent worker fundamentally prepared to meet the industrial challenge of this century, can by no means be characterized as modern. By U.S. standards the Japanese classroom is far behind the times. Not only are many of the buildings and barren classrooms traditional in design, the teaching methods and classroom atmosphere resemble nineteenth-century institutions more than twentieth-century schools.

Therein lies an element of considerable import. We would be remiss if we failed to recognize the traditional character of Japanese education and society in, ironically, the emerging era of high technology. The sophisticated electronic wizardry emanating from highly automated Japanese factories stands in sharp contrast to the rather old-fashioned, traditional classroom of many, if not most, of the Japanese public schools today. And it is precisely in that traditional school where the basic education of Japanese engineers and designers, as well as of the consumers, of the twenty-first century is being provided.

In a nation that has achieved international notoriety for its highly developed computer industry, the diffusion of computer-assisted teaching, and computers themselves, in Japanese schools seems incongruous. In contrast, computers in the classroom constitute the litmus test for evaluating the standards of a school in rapidly increasing numbers of U.S. communities. Even elementary schools with at least one computer are becoming common. American youth at all levels staring glassy eyed at the computer screen in the classroom symbolizes a modern school preparing for the era of high technology.

Not so in Japan. "MYCOM," the microcomputer, is gradually finding its way into the tiny homes and minuscule apartments of Japan. But computer penetration into the public schools has barely begun. For example, according to the pertinent office of the Ministry of Education, only 0.1 percent of the elementary schools and 0.9 percent of the junior high schools were equipped with computers in the mid-1980s for a grand total of 121 out of 45,054 public schools at the compulsory level.[1] From all indications, it will be quite some time before computer-assisted teaching, a popular concept in the United States, becomes widespread in Japan. There seems to be little disposition so far by Japanese teachers to employ modern technology currently flowing from Japanese factories for classroom teaching purposes.

How, then, can this nation ever hope to enter the twenty-first century with a classroom that resembles one out of the nineteenth? How can the

Japanese aspire to innovations in high technology with a classroom conspicuously devoid of high technology? How can they teach about high technology without employing it in the teaching process?

Perhaps these inconsistencies will be too great to overcome. The Japanese may be committing a colossal error in not modernizing their antiquated classrooms with the tools of the future such as computers and word processors. Perhaps they'll face their Waterloo in the twenty-first century by failing to modernize their traditional teaching methods whereby the teacher explains and the students memorize for the ubiquitous examination. The Japanese challenge of today may be just a passing phenomenon.

However, the Japanese have demonstrated over and over again that a traditional classroom can produce a worker who adapts readily to the requirements of modern technology. After all, from the available evidence applying any type of measuring instrument, Japan has achieved the rank of one of the leading industrial nations of the world today. Yet its classrooms are prime examples of the traditional school of yesterday. The contrast between the modern factory and the many older school buildings represents, ironically, another key to an understanding of the so-called Japanese economic miracle.

Japan has been capable of meeting the industrial challenge of the United States and the West up to now with a school system based on the most traditional methods possible. The typical class, especially at the secondary level as we have described, cannot be portrayed in any sense as a provocative experience. Innovative, creative, imaginative ideas are not encouraged. The cross fertilization of disparate opinions, the give-and-take of conflicting attitudes, the free discussion of varying notions are uncharacteristic of the Japanese classroom. Student participation is minimal.

The foreign language classes of English, yet to be considered, are good examples of the traditional classroom methods employed in Japan, yet they have a relationship to Japan's success in penetrating U.S. markets. The overwhelming number of classroom teachers of English employ the direct translation method, which is based primarily on translating written English passages into Japanese. Studying English in Japan is thus based heavily on a laborious memorization of grammatical rules and English vocabularies in their Japanese equivalent. Very little oral English is used during the English class. Few language laboratories with their tape recorders, so abundant in this country, are installed in the Japanese public schools. Such facilities could provide the students with an opportunity to hear spoken native English and to imitate correct pronunciation.

Nevertheless, written English tests in public schools can be quite intricate. They often require detailed knowledge of the techniques of the language, both written and oral. For example, first year junior high students are required to place accent marks correctly on the syllables of words that are rarely pronounced correctly in class. On occasion our children, native English speakers, have had difficulty on some English tests in the Japanese junior high school because they weren't sure where an accent mark belonged on certain words. The teacher, who seldom spoke English, knew exactly where it belonged. So did many of the other students. Other detailed exercises are included that have little practical utility in a class tantamount to a course in written translation.

Critics of foreign language teaching, especially non-Japanese English teachers who are themselves usually native English speakers, decry the old-fashioned Japanese approach with its overwhelming emphasis on memorization of rules and vocabularies. They argue that it is senseless to teach written English without a base in verbal skills. In other words, the criticism is that the traditional English classes, which dominate the schools, are grossly ineffective because they fail to provide verbal skills essential for an effective understanding of written English. The proof of the pudding lies in the fact that the high school graduate, after studying English for six years, can on the average barely understand a simply constructed question, let alone answer the question in correct English. Many Japanese teachers of English are not much above this level in oral English.

There is, however, more here than meets the eye. First of all, in addition to the very heavy academic demands in Japanese and mathematics, not to mention science and social studies, virtually every high school graduate has studied English for six years. English begins essentially as a required course for all students in the seventh grade, or the first year of junior high school, and continues through the twelfth grade. Projecting this on a nationwide scale, because about 95 percent of all students now complete high school, nearly the whole adult population will eventually have studied a foreign language, at the minimum, for six years. In addition, a fair number will have studied a second foreign language also.

When a comparison is made with foreign language requirements in the United States where only eight states require high schools to offer it but none requires students to take it, the heavy demands the Japanese place on their students in foreign language study become strikingly clear.

In U.S. high schools, which graduate only about 75 percent of the age group, few students study any foreign language more than two years. In Japanese high schools, which graduate over 90 percent of the age group, nearly every student studies a foreign language for the entire three years in addition to the three years of English lessons at the junior high school. Can anyone in the United States imagine every junior high school student in every community in the United States taking a test in a foreign language similar to the following sample (Figure 6.1) taken from the English test required for all junior high students entering the public high schools of Tokyo?

Part of the reason for the situation in the United States relates to the university requirements in language. Only 20 percent of all four-year public colleges in the United States required foreign language credits for admission when the report, *A Nation at Risk*, was published in 1983.[2] And, even though there has been a gradual trend to increase the minimum foreign language requirements for university entrance since then, they remain in sharp contrast to the language requirements for all students in the Japanese school. For example, the Japanese Ministry of Education's course of study reduced the minimum weekly English classes from four to three in the early 1980s at the junior and senior high school levels because of the heavy load. Nevertheless some schools continue to schedule it for four periods each week because English remains a required subject on virtually all high school and university entrance examinations. English teachers both at the junior and senior high school deplore the reduced time available in some schools to the teaching of English.

What does this have to do with the future Japanese worker? The international language of business and commerce is primarily based on English. The international language of science and technology is also heavily based on English. Every Japanese worker, the vast majority incapable of speaking English, has a basic understanding of written English and can, with the use of the dictionary, understand the content of manuals and reports published in English. Access to the international business, technical, and science community is thus made available in a sense to the entire working population of Japan, although in perspective relatively few Japanese workers have a need to deal in English in any form during their working career.

And that is precisely the point. How many Japanese out of the total population actually need to speak, read, or write English in their daily lives either at work or home? The number is greatly limited. And yet nearly all students are devoting three or four periods a week during six

1 次の1〜5のAとBとの対話の文章を完成するには，□の中にどの
ような語を入れるのがよいか。それぞれの下に示したア〜エのうちから，適切な
ものを選べ。

1　A: Is this your dictionary?
　　B: No, it's not □ . It's Mary's.
　　　　ア　yours　　イ　mine　　ウ　hers　　エ　me
2　A: I want to talk about tomorrow's party with you.
　　B: Can you give me some time? I need thirty minutes □
　　　　finish my homework.
　　　　ア　by　　　イ　in　　　ウ　for　　　エ　to
3　A: Can I walk to the station from here?
　　B: No. It's □ far to walk. So take any bus at the bus stop
　　　　over there.
　　　　ア　too　　　イ　enough　　ウ　only　　エ　never
4　A: Don't sit on that chair. One of its legs is broken.
　　B: Oh, □ it? I didn't know that.
　　　　ア　can　　　イ　does　　ウ　is　　　エ　has
5　A: Our teacher often speaks to us in easy English in his class. I
　　　　understand almost every word he says.
　　B: It's also easy □ me to understand him.
　　　　ア　at　　　イ　for　　　ウ　by　　　エ　with

2 次の対話の文章を読んで，あとの各問に答えよ。
　Mr. Smith:　It's time to go to see the game. Are you ready, Tom?
　Tom:　　　(From his room) I'm coming, Father.
　Mr. Smith:　Come down quickly. We don't want to miss the first pitch.
　　　　　　　(Tom comes into the living room.)
　Tom:　　　I'm here. Has Uncle George come?
　Mr. Smith:　No. He is busy now and wants to meet us at the ball park.
　Tom:　　　Mother hasn't seen a baseball game for a long time. I hope
　　　　　　　she will go with us.
　Mr. Smith:　I don't think so. She says your sister Susie can't stay
　　　　　　(1)
　　　　　　　home alone, and Susie doesn't like baseball. Well, I know
　　　　　　　your friend Jim likes baseball very much. Is he going today?
　　　　　　　Which team does he like? Does he like our team or the
　　　　　　　other team?
　Tom:　　　He likes our team. He'll be there today. Do you think
　　　　　　(2)
　　　　　　　our team will win, Father?

FIGURE 6.1 Tokyo Metropolitan Public High School Entrance
Examination, English (Excerpts)

156

Mr. Smith: I don't know, Tom, but it may win. I hope so. Let's go to the bus stop. The buses will be very crowded today. We don't have much time. The game begins at 1:30 and we are going to meet Uncle George there ten minutes before the start of the game. <u>Now shall we go?</u>
₍₃₎

〔注〕 miss 見そこなう　　pitch 投球　　alone ひとりで

　　　 team チーム　　win 勝つ　　be crowded こんでいる

〔問 1〕 <u>I don't think so.</u> の so が表している内容は，次のうちのどれか。
₍₁₎

ア she will meet your friend Jim

イ she will stay home with Susie

ウ she will ask Uncle George to come here

エ she will go with us

〔問 2〕 <u>He likes our team.</u> を読むとき，文中で最も強く発音する語はどれか。
₍₂₎

He likes our team.
ア　イ　ウ　エ

〔問 3〕 <u>Now shall we go?</u> の we は，次のうちのだれを指しているか。
₍₃₎

ア Mr. Smith and Tom

イ Mr. Smith, Mrs. Smith and Tom

ウ Mr. Smith and Susie

エ Mrs. Smith, Tom and Susie

〔問 4〕 次の(1)〜(5)について，(A)□〜(F)□ の中にそれぞれ1語を書き入れて，本文の内容に合うように，質問に対する答えの文を完成せよ。

(1)

Why do Mr. Smith and Tom have to leave home soon?

Because they want to see today's (A)□ from the beginning.

(2)

Does Mrs. Smith go to the ball park with her family very often?

(B)□ , she (C)□ .

(3)

Why is Uncle George going to the ball park without coming to Mr. Smith's house?

Because he doesn't have (D)□ to come to Mr. Smith's house before going to the ball park.

(4)

How are Mr. Smith and Tom going to the ball park?

They are going there by (E)□ .

(5)

When are Mr. Smith and Tom going to meet Uncle George at the ball park?

They are going to meet him at one (F)□ .

FIGURE 6.1 Tokyo Metropolitan Public High School Entrance Examination, English (Excerpts) (Continued)

157

3 次の文章を読んで, あとの各問に答えよ。

On the morning of New Year's Day, Mrs. Miller came into the children's room and said, "Get up, Frank and Ken. <u>Our dog, Tilly, has something to show you.</u> She had five puppies early this morning!"
(1)
"Five puppies!" shouted the boys. <u>Frank and Ken didn't know about it until then.</u> They were very happy.
(2)

They ran to the dog house. Soon they were looking at Tilly's new family. "Look, Frank! They are small red puppies," called Ken. "How many can we keep?" "<u>Mother and Father said we couldn't keep any puppies.</u> When they are six weeks old, we must find homes for all
(3)
of them," said Frank.

"But all our friends have pets already," said Ken. Then Frank said, "I've a good idea. ABC TV is going to invite to the TV station some fathers whose babies were born on New Year's Day. I saw it in the newspaper. Nothing was said about the kind of babies. If we tell everyone about our puppies on TV, we'll find homes for them. <u>I'll write
(4)
to the TV station.</u>"

<u>Two days later Frank got a letter asking him to come to the station
(5)
on Saturday afternoon at two.</u> <u>He read the letter over and over again.</u>
(6)
When the two boys arrived at the TV station, <u>eight New Year's
(7)
Day fathers were already waiting for the program to start.</u> A tall man came over and said to Frank and Ken, "I'm Mr. Casey from ABC TV. Please sit down here."

Soon the program started, and each father talked about his new family. <u>Then it was the children's turn.</u> "And now, everyone," said Mr.
(8)
Casey. "Two boys are here to tell us about five New Year's Day babies at their house." <u>All the eight fathers were very surprised.</u> "Yes, five
(9)
babies! They have a dog whose name is Tilly and she had five puppies on New Year's Day. Can you tell us more about the puppies, boys?" said Mr. Casey.

"Yes, there are five in the dog house. They are red with white legs. There are three boys and two girls. We can't keep them, so if anyone has a home for them, we'll be very glad," said Frank.

FIGURE 6.1 Tokyo Metropolitan Public High School Entrance Examination, English (Excerpts) (Continued)

years of public schooling and then at the university studying English in a traditional classroom through traditional methods based on the written forms of the language. It would appear under these circumstances that the requirements for foreign language study in Japan may be far too great, especially when contrasted with the recommendation by the National Commission on Excellence in Education that U.S. high school students preparing for the university should have as a minimum only two years of foreign language study. Compare that recommendation, which is far from being fulfilled, with the six-year study of English for over 90 percent of all Japanese students.

The study of English in Japan, however, extends far beyond the classroom of the school. The demand for private classes in English is overwhelming from elementary children through the adult community. Many university students thrive on the income from private English tutoring of elementary and especially junior and senior high school students, the so-called jukensei, preparing for the exams. Native speakers of English are in great demand to offer language lessons, sometimes at exorbitant fees, whether they know anything about teaching English, and most do not. Private English schools abound. English teaching in Japan has become an entire industry in itself as a result, in part, of the examination requirements.

Notwithstanding the fact that they have learned English in the classroom almost exclusively in its written forms, this huge pool of high school graduates who have studied English for six years in public schools and those completing university-level studies, many supplementing that with private lessons along the way, serves Japanese industry rather well. Because the employees at all Japanese firms have some foundation in English, and a fair number go well beyond the basics, a Japanese company can send many of its representatives abroad to live and work effectively in the English-dominated world of business, commerce, and technology. A good number of Japanese representatives abroad have enormous difficulty with spoken English during the first part of their stay as a result of the way they learned English at school. However, with their basic knowledge of written English and a foundation in grammatical rules and strange nuances, they can function fairly effectively from the beginning. And as their verbal skills improve with exposure particularly in English-speaking societies, many if not most soon become capable representatives of their firms overseas.

Japanese products have penetrated U.S. markets through the efforts of Japanese businessmen living in the United States using English. There have been, to be sure, communication problems. But with the tens of thousands of Japanese citizens living in the greater New York area alone, for example, the majority related to Japanese firms studying every market trend, every U.S. product, in the language of the host, the Japanese company is able to readily adapt its products and style of business to the local market place. The English that Japanese businessmen learned during their six years of lower schooling and in the university, even though it was concentrated on traditional teaching methods, served them well as they increased their share of many U.S. markets and opened up new ones.

In sharp contrast, U.S. businessmen sent to Japan to represent their companies invariably arrive without understanding a word of Japanese beyond *sayonara*, of little use upon arrival. Not only can they not speak the language; they obviously cannot read the ideographs even to distinguish in department stores, train stations, and elsewhere the correct entrance to the lavatory. Their understanding of Japanese markets and business methods is horrendously restricted, which in turn makes it exceedingly difficult for their firms to do business in Japan profitably. Inevitably many U.S. businessmen assigned to Japan must rely on a Japanese, who has spent a minimum of six years at Japanese schools studying English, to serve as a translator. Few, if any, Japanese businessmen assigned to the United States rely on an American to translate English into Japanese for them.

Although Japanese teaching methods in the language classrooms, and in other subjects as well, can be characterized as traditional, this should not be misinterpreted to mean that all Japanese schools are well-ordered institutions rigidly enforcing Spartan discipline. In many instances they are not. The Japanese school can be a noisy place. The hallways bustle with activity. In a fair number of classes, the students are not passively taking notes, that is, not until they reach the final year as junkensei before the examination to the next school level. There is, depending on the teacher, of course, a considerable undercurrent of buzzing going on among students during class, especially at the junior high school. In addition, the walls are paper thin, the ill-fitting sliding doors partly open much of the time, so that distractions both from within and without render it difficult at times to hear the teacher.

In addition, the classroom surroundings are drab: the walls often in need of paint, the lighting bad, the desks worn. The individual kerosene stoves with their long chimney pipes extending to the window throughout the cold winter months further detract from the overall classroom appearance. Even though there is a gradual shift from the old-style open-wick kerosene stoves to the more recent models of so-called kerosene clean heaters, central heating systems are simply beyond consideration in the Japanese school. The desks are movable, but they're usually arranged in traditional straight rows. All in all it has the atmosphere of an old-time classroom.

Notwithstanding the apparent contradiction of a top ranked industrial power gearing up to develop fifth, and inevitably sixth, generation computers, with a contemporary school system obsolete by U.S. standards, further analysis may point in a different direction. First of all, there is a historical parallel. The postwar reform of Japanese education in the late 1940s is of importance if we are to appreciate more fully Japan's competitive potential in the high technology race of the twenty-first century, in spite of the lack of modernization of the classroom.

By the end of World War II, the vast majority of urban school buildings in Japan had been destroyed. Most of the high school and even junior high students had been assigned to work in nearby factories. City children had long since been removed to the rural areas for safe keeping. The entire school system had already been closed for nearly half a year. Both the Japanese school and factory lay in ruin, the horrible legacy of unbridled militarism.

The American Occupation forces under General Douglas MacArthur (SCAP) post haste launched the painful process of assisting the Japanese to piece their factories and schools together again. From the ashes of the old, a new Japan would be constructed. A restructured Japanese society imbued with democratic principles and understandings would be produced by the new school. A new ethical system would permeate the classroom.

The Fundamental Law of Education promulgated in 1947 under American Occupation approval, some would perhaps unfairly say coercion, set the tone of the reforms. "We shall esteem individual dignity while education which aims at the creation of culture, general and rich in individuality, shall be spread far and wide." The aim of education will be the rearing of the people who shall "esteem individual value and be imbued with the independent spirit."

One of the salient features of the new education was the prominence given to individualism, a fundamental aspect of U.S. society and the school upon which the reforms were modeled. Although the Japanese leaders at the time endorsed the new foundation for democratic education, the emphasis on the concept of individualism introduced a degree of ambiguity, an inconsistency, with traditional patterns of group behavior and group loyalty. Still, U.S. military superiority had eclipsed Japan's misguided expansionism. The United States remained the teacher, the model, for the Japanese.

The average Japanese classroom teacher, long accustomed to managing her class as one large kumi divided into six or eight hans, found herself in a quandary over the new thrust toward individualism. Practical common sense manifested to her the necessity of marshaling the collective resources of her students. Japan lay in ruin. To recover, to run faster than the seemingly superior U.S. model in order to catch up, necessitated the combined efforts of all.

Prompted by the well-intentioned U.S. advisors with a most appealing reasoning, couched in irresistible democratic terminology, many Japanese teachers endorsed the new ideas by experimenting with modern progressive teaching theories emphasizing the needs and interests of the individual. The new ideas were based on the theories emanating from the great U.S. educational reforms instituted by John Dewey in the prewar period. The traditional one-way method of teaching gave way here and there to techniques utilizing student participation and student initiative. In many a classroom children were encouraged to speak up, ask questions, give opinions, confront each other with varying viewpoints. Criticism was applauded, free discussion promoted, individual student activity nurtured. The child was encouraged to take an active role in the learning process rather than be a passive note taker. The teacher-centered or subject-centered classroom was to be reoriented into the child-centered classroom. The traditional was to become the progressive. The future worker of Japan was to undergo a new type of democratic education based on U.S. ideals.

Alas, it was unnatural. The enchantment with pupil-teacher relationships American style was short lived. The intrinsic value and dignity of the individual has deep roots in Japanese social customs. Individuality per se does not. This distinction, as viewed by a non-Japanese, remains a key element of the social structure of this nation and an elusive concept difficult to analyze. It's important in this context.

The average Japanese in any endeavor has come to appreciate, through what could be described as an innate sense, the limitations of this precarious land and its people. They have proven to be, above all else, realists. Under the most adverse of geographical circumstances, they have proven over and over again that in unity there is strength. There is also comfort and refuge, a sense of security in group action rather than in individual initiative. One of the most appealing features of the society to the Japanese themselves, and one which inhibits the Japanese in their relationships with "outsiders," is the individual's relationship to the group, as has been explored.

At the same time there has developed in this land a respect for the worth and dignity of the individual, to an extreme say some Western critics. The interminable group meetings intended to arrive at an acceptable consensus by all before a collective decision can be made appears inefficient to the outsider. The concern for the individual viewpoint canoften obstruct constructive action. For example, on occasion the completion of a major superhighway can be held up for years until a neighborhood group protesting the noise levels in their area finally accepts some compromise. The will of the majority must not contravene that of the minority. A compromise is always sought to achieve group consensus and harmony, no matter the group, before action can be taken. The process can also result in inaction in its overconcern for minority viewpoints.

When the U.S. advisors emphasized the needs and interests of the individual as a basis for the new classroom teaching methods, the Japanese teacher in the initial postwar period found it extremely difficult if not unrealistic to handle 50 students or more in a class accordingly. The problem was further compounded by the severe economic depression of the late 1940s. How could basic mathematics, the multiplication tables, for example, be learned other than by the traditional method: memorize, repeat, drill, and test? How could such a large class of students learn the several thousand characters necessary to read a newspaper unless they were all studying the same lesson being led painstakingly through the predetermined list?

Many teachers found the new ways alien and far too difficult to manage. It grated on their sensibilities. Traditional teaching was much simpler and, to the average teacher, more effective in preparing for the examinations anyway. And examinations were the only known way to evaluate the 50 or so students in the class. Idealism soon gave way to realism. The typical classroom teacher spontaneously returned to the old one-way teaching methods. The government took the lead by producing a standardized curriculum. Tradition prevailed.

Not only were the new teaching methods originating from the United States, designed to strengthen individuality, found to be inconsistent with the traditional Japanese teaching methods; the new system of local control through locally elected school boards on the U.S. model came into conflict with Japanese custom. To the Americans, democratic education meant education "close to the people," eloquently explained to the Japanese public in the report of the first United States Education Mission to Japan, 1946, which set the basis for the U.S. reforms of Japanese education that ensued. Locally elected representatives from the community developing local school policy represented democracy in action. It epitomized grassroots democracy to the Americans.

Some Japanese officials interpreted the needs of Japan differently. The only natural resources of this country, the people, had to be cooperatively harnessed as a team to work together. Strength in unity is intuitive to the Japanese. In order to reconstruct a shattered society, all of the available resources had to be efficiently marshaled. A new emphasis on individualism could lead to disaster at a time when this nation was endeavoring to recover from the ultimate disaster, total economic collapse.

With the emergence of the locally elected school board system in 1948 came conflicting ideological pressures. Reacting to the rigid oppressive bureaucracy of the previous military regimes, the left-wing forces aspiring to gain political control of the nation through local school board control sparked heated debate. The left wing championed the U.S. reforms centered on local initiative and control. The conservatives in control of the government, forming close commercial relationships and military alliances with the United States, began to seriously question the U.S. reforms. The school board, intended by the U.S. reformers as a nonpartisan egalitarian instrument reflecting the local will of the community in the local school, became immersed in ideological controversy between the left and the right.

The newly acquired political strength of the conservative party shortly after the end of the American Occupation provided the framework necessary for the great Japanese educational reforms implemented from 1956 onwards of the American Occupation educational reforms. Simply stated, it meant a return to more centralized authority. The power and role of the central Ministry of Education was greatly strengthened. That of the newly initiated locally elected school boards patterned after the U.S. example were concurrently decreased. Japanese education was once again being planned from a national perspective, the traditional image of the school in this country, rather than from a local perspective, the traditional image of the school in the United States.

The Ministry of Education quickly grasped the initiative by producing a nationwide standardized curriculum for every subject at every level. Only authorized textbooks designed for that curriculum received governmental approval for use in the classroom. Teachers' manuals accompanying the authorized textbooks set the standard. The swing toward more centralized control was swiftly put into practice diametrically opposite to the American Occupational reforms, which viewed an "entrenched bureaucracy," the Ministry of Education, as an inherent obstacle to a democratic educational system and hence to a democratic society.

But the Japanese interpreted democratic education from a different viewpoint. They also saw the needs of the nation from a divergent perspective. Equality of educational opportunity, an elusive concept to be sure, was seen by the Japanese postwar leadership in its relationship to the new Constitution, ironically prepared and promulgated during the American Occupation of Japan. The key phrase in the Constitution stipulated that "all people shall have the right to receive an equal education correspondent to their ability."

Legal authorities within the government argued that this clause gave the Ministry of Education the mandate to equalize education throughout the nation by developing a common curriculum for the nation's schools. In so far as possible, every child should be studying the same curricula at the same general time. In this manner the Constitution's mandate that each child should have an equal opportunity for education would be followed. The Ministry of Education exists in large measure to ensure that opportunity on a nationwide basis, under this interpretation. The return to the more traditional central authority was thus uniquely couched in democratic terms of the American approved Constitution proclaimed during the American Occupation.

Education viewed from a national perspective, the traditional approach in Japan but rejected by many U.S. leaders, has had a beneficial effect on Japanese industry. Japan has come as close as perhaps any major nation in the world to achieving a mass elite through a national standard of education, which is in sharp contrast to the concept of local standards of education cherished by the Americans. The Japanese are endeavoring to reduce as much as possible the imbalances and disparities in educational standards and opportunities among the various prefectures, and indeed even among local communities within one prefecture, which are evident in the U.S. scheme of education.

Mainly because of this traditional national perspective on education, Japanese workers across the nation come out of the school with a minimum common literary and numerary standard. The national government sets that minimum standard. And it has been pegged at a very high level as the nation's leaders traditionally perceive this nation in an inferior catch-up postion struggling to come abreast of the leading Western nation, the United States, in the modern world.

Following the American Occupation of seven years, the Japanese quickly reoriented the national direction toward the traditional school. The classroom atmosphere became drab; the teaching methods were once again aimed at examination preparation; the curriculum was reimmersed solidly in the basics, sugaku and kokugo. The government set the standards. The great experiment in progressive education on the U.S. pattern never really began. The American Occupation barely made a dent in the traditional Japanese classroom.

Ironically, as Japan reemphasized traditional classroom methods, the economy spurted ahead. The nation's factories were modernized utilizing many of the most advanced industrial techniques of the United States. An economic miracle took place in Asia, the first of its kind. Japan, within 25 years, had risen from total economic collapse to become a supereconomic power.

Not only did the Japanese classroom become more traditional – memorize, repeat, drill, and test – as its factories modernized; it also reemphasized the traditional spirit of gambare – persevere, do your best, never give up. As a result the Japanese school produced a worker who was not only competent in reading, writing, and arithmetic through traditional teaching methods; he was also imbued with the spirit of perseverance, of sacrifice, if you will, while committing his loyalty to his group, the company. The combination proved to be a winner. It evolved into today's challenge to industrial America.

The existence of a traditional school system supporting a modern industrial sector is one of the apparent paradoxes of contemporary Japan. The demands of modern technology may require a high degree of specialization. Nevertheless, the function of the Japanese school is to produce a graduate with a sound general education in the basics, especially literary and mathematical. To achieve this objective, the Japanese so far have found little reason to change the traditional nature of their classrooms. The call for reform emerges periodically, but precious little takes place.

Nevertheless, the Japanese have not become complacent about the state of their schools. On the contrary, criticism is widespread. The government has launched a major campaign to reform the Japanese school system. This may seem odd to the Americans, many of whom feel that the Nation-at-Risk syndrome fits the United States and can be blamed on the deteriorating condition of U.S. public schools. Surely Japan, with its impressive balances of trade throughout the world, its impressive rates of productivity, and high literary and numerary standards is not a nation at risk. Surely its schools are not deteriorating, a condition that could threaten the country's very foundation.

But one must appreciate the Japanese mentality. There is indeed an underlying uneasiness that Japan is constantly a nation at risk, which it is. For example, Middle Eastern turmoil, which disrupts the flow of oil to energy-dependent Japan, can throw Japanese industry into chaos. American industry would feel the pinch, but it could survive with some limitations. Japanese industry would be imperiled. Even a sharp rise in the price of soybeans from the United States or a restriction in their export would have serious consequences for this food-dependent land.

Acting as if this nation were at risk, the prime minister has called for "sweeping reforms across the entire educational spectrum in preparation for the twenty-first century," in a state of the union message. Educational reform has become one of the three major platforms for improvement alongside economic management and administrative reform of the government. A blue-ribbon government panel has been commissioned to study the current system of education in order to prepare a series of educational reforms of the Japanese school.

How should Japanese education be reformed for the twenty-first century? How should the Japanese worker for the next century be educated differently from the way he has been educated in the Japanese school to live in this century? The prime minister has criticized the uniformity of Japan's schools. He contends they're too rigid and too bound to the university entrance examination. He calls for a school system more humanistic, with more emphasis on individuality and creativity. And he is correct in these assumptions. It also sounds statesmanlike. It is impressive when the prime minister of Japan calls for the internationalization of Japanese education.

But this kind of rhetoric has been going on for years. Many Japanese decry the system. Many people here attack the dominating role of the entrance examination. And a good many Japanese teachers are deeply disturbed by their inability, or lack of opportunity, to provide more individual attention to each student, to render the classroom more humanistic than the classroom of 40-plus students oriented toward the examination. But when it comes to actually changing the system with real reforms such as diversifying entrance requirements of major national universities, one wonders how many Japanese, including the prime minister himself, would support such a fundamental change.

There will be innumerable government panels and official reports on the reform of Japanese education during the next several years. There may even be structural change in the 6-3-3-4 system (elementary, junior high, senior high, and university) implemented during the American Occupation. The prime minister is hinting at such a change. But what transpires inside the classroom between the teacher and the student, the very core of the system will, it seems most likely, undergo minor changes. The traditional teaching method, it is predicted, will keep its predominant role in the Japanese classroom of tomorrow. The Japanese school is expected by the government and this society at large to produce a literate, loyal, competent worker well grounded in the basics of reading and writing. Any reforms that alter this tradition will be unacceptable.

Each company, then, must provide the specialized training required for the twenty-first century in each particular industry. It is the responsibility of the company, not the school, to equip its training programs with the latest technology available. It is in the company that the Japanese worker confronts the computer and modern technology. The division of labor between the school and the factory produces a capable work force in an era of high technology. The school must produce a literate, competent worker grounded in the basics. The firm, completely dependent on the school for its supply of adaptable workers, supplies the specialized training.

With this relationship between the school and industry, the Japanese have been slow in introducing technology such as computers in the elementary school or the high school. Vocational education, on-the-job training, is the responsibility of the company. Literacy and basic mathematics are the responsibility of the school. The division of roles has served Japan well. It is unlikely that this relationship will be significantly altered regardless of the so-called reforms of the school.

Can this combination continue to produce a winner into the twenty-first century? Can a blue-collar worker who has gone through a traditional school work effectively in a company engaged in high technology of the twenty-first century? Can white-collar managers, engineers, and designers who studied by the memorize-repeat-drill-test method lead a company engrossed in research and production of a new generation of computers? Can they both compete with the Americans?

That constitutes the challenge to the Japanese. But it also clarifies the challenge to the United States. Are our schools producing a graduate who is better equipped than the Japanese graduate to adequately meet the challenge of the high technology era? Are our workers, blue and white collar alike, well enough grounded in basic mathematics, reading, and writing to be gainfully employed in a technically oriented society? Do our workers demonstrate a spirit of perseverance? Do our company men and women harbor a commitment to their firm sufficient to make personal sacrifices for its general welfare?

These are questions of enormous consequence precisely because the answer is affirmative when applied to the Japanese worker. In the weekly seminar of senior Japanese businessmen conducted by this writer, which includes presidents, vice-presidents, and managing directors of various companies, as well as several high officials of the Japanese equivalent of the National Association of Manufacturers, the following three questions have been posed to them each year for the last ten years. And even though they are all critical of the Japanese school claiming there is much room for improvement, their answers remain unchanged.

1. Are your newly employed workers at all levels capable of reading and understanding written instructions essential to learn their new jobs?
   Every year the simple answer remains: Of course.
2. Are your new employees competent in mathematics sufficient to understand the requirements of their new jobs?
   The answer: A simple but confident yes.
3. Can you expect your new employees, both those just out of high school and those just graduating from the university, to serve your company loyally?
   The answer: Little substantial change.

No one can predict whether these basic traditional characteristics of the Japanese worker are adequate or even appropriate to meet the challenge of the high technology era. Indeed, there are distinguished U.S. critics who contend that the challenge to the future of advanced societies will be primarily entrepreneurial and innovative, rather than purely high-tech. They argue pursuasively that the rigidity of the Japanese school will prove inadequate and self-defeating in producing a graduate who can compete with a U.S. graduate under these unique conditions.

Only time will provide the answer. It would be presumptuous to predict whether this society and its schools can even sustain the traditional characteristics of its work force into the next century. We can only look to the past, however, and see that the Japanese classroom has played a central role in enabling this nation to catch up with its Western industrial counterparts, notably the United States, to remain competitive with them, and even to threaten to pull ahead. Consequently, to discount the role of the Japanese school in the next century, regardless of the changing demands of the age, would prove to be misguided as this traditional school produces its unique graduates who have proven historically to be suprisingly, and innovatively, adaptable to the needs of the times.

One thing is for certain. As the Japanese prepare for the next century, always the realists, they still view themselves whether justifiably or not in a secondary position to the United States, forever trying to catch up. For example, everyone of the businessmen in the weekly seminar just mentioned believe, without hesitation, that the United States will be the leader in innovative high technology in the twenty-first century. They reflect a common attitude among Japanese. Consequently they continue to recognize the necessity to gambare – work diligently – in order to stay in the race. They remain committed to the virtue of group loyalty. And of paramount importance they continue to place the greatest emphasis on the traditional classroom methods: memorize, repeat, drill, and test in reading, writing, and arithmetic, the basics.

Even though there are demands for educational reform as there have been ever since the end of the war, it's unlikely this traditional school will undergo any substantive revision. The Japanese school has served the needs of this nation well in the past. From all indications, the Japanese expect their school to serve them equally as well in the future as they challenge industrial America for technological leadership of the twenty-first century. As the prime minister said in his State of the Union message: "It is a fact that Japan's development and prosperity to date have been achieved by people trained in our outstanding educational system." The question remains: Will the prime minister of Japan in 2050 be able to make the same conclusion? It provokes another tantalizing question. Will the president of the United States be able to make such a statement about U.S. education in the middle of the twenty-first century?

7

LESSONS FOR THE UNITED STATES FROM JAPAN

Lesson: something learned by study or experience, a piece
of instruction, teaching.

— Webster

Can we learn anything from the Japanese school? Do their teachers
have anything to teach us? Historically, throughout this century of
industrialism as we have seen, the Japanese have invariably taken their
lessons from us. They have patiently and diligently learned much about
modernization from the United States. And they have obviously put their
lessons into practice. Could the student now become the teacher?

Any small nation devoid of resources like Japan that can achieve
supereconomic status rivaling and surpassing, in some instances, the
most powerful, richly endowed nations in the world assuredly has
something to offer the rest of us. There are indeed lessons for the United
States from Japan. By accomplishing an economic miracle under the most
adverse circumstances, the Japanese have had a truly instructive
experience. We Americans can learn and profit from their achievements
not only for our industry but also for our schools and our society.

We begin our first lesson from Japan with, appropriately, a brief
study of history. The Japanese have demonstrated during the pre- and
postwar periods the critical importance of the school in building a solid
foundation, the underpinnings, of a highly productive industrial society.
The school has been one of the primary agents within this society where

every worker has received, as it were, his preparation for a productive life. His literary and numerary skills, his attitude toward work, his determination, and his competitive spirit are all developed and fortified during the long school day, the long school week, and the extraordinarily lengthy school year.

In order for us to compete effectively with the Japanese in our domestic markets and in the international market place, we must reconsider the role and purpose of our schools that provide the preparation of our workers. As long as we were well in the forefront of industrial productivity, we could perhaps allow our schools a certain degree of laxness. But those days are clearly gone, probably forever. The shoe is on the other foot. We in the United States are no longer the clear challenger but the challenged as well. We must begin to modify our attitudes accordingly. And the classroom is the place to begin.

Our students must now be taught the realities of the day, as the Japanese have taught their students ever since their doors were opened to the West. The era of U.S. supremacy in industry and technology has been seriously challenged particularly by Japan. If we are to preserve our life styles, our customs and traditions, and perhaps even our cherished freedoms, we must teach our children that we are in a race that our competitors, especially the Japanese, take far more seriously than we do. The United States National Commission on Excellence in Education put it succinctly: "What was unimaginable a generation ago has begun to occur – others are matching and surpassing our educational attainments."

We run our schools much like a marathon racer who once upon a time ran far in front of the pack. We have failed to look over our shoulder soon enough to realize that one of the smaller runners has been catching up with us and that others are also moving up in the field. We have failed not only to realize the seriousness of our new position; we have failed to understand how the slower runner has become one of the fastest and, consequently, have lost the golden opportunity to profit from that experience.

In order to learn from the new runner now competing among the leaders, gaining a second wind in preparation to move on, we must first of all recognize the new lineup of the competitors. We must accept the fact that we are seriously being challenged. We must teach our youth that if we don't marshal every effort, every human skill, we may ultimately lose our lead. Regardless of our size and our previous records and trophies, impressive as they may be, we must "run scared."

But even then, we cannot match the quickened pace of our new rival merely by studying his stride or his fancy running shoes, which are probably imported from the United States along with much of the food he has eaten to sustain him in the race. These are the superficial. What we must study in depth are his commitment, his determination, his spirit, as well as his training techniques that have provided the very foundation for his ability to run among and, at times, ahead of us.

The metaphor of the marathon runner is apt. Our industrial society is engaged in a global race in order to meet the industrial challenge from Japan. We must first of all, then, prepare ourselves for the competition by changing our attitudes about the way our teachers teach our children. Both our teachers and students, as well as our adult leaders in government and industry, must be made aware of the seriousness of the challenge of those who would challenge us, in this case most notably the Japanese. We must teach our children that we are involved in the highly competitive international arena of industrial competition and that we may lose if we are not more diligent.

First, we must incorporate in our schools seriousness of purpose, in a word, gambare – perseverance. When the leader runs far ahead of the pack, it becomes admittedly difficult for him to maintain the diligence necessary to preserve the lead. Complacency, the seeds of the decline and fall of earlier Western civilizations, is a clear and ever present danger to the United States today as it was to our antecedents. Our students must be taught the earlier history of once great Western societies that were felled by complacency. They also must be taught the newly emerging world order. To ignore that is not only indulging in deceitful disservice to our youth; it is also failing to capitalize on the challenge from Japan to challenge our own society.

Our history books are replete with interpretations and descriptions of the greatness, as it were, the superiority of U.S. society. The illustrious contributions of the United States to the world in the modern era come bursting through the pages of our classroom texts. From music to literature to political theories to industrial might, U.S. accomplishments have been taken for granted in our teachings, as well as in our various media, which greatly influence our youth's social attitudes. A smug complacency of superiority is admittedly hard to counter in our schools.

The Japanese have interpreted modern world history in a similar way. Western superiority, especially American, comes through their classroom and the media as well. After all, there have been no internationally recognized figures in modern Japanese history to rival Kennedy, MacArthur, Einstein, or even Ben Franklin, all included in their teachings and the media as world figures to be emulated. At the same time there are no comparable internationally renowned personalities from Japan included in our textbooks or in our media. For example, in a poll conducted by this author, only eight out of 600 high school seniors in ten states across the United States knew the name of the Japanese prime minister. However, there can be no consolation therein.

The need to gambare has been endemic in Japanese schools as these people have realistically assessed their historical position in the universal order. They have capitalized on their trailing behind to instill a sense of urgency to catch up. That is the inspiration we must capture. We must instill in the mass of our students the sense of urgency, the motivation of one who is being hotly pursued, not the self-satisfaction of a leader comfortably ahead. That era has passed. Our school atmosphere is incompatible with the realities of the day. Our schools must be transformed into institutions with a sense of purpose, a sense of gambare. We must bring our classrooms into the real world.

We are deceiving ourselves and our students by not facing the exigencies of today. No single nation can maintain absolute superiority in the era of high technology. But we must now run much faster than we did before to compete among the leaders. This attitude of mind we must inculcate into our students because we are losing our clear lead in the race at this stage to be outdistanced, some caution, if we don't enliven our pace and intensify our efforts.

The foremost lesson we can learn from the Japanese school, then, is the determination to inspire our schools, our teachers, and our society with the spirit of gambare – perseverance, do your best – in every activity, not only in sports and extracurricular club activities where we excel, but in academic preparation as well. And one of the primary means of initiating this effort is by impressing upon our students the challenge to the United States by our competitors. Our schools must reflect that reality. We need the motivation of gambare in our schools. The lesson from Japanese history for the United States: replace complacency with determination and perseverance – gambare.

It would be comforting to dismiss the challenge to our industrial society as merely technical, that our superior moral traits and spiritual foundation are sufficient to overcome any competitive threat to our industry. It would also be wishful thinking. The level of U.S. crime, drug abuse, juvenile delinquency, divorce rates, and other social problems, especially in comparison to their level in Japan, puts that possibility to rest. In the modern free enterprise system of the West, our democratic form of government depends on the relative competitiveness of our industrial base. When the foundation becomes eroded, we must begin to run scared whether we like it or not.

The second instructive aspect of Japanese schools in which we would do well to take a lesson concerns the basics, the 3 R's. Admittedly the mass standards of literacy in Japan are simply too high to be matched by the United States. Our society is too diverse, including many foreign-oriented segments, to be able to achieve total literacy in our national language or in mathematics to the extent accomplished in Japan. Notwithstanding the plural nature of our society, the basic academic standards of our students, in comparison to those of the Japanese students, should and can be far higher than they are today.

The educational levels of our work force in the twenty-first century of high technology is of critical importance. As robots replace workers on menial, routine jobs and on more sophisticated work requirements, the labor force must be restructured for more mentally demanding responsibilities. Blue-collar workers will be increasingly displaced by white-collar employees, a wrenching process already well underway. A work force not grounded in basic mathematics will constitute a heavy liability on any firm competing with high technology products from a nation like Japan with a highly literate worker who has a good foundation in basic mathematics.

A report by the National Assessment of Educational Progress, a government sponsored agency, revealed the magnitude of the challenge to our nation of the information society:

> Higher order skills (mathematical) are achieved by a minimum of 17 year olds, and this proportion declined over the past decade. If this trend continues, as many as two million students may graduate in 1990 without the skills for employment in tomorrow's marketplace.[1]

Obviously we must enrich our standards in reading, writing, and mathematics but not just for our brightest students. In fact, they will often surpass the better Japanese student in creativity, innovation, and imagination. It is the mass of students below the bright ones in the public schools of the United States that, to put it gently, cannot match the standards of the average Japanese child in reading, writing, and especially mathematics. This is precisely where one of our major problems lies.

Far too many of the mass of students below the brighter ones, that is, the average and especially the below average, those who constitute the bulk of our blue- and lower white-collar classes, are graduated from our schools without a solid basis in reading and calculating. The energy of these students has manifestly not been properly directed in school. In many cases they have had little pressure or even encouragement to gambare in order to master basic mathematical computation necessary to perform work requirements in an increasingly complex industrial system.

Lately, though, we have become engrossed with the top end, that is, with trends in college entrance examination scores. According to a report by the U.S. secretary of education, the average score on the Scholastic Aptitude Test (SAT) dropped from 937 in 1972 to 893 in 1982 out of a possible score of 1600, and on the American College Test from 19.1 to 18.4 out of a possible 36. A state-by-state trend, not surprisingly, was the same: down. The one exception was our nation's capital, Washington, D.C., which moved up from an average 803 on the SAT to 821 during the same ten-year period. There is little comfort in that figure, however, because the higher average still remains 72 points behind the national average, which itself has fallen 44 points. And even though recent reports indicate that a gradual turn-around in the trends in SAT scores may finally have arrived, the road back just to former levels remains a long one.

The past decline in SAT scores indicates that academic standards, as determined by these multiple-choice, computerized national tests, had been deteriorating. And some would say the decline was dangerously precipitous. The *Nation at Risk* report supported this conclusion when it found that "about 23 percent of our more selective colleges and universities reported that their general level of selectivity declined during the 1970s, and 29 percent reported reducing the number of specific high school courses required for admission."[2]

The trend was confirmed in an unusual way during this writer's visit in 1985 to a large high school catering almost exclusively to minorities in one of our three major U.S. cities. According to an official of the school, representatives of colleges and universities from all over the country annually descend on that school, and others like it, eagerly seeking applicants to their institutions to fill the quotas made available for minority students in the freshman class. The students are well aware of this courtship by university recruiters and find little need to make an effort to study in preparation for the SAT exams. This particular high school even dropped the special course for SAT preparation offered after school at no expense for anyone interested, because of lack of interest. If these students want to get into a university, they can get accepted somewhere with poor SAT scores, even with scores below the national average. One minority teacher put it in an interesting perspective: "Minority students here are not being served well by quotas for university entrance. Neither are the universities."

One cannot help wondering what happens to these students once they get into the university with their low qualifying scores. One result, inevitably, has been the proliferation of remedial courses in reading, writing, and arithmetic, the old basics, throughout U.S. higher education. Others claim that grade inflation is another result. And the old standby, failure, takes a high toll of the fair number of unqualified university freshmen, not only from the ranks of minority groups.

A comparison with Japan is in order. The university entrance examinations during the past ten years have become more complicated, more intricate, and, as some critics would say, more absurdly difficult in an endeavor by the schools to select from among the huge pool of applicants who have been relentlessly studying for the examination. One wonders how many university professors today could pass the entrance examination to their own university.

Not only has the university entrance examination become more demanding than ever before; the academic standards of the lower grade levels have likewise been rising. For example, the Ministry of Education conducted nationwide tests in 1982-83 of fifth and sixth graders in four subjects. The tests were designed in so far as possible for comparability with tests administered to the same age group two decades ago. The results are indicative of the trends throughout Japanese schools. In nearly all subjects tested, a 20 to 30 percent improvement in scores was found (Table 7.1).

In the U.S. government report cited previously, the U.S. situation was described in a most interesting and highly revealing way:

> Each generation of Americans has outstripped its parents in education, in literacy, and in economic attainment. For the first time in the history of our country, the educational skills of one generation will not surpass, wil not equal, will not even approach, those of their parents.[3]

This passage highlights perhaps a far more serious condition than the decline in SAT scores reveals. The students who sit for the SATs constitute about the upper one-third to one-fourth of all high school

TABLE 7.1
Improved Scores on Nationwide Tests
(in percent)

Subject	Class	1982-83'	1963-64
Japanese	Fifth graders	67.6	59.1
	Sixth graders	73.2	60.7
Social studies	Fifth graders	72.1	58.8
	Sixth graders	72.8	64.0
Mathematics	Fifth graders	64.6	44.8
	Sixth graders	70.0	35.2
Science	Fifth graders	73.4	64.0
	Sixth graders	68.8	58.0

Source: Asahi Shimbun, Tokyo, September 29, 1984.

seniors. These declining scores during the past decade then, are only for our best high school students, not all of our high school seniors, the majority of whom choose not even to sit for the exam. When you factor in the 25 percent of all youth of high school age that drop out of the school, many before reaching the later stages where high school students take the SAT or equivalent tests, then you can see that the decline in the SAT scores related only to the student elite, if you will, among our 17 and 18 year olds.

If the standards of our elite have been declining, what must be happening with the others, the average and below average student, and the very bottom 25 percent of that age group that are no longer enrolled in school? What about the 42 percent of the high school students who dropped out of school before graduation in our second largest school district of Los Angeles between 1979 and 1983?[4] A vital question concerns the standards of our general population. Alas, statistics are not accessible because many within this group are not available for testing. Perhaps their literacy and numerary standards have been rising, while the elite's have been falling. Perhaps that's wishful thinking.

Far too many of our students are not required to achieve in school a literary and mathematical level sufficient to secure gainful employment in an industrial world being recast for the next century of high technology.

The national report on U.S. education, the *Nation at Risk*, verified this state of affairs. Approximately 25 percent of all recent recruits into the U.S. Navy could not read at the ninth grade level, the minimum needed simply to understand safety regulations. In contrast the Japanese public can rest assured that the Japanese school is not producing an illiterate recruit for the Japanese Navy, or for any other sector of employment. Rather, the Japanese school is preparing en masse the future worker with the basics that should enable him to fit in and adapt to the new era of technology, and the school is doing that more efficiently than perhaps any other society in the world today. That is the ultimate challenge from the Japanese school that our society must meet.

Another study on the performance of U.S. youth from the Education Commission of the States reported that:

> Well over 90% of the 17 year olds could perform simple addition and 85% to 90% could perform subtraction. Between 80% and 90% could multiply and divide. Computations using decimals, fractions, and integers were more difficult, but percentages were still high.[5]

Are these statistics, couched in guarded terms, indicative of a labor force being prepared to work in the factoryless society of tomorrow? Are these future workers of U.S. industry equipped with minimum competencies to find employment in the electronic society of tomorrow, which has already emerged today? When you compare the performance of U.S. 17 year olds in "simple addition and subtraction," (and remember again this does not represent all 17-year-old youth because many have dropped out of school by this age) with the mathematical requirements of 15-year-old Japanese students preparing for Tokyo City public high schools, as illustrated in Chapter 4, the magnitude of the educational challenge from Japan is impressive. Clearly the Japanese can teach us a lesson in the basics.

This does not mean that we should turn our classrooms into "examination hells," as critics brand the Japanese school for the years before the examinations for the high school and university. Clearly the Japanese in their purblind enthusiasm have gone too far in that direction. Nor would anyone suggest that U.S. parents send their children to school six or seven days a week, five days in the regular public schools and the others in supplementary schools. The widespread use of yobiko and juku during the evenings and/or weekends distorts a child's tender years leaving too little time for nonacademic activities. The academic pressure on the average and below-average Japanese child is simply too heavy, especially at the upper levels of each school unit, whereas the academic demands on the average and below-average child in U.S. schools, across the board, are, in far too many instances, too light.

Nor would we support a classroom with 40 to 50 students, a standard range in Japanese schools. Nevertheless this leads one to question why we, with our smaller classes, cannot produce far better results in the basic subjects with our slower students. In other words, if the Japanese school can achieve total literacy with inordinately large classes, why can't our schools come much closer to that standard than at present with our smaller classes? Should we not be far more academically demanding of our classrooms?

If we really accepted the educational challenge from Japan, which underlies their industrial challenge, we could raise the academic standards of our schools to be more in line with those of the Japanese school. It would take a massive effort. But if it is true, as many critics proclaim and statistics indicate, that we are in danger of losing our lead in the global industrial and economic competition and the high technology stakes, then it is essential that we undertake that effort promptly. The goal of our schools should be obligatory literacy and numerary standards for our secondary school graduates so that they can perform basic requirements at home and work. No one should ever pass through our schools into our society without achieving far more than the ability to read and "understand safety regulations." The Japanese school has gone far beyond that minimal level in producing en masse high school graduates who can perform basic requirements at work in an age of high technology, of a service economy, of an information society. We must endeavor to compete with them by running far faster than our present pace. It's a new and challenging world for us. We must rise to the occasion.

Ironically, while the Japanese classroom must reduce somewhat its inordinately high demands or face further student disruptions that could lead to far more serious repercussions than they face today, the United States must move in the oppposite direction. The Japanese simply cannot contain too much longer the reaction of those students who can't keep up with the public school standards. But it must be remembered that most of those falling behind will still perform better in mathematical concepts or reading skills than those students falling behind in U.S. schools. In other words, even the standards of Japanese dropouts are superior to those of U.S. dropouts, although this is of little solace to the Japanese.

At the same time we can no longer tolerate the poor mathematical and reading ability of far too many of our secondary school graduates and even, according to some reports, of a number of those who enter our universities. Remedial reading and mathematics courses have become commonplace at the first year level in many such institutions. The Japanese wouldn't tolerate such standards for their high school graduates. How could they possibly remain in the international industrial race? They are well aware that they couldn't. And our concern should be that with such low mass standards in the basics in many of our schools, we may not be able to either.

The third lesson to be learned from Japan is that money is not the basic solution to the problems of our classroom. Too often the more we spend on education the less we learn, both literally and figuratively. The Japanese school system is run on the barest essentials. There are few frills. What we call basic would be a luxury in Japanese schools. Heating is a good example. Rare is the school equipped with central heating in Japan, a northern country with heavy snows and bitter cold winters. Even in the affluent suburbs of the major cities, the classrooms until very recently were equipped with simple, rather unsightly, kerosene stoves. As in the story books of the past, the students who sat nearest the stove were warm while those farthest from it shivered or kept their heavy sweaters on all day. The hallways, gyms, and toilets are cold and drafty throughout the winter months.

A prime example of the Japanese attitude toward school facilities can be seen in our local area. When a new elementary school was built in the mid-1970s, amid a middle-class residential area in which almost all houses with land were selling for the equivalent of over $150,000, many for much more, the new building was designed like a simple L-shaped box. But even this was far superior to the previous building where our first child began her Japanese schooling. That one, during its last year, was literally propped up with large, unsightly supports. For heating, the new structure was equipped with individual coal stoves in each room. The children were assigned according to their hans to carry the coal in buckets to the classroom each day. The teacher made the fire. It often went out. Several years later kerosene stoves replaced the coal stoves but the unsightly chimney pipes remained as the classrooms were modernized at a minimum of expense, and comfort.

No parent at the PTA meetings ever questioned the heating system, or lack of it, for the new school. They were well aware that even with the primitive method of heating the classroom, some teachers keep a window slightly open except on the coldest days. Even then the ill-fitting simple sliding windows and doors allow the cold air to seep into the room both from the outside and from the unheated hallways. The Japanese classroom is not designed for warmth and comfort, nor to be expensively outfitted.

While the new elementary school was under construction, the local authorities built a new city hall. The contrast between the two was shocking. Whereas the new school was a simple structure with stark straight lines, the city hall took the form of an elaborate, expensive, intricately designed piece of impressive architecture with wide flowing stairs, unusual entrances, unique terraces, and elevators. No one, except perhaps a Western observer noticed the differences between these two public buildings.

However, outside the new Spartan-looking elementary school building, at one edge of the playground, was an outdoor 25-meter long in-ground swimming pool. Perhaps it was to be expected. The number of Japanese city schools from the elementary level up equipped with swimming pools, a facility considered a luxury in U.S. schools, is truly impressive. Although simply constructed with barely any additional equipment, swimming pools are common enough at Japanese urban schools to conclude that even though they are not considered essential, they are thought to be one of the basic facilities of a school.

The other unique, somewhat unexpected feature of many Japanese schools, even at the elementary level, is a grand piano or a fine upright. The incongruence of a good piano with its splendid tones, nearly always looking brand new, placed in a rather barren, often shoddy looking music room of a local junior high school cannot help attracting the attention of a foreign observer. The combination of a swimming pool and a quality piano in a public elementary or junior high school immersed in basic academic subjects indicates that there is a strong effort to provide a balanced curriculum in the local school.

Even though from the U.S. perspective, the Japanese school falls far short of an overall balanced school program between the academic and nonacademic, both the sports program and the music standards of this school system compare favorably with those in any country in the world. And, as with their academic program, it is the mass of average students in the Japanese school that is put through what could be called a quite rigorous program in physical education and music. All children in every grade will go through a swimming program in schools with pools. In those without pools, a very strenuous program in physical education in the large gymnasium and playground will be carried out for all. In addition, in virtually every elementary school, all children will be taught to play one or more musical instruments such as a simple flute or woodwindlike instrument. Even music standards are impressively high.

The basics of the Japanese school, then, tend to be somewhat different from ours. We think as essential to our schools such items as a cafeteria, an auditorium, a student counselor, a remedial reading teacher, a football team, or, in many a suburban elementary school, rugs on the floor. All of these basics in the U.S. school are considered a luxury, or rather a nonessential, in Japanese schools and are rarely provided for in the school budget. Rather, educational funds here are allocated for such "big" items as a large gymnasium, found in virtually every elementary school through the high school, which doubles as the auditorium for ceremonies, a pool, and a fine piano.

Teaching materials in Japanese schools are also simple although most classrooms are equipped with a TV set. Its use is limited. A number of teachers, however, like to use the overhead projector because it facilitates board work. Supplementary books are few. Even the school libraries are poorly stocked. In a large number of the schools, the walls need paint. The desks and chairs are often badly worn. In fact, the average Japanese teacher would simply be overwhelmed with the facilities and the general condition of typical suburban and small town schools in the United States.

Ironically, for a school system that places an inordinate emphasis on the written word, school textbooks are surprisingly simple and inexpensive. An elementary school Japanese reader costs about $1. Hardbound texts are seldom issued. In contrast to the typical Japanese classroom textbook, U.S. texts are often hardbound, colorful editions costing five to ten times more. The textbook budget causes no heavy drain on the Japanese school budget. Until the 1970s, students had to pay for their own textbooks in the public schools. Although the debate continues whether school textbooks should be issued free to the students, clearly the financial burden on the parents would be minimal if it shifts to them.

Also in sharp contrast to the U.S. schools, supplementary professional personnel attached to the school are rare. For example, as mentioned above, guidance counselors or remedial reading teachers, common in the United States, are virtually unheard of in Japanese schools. The teacher serves as the guidance counselor, the remedial teacher, and in every other capacity as well. The classroom teacher in

Japan has little professional help to turn to within the school except for a fellow classroom teacher. Personnel expenses beyond the classroom teacher are minimal.

In spite of the very heavy burden placed on the Japanese classroom teacher with large classes, a demanding curriculum to cover, parental pressure for examination preparation, and a five-and-a-half-day school week, the salaries of teachers are modest. A beginning teacher in Tokyo, one of the most expensive cities in the world, starts his career at the equivalent of about $10,000 a year, including bonuses. And yet there is great demand by university graduates to enter the teaching profession. There is, as we have seen, no shortage of qualified mathematics teachers in Japan because university engineering graduates in private industry do not command initial salaries much higher than salaries of a classroom teacher. In other words Japan is able to staff its classroom with qualified teachers at minimum expense from among a huge pool of applicants.

Another reason teaching remains fairly attractive, in addition to its competitive salary vis-à-vis the industrial sector, relates to the prestige it holds within the society. The Japanese teacher has traditionally held a respected position, particularly in the rural areas. And although the lure of teaching has been diminished somewhat over the years, the title of "sensei" still commands a degree of respect the word "teacher" can never acquire. That sensei (teacher) is used in the same manner for the elementary teacher and for the university president places the regular public school teacher in a unique and still fairly prestigious category.

Personnel expenses for school maintenance are also held to a minimum, in part through the participation of students in the cleaning process. Few children in U.S. schools are, for example, required to clean the floors of their classrooms and hallways before leaving each afternoon. In most cases the U.S. child is expected to merely pick up the paper around his desk and put his desk and chair in place. Cleaning the floor on hands and knees at the end of the long day is an old tradition in Japanese schools. It is intended to be an instructive as well as hygienic aspect of the Japanese school. It also reduces janitorial expenses.

From any standpoint – facilities, personnel, textbooks, buildings – the Japanese school is one of the most frugal institutions among all economically advanced nations. Remarkably, the academic standards are among the highest. The Japanese experience demonstrates that to be effective schools do not have to be costly. The most expensive item in Japanese education is the land required for the site of new buildings. This, of course, is inevitable in a small country with limited useable land supporting a large population. Land prices are exorbitant. But once the building, which is often of modest proportions simply designed, is in place, the operational expenses are kept minimal.

Clearly a supereconomic power like Japan could afford far better school facilities if it felt the need to provide them. However, an older tradition prevails – education is most effective when it takes place under Spartan conditions. Learning and comfort are not related. Color, brightness, attractive surroundings are irrelevant to the learning process. Simplicity is conducive to learning, according to the Japanese way of thinking.

The fourth lesson to be learned from the Japanese school relates to expectations. The Japanese public, the Japanese government, the Japanese teacher – all elements of the society – expect the school to be an effective agent within the infrastructure of the nation. It is taken for granted that the raison d'être of the school is to produce a literate graduate across the board who has a basic understanding of mathematical concepts. Anything less is unacceptable.

What this means is that Japanese industry in every sector expects the new employee coming from any school anywhere in the land to have minimum competencies in the three R's. And the vast majority of graduates go considerably beyond the minimum standards. The leaders of the Japanese industrial world expect the school to produce a person who can function effectively in the factory or the office. Anything less is unacceptable.

This society also expects, nay demands, its schools to maintain a reasonable atmosphere of discipline. Consequently, the rise of student indiscipline during the 1980s, although not nearly the magnitude of student indiscipline in the United States (especially in cities comparable to a massive metropolis like Tokyo), has produced a nationwide reaction. Reports revealing that classroom disturbances at the junior high school level have been increasing, although amazingly few high schools experience student disruptions, send ripples throughout the society sparking responses at all levels.

The Ministry of Education has set up study committees on student indiscipline. The local prefectures and many communities followed suit. The PTAs, the Japan Teachers Union, and various other supporting groups throughout the society have all been studying the causes of the increasing incidences of classroom indiscipline. Even the national association of lawyers appointed a committee to study the situation. The Japanese society at large is seeking a solution to this problem. The level , of toleration of student indiscipline has been historically low in this country because the degree of expectations has been traditionally high.

The lesson to be learned from the Japanese school is that the United States does not hold high expectations of its schools as the Japanese do theirs. If Japanese schools produce graduates who are not functionally literate both in letters and numbers or who are not equipped with the minimum essentials for satisfactory employment in their transforming industrial society, the Japanese take concerted action to rectify the situation. It cannot be overemphasized that Japanese education is an "affair of state" in the broadest sense.

During one of my visits to U.S. schools interviewing teachers and administrators about the problems of their school, this writer heard one teacher from a middle-sized community express an extremely astute observation about U.S. society's expectations of its schools. He said that although the academic standards of his local school were not very high, especially in comparison to the standards of the football program, they were about as high as the community would support. To strive for much higher academic standards, to raise the passing grade level, to make significantly greater academic demands would result in a community backlash against the schools thereby defeating the very purpose of the effort.

What this teacher's frank opinion reflects is that in a fairly typical community, many if not most of the local citizenry aren't too concerned with the academic performance of their schools. There are, to be sure, some deeply concerned people in every U.S. community, but most are probably more disturbed over discipline, drugs, alcohol, and other problems than over reading, writing, and arithmetic. If education officials in each community established a fairly demanding high school standard for graduation, in which many if not all of those students who really didn't deserve a high school diploma were failed, there would be sufficient opposition in the average community to reform that practice or to replace the school board in the next election. The U.S. public has historically supported the public school, but it has seldom championed the cause of high academic standards in it.

That takes us to the heart of the problem – the attitude toward the school held by the average U.S. family living in the average community. Complacency may be the best description of it. And this points out the importance of U.S. leaders, especially at the local level, and the very academic community itself. Rather than lowering university standards, as has been reported, university leaders should be demanding higher standards to meet the needs of an increasingly complex society in an age of technology. Surely they must be aware of the industrial challenge of our competitors. If local colleges and universities, which the majority of students of higher education attend, became the centers of educational attainment setting examples for local high schools, a real beginning in the long struggle to raise the standards of U.S. education from top to bottom could get underway.

To put it frankly, the Japanese public in any community would not tolerate the reading, writing, and computational standards of 17 year olds as reported in the previously cited study of American teenagers. If a nationwide study revealed simply that among all Japanese 17 year olds, "85 to 90 percent could perform simple subtraction," or if many millions of adults in this society were functionally illiterate as reported in the United States, the Japanese government would undertake an immediate nationwide campaign to rectify the situation. Otherwise, it could not survive. The expectations of the school by Japanese society are very high indeed. Those of the United States, in comparison, are far too low.

School discipline holds another Japanese lesson for the United States. Consider the overall situation. The Japanese teacher has 40 to 50 students in a classroom built for 30. The environment is often drab at best. The lesson requirements are set by government and are extremely difficult for the below average child who must make a herculean effort to keep up. The student may come from a *danchi*, a crowded apartment house, with three tiny rooms. Such housing was once branded as "rabbit hutches" by a European diplomat in a most undiplomatic but absolutely frank description that captured national headlines. Everyone understood it. And surrounding that housing complex will be precious little space for play and relaxation, both of which come at a very high premium in heavily populated Japan. If the student goes to school on a morning train, he experiences a crushing ride as commuter trains are solid flesh door to door.

These conditions provide a natural setting for student delinquency in the massive urban areas of Japan. And yet student indiscipline as a result of drugs, alcohol, and sexual misbehavior remains at a very low level in comparison to that in many schools in the United States. The Japanese are clearly in another league from the Americans concerning school violence; luckily for them, it's the minor leagues. Nevertheless, this nation is deeply concerned about the disruptions of the secondary classroom. In other words this society is determined to take concerted efforts to solve the problem of student indiscipline before it becomes uncontrollable. The expectations of the Japanese school would allow nothing less.

Indiscipline in school also includes such lesser evils as petty thievery, vandalism of school property, and even absenteeism and tardiness. In all of these, the Japanese school maintains a far higher standard than the U.S. school. None of these can be considered a serious problem in the Japanese school, although damage to school property in a few troubled city schools has reached the highest level in the history of the nation. Even there, the extent of the problem would be the envy of principals in many so-called troubled schools of our inner cities where lethal weapons are at times carried into the school by students, something a Japanese principal would find incomprehensible.

Too many U.S. schools tolerate student indiscipline at a level that would bring down the local government and threaten the national government as well in this country. For example, another U.S. government paper entitled "Disorder in Our Schools" reported that in an earlier year, 282,000 students were physically attacked in U.S. schools each month on school premises. During each month 1,000 teachers were also assaulted seriously enough to require medical attention, and 125,000 teachers were threatened with bodily harm.[6] In contrast, the Japanese National Police Agency reported that a record 2,125 cases of school violence occurred in Japanese schools in a one-year period with less than half involving incidents against teachers. Reflecting the academic demands for high school entrance examinations, an overwhelming number of incidents, 95.7 percent, took place at the junior high school level.[7] The usual type of violence took the form of a student, sometimes armed with a wooden stick, attacking a student or a teacher. No other weapons were reportedly involved. However, as the nation entered the middle of the 1980s, school violence had already decreased by 23 percent in one year, indicating that the peak in school violence in Japan may have been reached.[8]

Although critics of government reports claim the U.S. figures cited above are dated, violence in U.S. schools today continues to plague the classroom to a far, far greater degree than it does in Japan. The U.S. Supreme Court, for example, based a 1985 ruling (giving school officials greater authority in combatting school violence) on prevailing conditions and argued that "drug use and violent crime in the schools have become major social problems."[9] Statistics support that contention. For example, in a survey of a number of Boston's high schools conducted by a local commission, half the teachers and nearly 40 percent of the students had been victims of crime during a one-year period. Three of every ten students said they have carried weapons to school, one of the most startling discoveries, and four of ten reported that they often felt afraid for their safety while at school and avoided bathrooms and certain hallways if at all possible.[10] During only the first four months of a recent academic year, 1,000 weapons, including 76 handguns, were confiscated from students in New York high schools.[11] In Philadelphia schools during a one-year period school principals reported 2,449 serious incidents, including 348 cases of weapon possessions.[12] In Prince George's County, outside our nation's capital, when an expulsion policy for carrying concealed weapons or distributing drugs was initiated during the 1984-85 academic year, 196 students were expelled including 143 for carrying concealed weapons.[13] No principal of a school in Japan faces those kinds of problems.

Absenteeism is another major problem of the U.S. school, as a survey of school principals revealed. An absentee rate of 15 percent daily in large urban schools is not uncommon. Schools in Philadelphia may have 37,000 students absent every day. The absentee figure reaches 71,000 for Chicago, 100,000 for Los Angeles, and 150,000 for New York each day.[14] Absenteeism in the public schools of Tokyo, Osaka, Nagoya, and other large cities is minimal, in comparison, yet it receives increasing attention.

On a number of school visits to U.S. high schools by this researcher, police assigned to the school on a full-time, permanent basis were seen patrolling the halls. At one school, the officer was overheard testifying to the assistant principal for discipline about an attack on the second floor hallway. All school police had guns in holsters. The city of Detroit, in response to the rise in school violence, posted several five-member police teams using handheld metal detectors to check students in strife-torn high schools for weapons. In the first one-month period, of 600 students suspected of carrying weapons, 35 students were arrested and 12 weapons were seized. Ironically, because of budget problems, the city had to reduce the number of security officers from the incredible number of 228 to 70.[15] The following year, 120 students were shot, and officials confiscated 60 guns from students.[16] In comparison, the Japanese are still "babes in the woods" in the matter of school indiscipline.

Regarding drugs, the situation in the United States is similar to the incidence of violence and is, of course, related to it. For comparison purposes, the Japanese National Police Agency reported that 138 high school students and 67 junior high school students from throughout the nation were taken into custody for drugs during a one-year period.[17] Although similar statistical data from the United States is not readily available, one can assume that the comparable number of teenagers arrested, perhaps even in just one major city, for drug abuse in one year would be many times the number arrested in Japan. For example, *U.S. News and World Report* claimed that "an estimated 20 percent of all young people between 12 and 17 are regular users of illegal drugs."[18]

Teenage pregnancy continues the list. *Time Magazine* featured the problem, Children Having Children, by reporting that one million American teenagers become pregnant each year. If present trends continue, "fully 40 percent of today's 14-year-old girls will be pregnant at least once before the age of 20." The contrast between the United States and Japan is itself pregnant with revelations. For example, approximately 10 percent of female American teens become pregnant, whereas "Japan enjoys a startlingly low teenage birthrate" of 3.4 births per 1,000, or 0.34 percent. And this is in a nation where the pill is severely restricted. In addition, American researchers reported that 43 percent of 17-year-old American girls had already experienced sexual intercourse compared with 7.8 percent of Japanese high school senior girls.[19] Although the Japanese Ministry of Health and Welfare is alarmed with the recent increases in teenage pregnancies, any American official would envy the problem the Japanese face.

The Japanese are beginning to get a bitter taste of student delinquency, which has evidently reached alarming proportions among U.S. youth. Although some reports indicate that a peak may have been reached in Japan, because of their expectations of the school, the Japanese are alarmed from top to bottom of the society over the problem here. For example, incidents of school violence, expulsions (a total of 108 throughout elementary and secondary schools in one year) and suicide have been decreasing while bullying and absenteeism have been increasing.[20] Curiously the concern here now centers on the issue of so-called bullying which takes the form of teasing that, in extreme cases, causes severe psychological effects among weaker children who find themselves excluded from the group. But in the overwhelming number of cases common in certain lower ranked schools, bullying takes on a completely different dimension from the bullying that goes on in many a lower ranked American inner city school facing problems of school vandalism, intimidation, gang feuds, not to mention the severe problems of drugs and teenage pregnancy. The Japanese at all levels expect much more from their schools, concerning both academics and discipline. And they get that much more than the U.S. public. We simply expect and demand far too little of our schools.

Even the weekly schedule of classes strikes a sharp imbalance with the Japanese schools and indicates how little we demand of our students in contrast to the Japanese. According to the *Nation at Risk* report, the average U.S. school provides 22 class hours a week of academic instruction. Some schools offer only 17.[21] The Japanese student at the junior high school, for example, attends class according to the following schedule, which shows a much heavier weekly load of classes. Many here in Japan say too heavy.

Several aspects of the weekly schedule should be pointed out to the U.S. reader. One is the inclusion of a foreign language, English, in the regular course of studies three times a week at the junior high level for all students. In some schools the activities period, meant to be a free class, is used for an extra hour in English. Few U.S. students study a foreign language at the junior high school level. Another difference is the Saturday morning classes. No U.S. community requires Saturday attendance. The Japanese school day is even longer than that in many of our schools. But of greatest importance is that this heavy weekly course load continues from September 1 to July 20, or from five to six weeks longer than the schedule for a U.S. child. In other words all Japanese children have a longer school day and considerably more classes each week. And they attend school many more weeks each year than their American counterparts. The Japanese school has a demanding schedule for all.

In order for U.S. schools to respond to the far more demanding expectations necessary to raise the standards, both academic and disciplinary, the parents and the society at large must give the school much more support and concern than one witnesses when studying educational issues in the United States today. Japanese parents on the whole take an active interest in the school and play not only a supportive but also a demanding role. The parents, especially the kyoiku mama, maintain the academic pressure on the school. Large attendance by parents for school events is expected. Well over half the mothers often attend the classroom observations. It is the same with the teacher-parent interviews at school. Classroom teachers know that most parents in this overwhelmingly middle-class society stand squarely behind them. There are exceptions at the comparatively few troubled junior high schools, but the vast majority of teachers can rely on parental support.

Another critical lesson to be learned from the Japanese school concerns the relationship between the individual and the group, and the commitment of one's loyalty to it. We from the United States have

Junior High School
First Year Sample Class Schedule

Time		Monday	Tuesday	Wednesday	Thursday	Friday	Saturday
	Day						
8:30-8:45		Homeroom					
8:50-9:40		Class Activity	Mathematics	Japanese	Geography	Science	Morals
9:50-10:40		Mathematics	Calligraphy	Music	Japanese	Physical Education	Mathematics
10:50-11:40		Japanese	Physical Education	Science	English	Home Arts	Music
11:50-12:40		Geography	Japanese	Physical Education	History	Home Arts	Homeroom Cleanup Dismissal
12:40-1:25		Lunchtime					
1:30-2:20		Science	English	Clubs	Art	English	
2:30-3:20		History	Extra Activities	Clubs	Art	Extra Activities	
3:25-3:35		Homeroom					
3:35-3:50		Cleanup					
3:55		Dismissal					

traditionally viewed Japanese society in terms of its close-knit social relationships. Our image of the Japanese pictures them as lacking in individuality, consequently blindly following their leader. Sacrificing one's personal desires for the benefit of the group typifies the U.S. view of Japan.

There is an element of truth in this characterization. However, what we fail to recognize in the relationship between the Japanese individual and his group, that is, his kumi as a student and his company as a worker, is the sense of participation that underlies his commitment. The Japanese people, highly educated and fairly well read in history, both Eastern and Western, do not follow their leaders willy nilly, blindly sacrificing their individuality for the welfare of their group, either the kumi at school or the kumi at the company. This is not a nation of lemmings.

The uniqueness, and a lesson for us, is the way in which the individual commits his loyalty to the group. The emperor, the prime minister, the company president, or the classroom teacher cannot and does not order the Japanese to be loyal. There was an interlude in Japanese history when this was to a certain extent possible. But Japanese society has functioned primarily on the voluntary commitment of oneself to the group. That is one of the most critical aspects of this society.

We in the United States must work toward this goal – the voluntary commitment of oneself, the loyalty that implies sacrifice to the welfare of the group – in order to promote the well-being of our industries and the well-being of our society. This commitment does not mean blindly following the leader or the department manager. It does not involve meek acceptance of orders from the foreman.

Rather, based on the Japanese model, it means active participation in small intimate groups to arrive at a group consensus. It means that decisions do not routinely come from above to be dutifully followed by the members of the group. It means that all members of the group from the leader to the newest and youngest member must, at the earliest stages of discussion, be involved in the decision-making process through early consultations. It means that group action, group attitudes, should be based on the general consensus of the group.

Loyalty to the group in Japanese society is based to a great extent on the individual's sense of participation, the satisfaction that he has been part of the process of deciding on the group's actions or its attitudes, whether or not his particular viewpoint won out in the end. It also stems from the individual's belief that he as an individual benefits when his group functions effectively. It's pure practical common sense to the Japanese. When the group, that is, the Japanese company, prospers, the employees prosper. When the company fails, the employees suffer.

When the group functions harmoniously in Japanese society, which it does to an impressive degree, the distinction between the group leader and the members of the group become somewhat blurred. The leader is not the boss, in the usual meaning of the word. Instead, the leader is the harmonizer whose responsibility is to bring about a general consensus of the group. When the members gain the satisfaction of participation, they are ready to commit their loyalty to the group. Not before.

Critics of the "herd instinct" of the Japanese argue that the group stifles individual initiative and creativity. Among some groups throughout the society, there is, of course, some truth to this assessment. But the system also encourages individual initiative when new ideas are actively solicited by the leader for the furtherance of the group's success. After all, a loyal member of the group will do all he possibly can to promote the welfare of the group. Therefore during the long discussions, the *hanashiai*, new ideas are often encouraged. And, when justified, they are rewarded by the group's recognition and acceptance. Japanese industry could not have arrived at its present position, nor can it face the era of high technology, if individual originality had been overly restricted by the group.

The lesson the United States can learn from Japan is that we must strike a more harmonious balance between the individual and the group, the worker and his company. Those who manage our factories must view their employees as individuals whose loyalty to the company can only be gained if they have a sense of participation. Those who work in our factories must view management as individuals who are concerned with them and who are actively seeking their ideas and their loyalty. On both sides it involves an element of sacrifice for the harmony and welfare of the group.

Surely the ancient leader of Japan, Prince Shotoku Taishi, had a wise message not only for the early Japanese but also for contemporary Americans. His simple advice is worth repeating: "But when those high above are harmonious and those below friendly, and there is concord in the discussion of business, right views of things gain acceptance. Then what is there which cannot be accomplished?"

The final lesson to be learned from the Japanese school concerns the significance of the concept of challenge itself. The Japanese thrive on challenge, on competition. They rise to the occasion when challenged.

They can discover a challenge in trivial matters, and they become highly motivated when challenged. This nation of people, proud of its heritage, proud of the accomplishments of its ancestors, is particularly adept at turning adversity into challenge. To catch up has been the great stimulating challenge propelling the nation ever onwards, and upward.

Americans are up against a stalwart competitor who thrives on competition, on the challenge of being a runner-up. The Japanese have benefited enormously by taking seriously the old saying, "Better the follower than the forerunner." The Japanese throw themselves wholeheartedly into the ring. Nothing is halfway, lukewarm. It's all or nothing. The postwar challenge has been primarily an industrial competition. It has breathed renewed vigor into this society.

The Japanese school is a highly competitive institution nurturing a keen sense of challenge. Academically it can be merciless. The constant posting of examination results lays bare the standing of every student in the class. The ranking, the order of performance, is thrown open for everyone to see. The individual challenge is to work harder to move up or to remain diligent to stay at the top.

Group competition is also of great importance in the Japanese school. Every opportunity is utilized to create a competitive situation. Teachers use study situations in which the hans compete among themselves within the kumi. The various kumi compete with each other within the same grade level. And even the entire school population, students, teachers, administrators, and parents as well, become involved in the great annual challenge, the *undokai*, the sports day, held on every school playground. Let us complete this chapter with a look at how the Japanese school utilizes play as a challenge.

For many weeks before the undokai all students become involved in preparing for the many scheduled events, from racing to dancing to games. During the last few days before the event, the school is literally inundated with undokai preparations. It absorbs everyone. The process involves dividing all the students from the youngest to the oldest into two teams, the Reds and Whites, by splitting each kumi in two. A simple red band on the sports cap distinguishes one group from the other as the school buzzes in anticipation of the great challenge between the two sides. Every opportunity is employed to sharpen a keen sense of competitive readiness for the big event. They practice the events daily.

The undokai begins at 8:30 a.m. with greetings by the principal to the mass assembly of students in the center of the playground. He will invariably stimulate the competitive spirit by challenging the students waiting patiently, all dressed in identical sports wear except for the hats, to gambare – do your best. Then begins the mass calisthenics entered into by some of the many parents who come with their *obento*, the box lunch, prepared to stay for the day. With these preliminaries out of the way, the events begin.

The competition is divided according to grade level so that third grade boys compete only with third grade boys in their races; second grade girls are competing in the 100-yard dash only with girls the same age. Boys from the same class will compete with each other on the two-kilometer race. And so it goes throughout the day. Race after race takes place interspersed by acrobatics, a kind of mass athletic dance, a few games, an event for PTA parents, an event for teachers, and the lunchtime break. A carnivallike atmosphere, depending on the weather, prevails throughout the day.

The undokai is a marvel of precision, for the Japanese school at play functions like a precise instrument. In a school of 1,000 students, in which every child participates in four or five competitive events, a logistics plan of major proportions must be carefully worked out. The movements of 200 fifth graders on to the playing area for their event, the running of that event, and then moving the group off again to their seats arranged around the field requires detailed preplanning as well as exacting implementation. Otherwise, it could become chaotic. It never is.

Each child in an elementary school undokai from the first grader on up must know where he should be at exactly the right time for his events. He must move with his kumi to the waiting area on time, move out through the gate promptly on command to his starting place, bolt off with the crack of the starter's gun, and run with all his might around the track. He then must patiently wait until all the others in his kumi have run in that event before moving off the field to his seat. The schedule must be adhered to.

Overhead, hanging from a second story window of the school, little noticed at first, is a large scoreboard divided colorfully into Reds and Whites. Throughout the day, a careful count of the winner of each event according to the color identification on the cap will be kept on the scoreboard. Throughout the day with each event, both students and parents cheer the Reds or the Whites on to victory as the score builds up. Gambare! Gambare! Every child does his best until the winning side is declared. A final ceremony recognizes the winners of the day's competition, that is, half the student body.

Although the undokai has a carnivallike festiveness about it, there are lessons to be learned even from the Japanese school at play. First of all everyone participates. It is inclusive. Every fifth grade child, fat or thin, runs the 100-meter relay race. Amazingly, few are fat. Secondly some of the events will be group events in which, for example, four students balance a huge red or white ball on a stretcherlike carrier with four handles while running a 50-meter race against another set of four. Each must coordinate like a team to win the race. Or first grade children must pick up balls scattered on the ground and throw them into their team's basket atop a pole to see which side can get the most balls in during a five-minute frenzy of activity. Everyone joins in the slow dramatic counting of the balls to determine the winning side. The acrobatics include mass performances in unison as well as small group stunts.

And so it goes throughout the day. One competition follows another. The Japanese child learns, in part through the undokai, that there is a challenge in every activity of the school, be it inside the classroom or outside on the playground, at study, play, or work. It is this keen sense of the challenge, the enthusiasm for competition, that the Japanese child develops in school through all of these activities. Life is a continuous challenge. To meet it one must gambare – persevere, never give up. It's a simple lesson, a challenge, of the Japanese school and Japanese society that Americans can learn from.

8

LESSONS FOR JAPAN
FROM THE UNITED STATES

After a century of endeavoring to catch up with the West by looking primarily to the United States for the model, Japan, now challenging her teacher, faces a unique situation. Can Japan still learn anything from us? Do we have anything of educational value from which Japan can benefit? Are there any lessons remaining in the U.S. classroom for the Japanese classroom?

All prudent nations can benefit from the experience of others. The wise can always learn from their neighbors whether it be from the positive elements to imitate or pitfalls to avoid. Japan can still learn much from the United States today to enrich her schools and enliven her society, as she did previously, both from the positive and negative features of U.S. schools and society. The challenge, as in the past, is to be able to distinguish between the two.

One of the most visible differences between U.S. and Japanese schools concerns the number of students per class. Rarely is the U.S. teacher burdened with 40 students in the classroom as is the typical Japanese classroom teacher. Little change can take place in the Japanese classroom until the maximum number of students per teacher is reduced. In this peculiar sense, the Japanese can take a lesson in arithmetic from the Americans.

The classroom in Japan has traditionally catered to a large enrollment. Teachers in Japan have grown accustomed to such conditions although the organized teachers movement has continually pressed for a reduction in class size. The major teachers union currently has been demanding that the approved number of 40 students per class at the elementary and junior high school and of 45 at the senior high school be immediately enforced rather than waiting until the scheduled date of 1992 for full implementation. When Japan struggled as a poverty stricken country, when her per capita income was among the lower scales in the world, when she was confronted with an economic disaster at war's end, there was justification for large classes numbering 50 or more. In order to finance a mass school system under the prevailing conditions, there was no alternative.

Japan, however, is now among the affluent. It is clearly a recognizable supereconomic power. The national treasury has multiplied many times since the destitute years. The yen has become an international currency. Japanese investments throughout the world have reached substantial levels. Japanese corporations operate on a global basis.

And yet at home the teacher is responsible for a number of students typical of an underdeveloped nation rather than of a major economic power. Tokyo is a prime example. The standard public high school class in nearly every subject in this great commercial and industrial center of the Orient contains 48 students. The size of the classroom itself should accommodate about 30. The classrooms are bursting at the seams with the students becoming taller and broader each year as their diets include more bread, meat, and potatoes, and less rice and fish. There can be no rationale for tolerating the high student-teacher ratio that exists in Japan today. The burden on the Japanese teacher, although carried with remarkable efficiency as well as forebearance, is far too great in comparison to that of the average U.S. teacher. How our children's Japanese teachers would have envied a U.S. classroom with the usual number of students under 35, still considered excessive by many U.S. teachers and their unions.

Once the number of students per class is reduced to a more reasonable level commensurate with Japan's ability to finance it, which is considerable, an attempt should then be undertaken to diversify the teaching methods. No one can deny that Japanese teachers are efficient and capable, in comparison to their American counterpart, in the process of dispensing information for test-taking purposes. No one can fault Japanese teachers on their ability to manage 48 students in one class and maintain an impressive mass standard in subject matter tests, in comparison to any other nation in the world.

But what is absent in far too many Japanese classrooms, as we have seen over and over again, is the searching and probing for the spark of creativity, innovativeness, and originality. Too few Japanese teachers recognize, stimulate, and reward the creative response, the imaginative thought, the original idea that may deviate from the planned lesson. Unfortunately even to the considerable number of teachers who express a genuine interest in developing creativity among their students, there is simply little time and opportunity for such an endeavor. In the tightly packed daily schedule aimed so intensely at examination preparation, the classroom teacher simply cannot devote much energy to creativity or personality development.

The Japanese teacher should become more aware of the difference between instruction and education, referred to previously. Instruction implies the dissemination of knowledge. Education goes far beyond that. The development of independent thinking, the molding of character, and the formation of personality – all highly elusive concepts to be sure – are incorporated in the true meaning of education. The school is thus viewed in a much broader context than the mere preparation for examinations leading eventually to industry. It signifies the overall enrichment and fulfillment of life.

In no sense does this imply that the average U.S. teacher is adept at "educating" her students by recognizing, encouraging, and developing creativity or character in the classroom. But Japan should take lessons from the most positive elements of the U.S. school. And certainly a greater effort at nurturing creativity, originality, and personality is made in the U.S. classroom than in the Japanese classroom.

If one were somewhat crudely to evaluate the average teacher, based on innumerable classroom observations in Japan, the United States, and many other countries as well over the past three decades, the report card would look something like this. On instruction, the Japanese teacher would receive a grade of A to B; the U.S. teacher, a B to C. On education, as loosely defined above, the U.S. teacher would receive a B to C; the Japanese, a C to D.

As so often is the case in matters of the school, there is more here than appears at first glance. A highly structured classroom, such as that in Japan where the average teacher follows fairly closely the teacher's guide and the texts, both standardized by governmental approval, can ensure a high level of instruction throughout the land. The test results continually prove the success of this approach. Consequently, even in the hands of a teacher who does not have the stimulating character or personal qualities of a good teacher, the results can be and are impressive. In other words, those Japanese teachers who would do poorly in a fairly unstructured classroom where individual initiative and skill is critical (and many Japanese teachers observed fit into this category) can be quite successful in the Japanese school in instruction for examinations. Most teachers can function effectively under this system.

Unfortunately a good many U.S. teachers also do not have the stimulating character and personal qualities of a good teacher. Make no mistake about it; teaching is one of the most demanding professions, which only a minority of teachers perform well in any country. The situation is aggravated in the United States because, it is authoritatively reported, "Too many teachers are being drawn from the bottom quarter of graduating high school and college students."[1] Thus in the United States, with its rather unstructured classroom where a clear path toward specific goals aimed at high school and university examination preparation does not dominate the teacher nor the teacher's guide, this type of teacher can prove ineffective at instruction. Far too many of the students in the U.S. classroom under this teacher do not obtain literary and numerary skills sufficient for gainful employment. Instruction is critical for the basics.

In other words, in the hands of the regular classroom teacher, the vast majority having ordinary character and personal qualities, fairly structured teaching methods can produce a literate graduate. Japan is the outstanding example among all developed nations. Under the same type of teacher in an unstructured classroom setting, far too many graduates cannot read, write, and calculate sufficiently to live a productive life. The United States is the outstanding example among the developed nations of the world.

Japan must not reform her schools to the degree that the structured classroom becomes so unstructured that the ordinary teacher cannot maintain basic standards necessary for the graduate, every graduate, to achieve the basic essentials necessary to live productively in an era of high technology. At the same time the overemphasis on rote memory and test taking, which can stifle individual creativity, sensitivity, and imagination must be curtailed. It's a fine line that no country has noticeably succeeded in keeping in focus. But the Japanese have not yet really addressed the problem. A simple but highly provocative letter by a teenager to the editor of one of Japan's great daily newspapers, which can be read with understanding by nearly all Japanese adults, illustrates the situation perfectly.

I worked out this year's questions on the Unified Entrance Examination for National Universities (as published in the paper the day after the examinations were administered). I then calculated my score at 462, a failing grade.

At the present time I am an 18-year-old freshman at a national university in Tokyo. Last year when I took the Unified Entrance Examination I scored a total of 903 points, sufficient to enter this university. I carry a normal load of courses and earn average grades. I now realize how rapidly my ability at taking tests has fallen since last year. Many of my friends have the same feeling.

Frankly I think that cramming of information and knowledge like that required to pass the Unified Entrance Examination is unnecessary for university studies. This is especially true for majors in humanities and social studies who must cram for the physics and chemistry sections of the examination.

The last year in high school and the following two years are critical ones for determining what one wants to do in life. Devoting so much time cramming for tests during this period seems like such a waste of time. There really should be a reexamination of the entire entrance examination system.[2]

This poignant but simple letter by a teenager, who undoubtedly will enter some Japanese company as a loyal, literate, and competent employee, points out one of the great ironies, and weaknesses, of the school system. The Japanese teacher has before her a group of students that has achieved one of the highest mass standards of literacy and mathematics in the world. Her better students can read, write, and calculate across the board at least on a par with, if not better than, their counterparts in the U.S. classroom and, in comparing the average and below-average students, can far outperform them. Moreover a large percentage of her students are fairly well motivated. Not only that, the school has strong support from the parents.

In other words, the basic academic standards of the Japanese class are ideally suited for developing creative, original thinking rather than rote memorization of factual information. This is in contrast to many U.S. classrooms where one-fourth or one-fifth of the students, and in some instances a far higher percentage, may not have acquired basic reading, writing, and numerary skills. It is extremely difficult even with the smaller classes in the United States to develop and encourage originality and creativity when many a U.S. teacher must devote so much time to the slower students who never master the basic skills. In spite of that, a considerably greater effort is undertaken in the U.S. classroom to motivate the inner spark of creativity that many teachers feel exists in every child.

It surely exists in the Japanese child as well. The young man who wrote that letter reflects a potential creativeness masked by the school. But precious little attempt is made to search for it and nourish it. There simply are too many students in the classroom. And the official course of study requirements are too demanding to enable the average, mortal Japanese classroom teacher to devote time and energy to the admittedly elusive goal. She must concentrate on completing the required course of study on time. Otherwise, she's failing to do the job expected of her by the school authorities, both locally and nationally, and the parents.

If given the encouragement and opportunity to do so, Japanese teachers are also as capable of nourishing student character and personality as their U.S. counterparts are. The teaching corps in this country is not only academically competent in subject matter; it exhibits a high degree of commitment to the job, devoting many hours of extracurricular duty few U.S. teachers or their unions would tolerate. For example, in a survey made in Tokyo, it was discovered that 30 percent of teachers in the 35- to 44-year-old nonadministrative class at the compulsory school level return home from work each evening about eight o'clock as a result of after-hours school duty.[3] This is a remarkable dedication to the job. It smacks of zanygo, the practice of overtime work in the corporate offices of Japan.

If the immense energy and commitment of the Japanese classroom teacher could be released through a reduction in class size from the unbelievable amount of paperwork required for such a large number of students, that teacher could redirect her time for other critical matters. Character development requires that the teacher take a more personal interest in each child. Personality development requires individual attention by the teacher. Under no circumstances can any teacher in any country, regardless of her devotion to duty, consider the child's personal development when there are 48 students in each high school class, 45 in the junior high school class, and 42 or 43 in the elementary school classroom.

When Japan underwent the catch-up phase of her historical development, a school dominated by instruction for examinations and an industry dependent on Western discoveries, methods, and original ideas were understandable. Her international reputation as the clever imitator was well deserved. Throughout Japan's modern history she has made few original contributions in any endeavor except for the Japanese arts. It is often pointed out that Japan has produced only four Nobel Prize winners compared to 126 awards to Americans and more than 200 to Europeans (Table 8.1). This disparity is remarkable in itself because the mass standards of mathematics in particular are among the highest, if not the highest, in the world. On the face of it, surely the Japanese should have produced a score of mathematicians worthy of the Nobel Prize. That one of the two living Japanese who have received the Nobel Prize works in the United States as a researcher for IBM tells a story in itself.

But a step into the math classroom in any Japanese high school will clarify the situation. Seldom does the mathematics teacher go beyond the concepts required for the examination. As we have seen, it is a process of drill, repeat, and test. The problems have become notoriously complex. The level of mastery in solving intricate problems is, to be sure, most impressive. But the application of mathematics to unique situations requiring imaginative or original thinking is rare indeed. The pity of it is that the Japanese student is surely capable of such efforts. The school, however, does very little to develop that skill. Some critics argue that the Japanese classroom, in fact, stifles creativity. The theme is a popular one among the avant-garde.

The Japanese teacher, then, deserves recognition for the ability to attain a very high standard in examinations in nearly all subjects with a large majority of the very large number of students in the class. What that same teacher has failed to do, or simply cannot possibly undertake under the prevailing circumstances of large classes and demanding course

TABLE 8.1
Nobel Prize Winners, 1901-82

Country	Total
United States	126
England	63
Germany (East and West after 1945)	49
France	22
Sweden	15
Soviet Union	10
Holland	9
Switzerland	9
Austria	8
Denmark	7
Italy	5
Belgium	5
Japan	4

Source: White Paper on Science and Technology (Kagaku Gijutsu Hakusho) 1982, Kagaku Gijutsu Cho, p. 41.

requirements, is to consider the development of character and personality or to stimulate creativity, originality, or analytical thinking among her students. And many Japanese teachers and students are capable of achieving such lofty goals.

At the same time, with such large classes of students, those who cannot keep up with the relentless pace of the classroom are placed in a very precarious position. It is physically impossible for the classroom teacher to provide the necessary guidance to the slower students, especially at the upper grade levels where examination preparation exerts its increasingly demanding influences on the classroom. It is, of course, the slower students who require more individual attention than the others. And it is precisely this group that receives too little concern in the schools of this land.

The academic pressure on the slower students in the Japanese classroom is very heavy indeed. The constant testing leaves little to the imagination. The slow student is continually revealed for what he is, the bottom of the class. The frequent posting of test results exposes to all the rank order of achievement. All students know where the others stand. It is inevitable that the slower student's lack of ability is frequently reinforced in a school system dominated by examinations. The shame of it is that there are few provisions to guide that kind of student. Nevertheless, what is very impressive about a neighborhood Japanese school, which should not be lost sight of in this analysis, is how fast the slower learners in this nation learn. It indicates that the so-called slow learner in U.S. schools could and should do far better than has been heretofore demonstrated.

But the Japanese pay a price for their inordinate pressure on all students to learn. The slow learner, in increasing numbers, is not allowing the teacher nor the general public to forget his plight so easily. It is primarily within this group at the junior high school level where the growing incidents of school disturbances occur. It is this type of student that, as graduation time approaches, harasses those teachers who simply forgot him during the classroom hours or who pressured him to study harder without providing the guidance necessary for him to better cope with the math problems designed for the bright students. It is this type of student who disrupts the class or graduation ceremonies. The moment of revenge on the school has finally arrived. It's surprising, in fact, that the number of such incidents is not far greater, although the alarmed Japanese public does not view it that way.

The Japanese can learn something of value from the U.S. approach to school guidance. No one would expect the Japanese to employ a fulltime, professionally trained guidance counselor assigned to a junior high school, a common and expensive practice in most U.S. communities requiring the employment of a corps of counselors, who often do not teach within the regular academic course offerings. Rather, what the Japanese can learn from the U.S. approach is the rationale underlying student guidance. One of the basic principles is that the slow learner has the right to receive something of value from the school in a democratic society. It is the responsibility of the school, therefore, to devote a certain amount of its resources to provide special guidance to the slow learner so that he can find his place in school and in society. It is extremely difficult, nearly impossible, to accomplish this with the large classes usual in Japanese schools.

There is, clearly, a predicament here on both sides of the Pacific Ocean. It exists, of course, in every country. Should academic standards be emphasized at the expense of the slower student who can't keep up? Or should the pace of the teaching be slowed to more adequately accommodate the slower learner? How to strike a balance represents a universal problem in modern democratic school systems. Some in Japan criticize the former trend in their schools. In particular the Japan Teachers Union has focused on this popular theme at many of its conferences squarely blaming government for encouraging and abetting this distortion of Japanese education.

Some in the United States criticize U.S. schools for the latter, claiming that the classroom standards have been lowered to meet the standards of the slower student rather than those of the more academically talented. The *Nation at Risk* report repeatedly commented on this theme under the title of "Expectations."

> During the past decade or so a large number of texts have been "written down" by their publishers to ever-lower reading levels in response to perceived market demands. In some metropolitan areas basic literacy has become the goal rather than the starting point. And the ideal of academic excellence as the primary goal of schooling seems to be fading across the board in American education.[4]

Obviously neither Japan nor the United States has solved this dilemma, if indeed it is solvable. The Japanese must forever be alert not to let their overall school standards fall to the point where "academic excellence as the primary goal of schooling seems to be fading." It is inconceivable, however, that this could happen in Japan, an enviable state of affairs. But the opposite has already taken place in which an emphasis on academic excellence has taken precedence over the concern for individual growth and development of character and personality.

This whole issue centers to a great extent on the all-embracing role of the examination in Japanese education. As long as education is seen in its singular purpose, examination preparation, the classroom teacher cannot provide the guidance necessary for the slow learner. However, no one with an understanding of Japanese geopolitical limitations would suggest that the emphasis on examination preparation be eliminated. That could lead to disaster. The university entrance examination is the backbone of the system underlying the very high standards of the classroom on which Japanese industry must rely to maintain its competitiveness. And the nation depends on that. But surely some reorientation of examination preparation at the lower levels is long overdue.

For example, the complexity of the senior high school entrance examination as illustrated by the Tokyo example in mathematics is approaching, perhaps has already passed, the abusive level. The abstractness of the questions is geared for the brightest. Nevertheless, the regular junior high school classroom teacher must subject all of her 40-plus students to the task of preparing for that examination, even though the slower students can't follow up to half or more of that very advanced course content. The same conditions exist in every prefecture. Something must give.

The time has come for Japan to "bite the bullet," beginning with the high school entrance examination. Secondary education for all has virtually been achieved with about 95 percent of the age group continuing from the junior high school, over a quarter of them entering private schools. The current situation should be recognized through codification in the form of incorporating high school entry into the compulsory schooling provisions. The change should include the abolition of the high school entrance examination at the age of 15, with major consequences.

The word compulsory, however, when applied to high school entry is misleading and unfortunate. It implies coercion. It shouldn't. The U.S. approach to the high school has been traditionally couched in democratic terms. The public high school developed throughout the United States, in part, as a right of every child. It should be considered so in Japan. It becomes the responsibility of the Japanese government, in its obligation to the public, to provide with public funds the opportunity for every child to enter high school without examination. Technically it would fall under the category of compulsory education. Nevertheless, reflecting the contemporary status of Japan as one of the major democratic nations in the world, free secondary educational provisions for all should be considered as a fundamental right of every citizen.

The many consequences of such action must simply be faced. It should not be postponed any longer. The cost admittedly will be enormous primarily because of the exorbitant cost of land in this small but heavily populated country. Currently much of the financial burden is shifted to the individual family. In the case of a slower student, the family must enroll their offspring in a low-standard private high school paying tuition and, sometimes, commuting expenses to distant areas. If lucky, the applicant may be accepted by a lower-standard public high school. In too many instances, debilitating daily commuting journeys are required.

The principle that every child has a right to attend a neighborhood public high school follows this line of reasoning. Currently neighborhood friendships among teenagers are tossed asunder, as we witnessed when our daughter's junior high friends were dispersed all over this huge metropolis to Tokyo upon graduation. Each family is forced to find a high school, either public or private, that is suitable for their child and that is willing to accept their application based on examination results. Patterns of long-established friendships were consequently abruptly changed. All junior high students in the neighborhood realized that an era in their lives was coming to a close with the graduation ceremony. At age 15, this disruption in the socialization process is surely premature.

Internal reorganization of the local public high school then becomes of prime importance. The Japanese have never fully addressed themselves to the problem of the postwar high school. It remains a key unresolved topic within the system. How to provide a democratically structured secondary school while maintaining the traditionally high academic standards of this nation represents the challenge. It is, to be sure, not simply a Japanese problem but rather a universal problem in education and should be considered from a broad comparative perspective. No country has solved the issue to everyone's satisfaction. However, a glimpse into secondary patterns in Europe and in the United States could provide some direction.

There are, then, two Western models, the traditional European and the American. The European model, currently undergoing extensive reforms in most countries, was based on a dual system; a long academic secondary school program designed for the bright student who could pass a very difficult entrance examination. The overriding goal of the school was the preparation for the university entrance examination. Those who could not pass the rigorous academic entry requirements were assigned instead to a separate and much shorter general-vocational secondary school program geared for their abilities. It had a much less academically oriented curriculum and a variety of general and vocational subjects. Thus the two types of schools, sometimes further divided into three – academic, general, and vocational – were designed to meet the needs of the various types of students.

The Americans in their interpretation of egalitarianism shunned the European diversified secondary school system on the grounds that it undemocratically separated children according to their social class background. Upper-class children dominated the academic schools such as the British grammar school, the German gymnasium, and the French lycée, which led to the university; lower-class children dominated the other schools, which led to early employment in factories or menial labor. To the Americans, the European schools were viewed as instruments that perpetuated social class divisions favoring the elite classes. The alternative was the birth of the U.S. comprehensive high school during the great progressive education movement of John Dewey. The reform provided both the academic and vocational curricula under the same roof for all students, the academically talented in college preparatory classes and the manually oriented student in vocational courses. Certain subjects such as American history and government, physical education, music, and art would be taken in common.

The Japanese high school is a unique combination of the two. Its curriculum, its goals, and its emphases resemble the academic high school of the European model with an overriding priority given to the preparation for university entrance examinations. Its all-encompassing student body, however, resembles that of the U.S. comprehensive high school model. The Japanese have thus created a hybrid in which the overwhelming majority of its secondary school population is subjected to a school curriculum more appropriate, as in the European academic secondary schools, for the brightest. There is little flexibility or variety in the Japanese high school.

The results, it must be recognized and admired, are impressive indeed. The academic standards of the masses, that is, over 90 percent of the cohort who are graduated from the high school, are among the very highest if not the highest in the world. A price must be paid, and it is in terms of the slower student who has been brought through the system under immense pressure. If the standard academic requirements are not eased, if the school curriculum does not offer more courses appropriate for the less academically able, the level of school violence especially around graduation time may again grow in intensity. The Japanese simply demand too much from the slow learners, in sharp contrast to conditions in the United States. A reaction seems inevitable.

Japanese high schools, to begin with, should provide a greater variety of courses especially in mathematics to provide more adequately for both the bright and slow students. For the bright student, more emphasis should be placed on creative mathematics, that is, the application of mathematics to unique situations or conditions and on creative writing, the application of the written word to imaginative thinking. But of great importance must be the sharp reduction in the highly abstract exercises in mathematics that the slow students are subjected to as part of their course of required studies. Rather, more simplified exercises based on requirements of daily life should form the basis of the mathematics curriculum for the slow learners. These requirements should be the minimal standard for high school graduation. Slow learners may attend courses adapted specifically for their needs. This, too, is a long over-due reform. Separating students according to academic ability into different schools on the European model certainly has a social implication. Only the Japanese can decide if such separation is appropriate for their country.

The government must take the lead in this reform, along with other changes of the school, so that this society can more fully enjoy the fruits of its success and so that the excesses of the Japanese school can be brought into balance. The first reform for all subsequent improvements of the Japanese classroom must be the reduction of the allowable class size in all public schools to an absolute maximum of 35. At a later date consideration should be given to the possibility of further reducing the number to 33 and again to 30. Financially there can be no excuse for delaying this critical reform. And all the others are dependent upon it.

The second reform would be to reduce the school week by abolishing Saturday morning classes on the U.S. model. The long-term benefits gained from operating a nationwide school system for three and a half hours on Saturday is debatable. Just the extra commuting burden and expense on the part of all students and teachers for the half-day session are questionable. By retaining the extraordinarily long school year and the short vacation, from July 20 to September 1, the government could eliminate the half-day Saturday class without risking any serious reductions in the academic standards.

Japanese industry for the past several years has been very gradually moving toward a five-day workweek in several major industries on a once- or twice-a-month basis. Apparently it will take many years before a full two-day weekend holiday can be fully implemented. The school should be moving gradually in the same direction. If the Japanese worker gains the two-day weekend off, and it will eventually transpire, surely their children deserve the same treatment. The mentality of catching up must undergo some revision. It is time that the Japanese give their children and their hard-working teachers the weekend free from school. It would be one sign that the government is seriously concerned with the overemphasis on academic requirements of the school.

One of the major arguments against a five-day school week presupposes that a good many children will not use Saturday as a day for relaxation apart from study. Rather, too many children (say some teachers, parents, and government officials) will spend that day in one of the proliferating private schools, the yobiko and juku. During their day off from school, they will devote their energies preparing for the examinations by intensively poring over mock tests. A free day from school on Saturday will have the provocative effect of intensifying examination preparation instead of reducing it for far too many students to make the change acceptable.

Not only would Saturday off from school result in an intensification of study in mathematics and Japanese, the two pillars of all entrance examinations, it would probably increase the private study of other subjects. The demand for private lessons in English, calligraphy (shuji), and piano, all three especially popular among Japanese girls, would be even further increased on Saturdays. Consequently, a major result in reducing the school week to five days would be to greatly increase the income of private schools and private teachers at the expense of the students, not merely financially but emotionally and physically as well. Carrying this line of reasoning to its ultimate conclusion, its proponents say that the Japanese Ministry of Education should continue Saturday classes to protect the students from an intensification of study.

One of the proposals to adjust the school workweek of the teachers to conform to the working conditions of industry, as the five-day workweek is implemented very cautiously in stages, reveals the traditional Japanese attitude toward both work and school. Under this approach, the school would continue on a regular five-and-a-half-day schedule. Teachers, including those at the elementary level, would work only five days a week. The students, nevertheless, on the grounds that Saturday off would intensify cramming for entrance examinations, would attend school for the full five and a half days. Japan must surely be one of the few nations in the world where such convoluted reasoning has considerable legitimacy.

If no other revisions of the school curriculum are implemented, rather than contributing to the general well-being and growth of the child, a five-day school week would surely result in the widespread use of Saturdays for private study. But other reforms must accompany both the reduction of classroom numbers and the shortened school week. The next step calls for the Ministry of Education to slow the academic pace somewhat by curtailing the requirements of the course of study. This is particularly true in mathematics. The current level is too exacting even for the average student. The pressure to keep up with the standard on the part of slower students and their teachers is too heavy. Americans do not extract such a high price from their teachers or students.

The Japanese have gone too far in this direction. A course correction is long overdue. The early symptoms in school violence, even though it doesn't approach that in the many big U.S. city schools, should indicate to all concerned Japanese, and there are many, that something must be done to better accommodate the slower students. A five-day school week and abolishment of the high school entrance examination will help. Such changes will reduce pressures on those students who are less academically inclined but who, nevertheless, have an inherent right to an education commensurate with their ability. But it won't solve the major problem. The heart of the matter remains the university entrance examination.

A very important lesson Japan can take from the positive elements of U.S. education concerns the uses of testing. In a school system like Japan's, so dominated by examination preparation, any improvement in the use of examinations would be of great significance. The intense memorization of material for all examinations in the Japanese school reflects the object of testing. The primary purpose of the examination seems to be testing the student's ability to memorize huge doses of information. Under these circumstances drilling, repeating, the heavy uses of mock tests, and the proliferating supplementary yobiko schools are inevitable consequences.

If the very nature of the examination were revised, it could exert a tremendously beneficial effect on the entire school system. The character of the classroom itself could undergo a vital change. And that change, if properly executed at all levels from the Ministry of Education to the local school level, could be in the direction befitting a leading industrial and commercial power like Japan. The widespread use of examinations is fundamental to the Japanese school system. It could be harnessed to more productive goals beyond maintaining basic standards in literacy and mathematics.

The reform of examinations could be accomplished by redesigning them to test critical and analytical thinking rather than pure rote memorization. To achieve this end, a good part if not most of the examination would have to be reoriented from purely factual questions. Rather, the heart of the examination should be structured so that students would be required to read selected passages in each subject area including mathematics and science. Interpretative and analytical questions based on the passages could be designed to test the student's ability to reason, to draw conclusions, to infer, and to analyze.

One of the characteristics of this method of examination is that the student cannot study in the traditional manner. The memorization of enormous amounts of data will not enable a person to critically choose the correct answer to questions based on the reading of assigned passages. The critical eye can pick it out. The uncritical eye stuffed with factual information will have no advantage. In fact, such preparation may prove a disadvantage when examinations requiring analytical thinking and reasoning are employed (along the lines of the SATs).

The university in Tokyo where this writer teaches has been employing this type of examination for years. It is one of the few institutions in Japan to experiment with differing approaches to entrance examinations. The pioneering efforts were carried out, appropriately, by a U.S. psychologist on the faculty shortly after the war. The Japanese students find it novel. Most of them have never encountered such an exercise in testing. They're taken by surprise over a "test you can't study for." What they mean is that pure memorization of massive doses of factual knowledge is of limited help. They have all studied diligently for a test requiring knowledge of facts rather than the ability to analyze. The new experience in test taking proves disconcerting to many, although most recognize and approve the unique purpose behind it.

At a period in world history when technological developments based on the computer are hurtling the advanced countries into a new era, the memorization of massive amounts of formulas will have limited practical value. That kind of material can be stored in the computer to be retrieved with the punch of a key. What has become of prime importance is the application of knowledge in heretofore unknown situations. Examinations designed to test the student's ability to apply knowledge in unique circumstances should become the core of testing. Japan must develop the essentials of high technology in order to remain competitive.

The need for developing analytical reasoning is critical in Japan. One of the glaring weaknesses of Japanese students is the shortcoming in their ability to respond with critical conclusions, to analyze persuasively passages of readings, or even to ask pointed questions when they are puzzled. For such a highly literate student well versed in mathematics, to simply sit passively in class taking notes verbatim seems dreadfully wasteful.

In contrast, in a respectable number of U.S. classrooms one often hears teachers probing their students: "What do you think about that idea? Why do you believe that? Does anyone disagree with that opinion? Are there any other ideas?" Obviously the purpose is to develop critical thinking and logical reasoning in an effort to challenge student reaction, to encourage the cross-fertilization of differing viewpoints in a critical manner. Such teaching is far more prevalent in the U.S. classrooms than in Japanese classrooms, although there is much to be derived in the United States as well.

Analytical thinking is perhaps one of the most demanding challenges of any student and teacher in any classroom. Not too many teachers anywhere are successful in cultivating critical reasoning. Not too many students in any country are truly capable of analytical thought. Nevertheless, in the classroom of this author, where the bright students from the United States have studied together with the bright students of Japan for the past 25 years, the bright U.S. student has consistently exhibited a greater capacity for analytical reasoning than his counterpart, the Japanese university student, has. Test the two in mathematics, and the Japanese will invariably be ahead, often considerably so. Assign them an exercise in critical analysis, of reaction to an unusual set of circumstances, and the U.S. student will consistently respond more persuasively, not to mention uniquely so, than the Japanese student. Interestingly, the Japanese student, himself, is aware of his weakness in creative, independent thinking. He also often blames the intense examination preparation, in which enormous doses of factual information must be routinely memorized, for this deficiency.

We have encountered unique students in our classes over the years: the Japanese students who came through the preuniversity studies in the traditional Japanese school and who also studied at a good U.S. high school and for one or two years at a U.S. university. In other words, these students are well versed in the basics because of their Japanese schooling and are fairly articulate, inquisitive, and somewhat imaginative as a result of their U.S. university studies. The unique combination incorporates the best of the two systems yielding an able student.

The university entrance examination could be redesigned to develop such a unique blend of the best of the two systems. If the exams at all levels were redesigned so that they required critical analysis as well as a reasonable amount of factual knowledge, the character of the Japanese classroom could undergo a positive change. So would the graduates of the system, the Japanese people. This nation with its extraordinarily high standards of education among all levels of the society is perched for new accomplishments. That effort should be directed at nothing less than developing a new incentive for innovation and creativity through the use of examinations. There are indeed very creative approaches to the construction of examinations that reduce the need for rote memorization of facts while increasing the need for analytical skills. The Japanese have tried few of them.

When the overriding role of the university entrance examination is finally brought into balance, and one cannot help thinking that the common sense of the Japanese will ultimately bring this about, then the reform of the Japanese university system must follow. So far, Japanese higher education has not been considered because the primary concern of this book has been the Japanese public school. There is another reason as well. To put it bluntly, the Americans have little to learn from the Japanese university. But the Japanese have much to learn from the U.S. university. Therefore the issue is only appropriate in this final chapter concerning what Japan can learn from the United States.

A familiar saying is that it's very difficult to get into the Japanese university, but it's easy to graduate from it and that it's very easy to get into a U.S. university, but it's difficult to graduate from it. The first part is very close to the mark. The second misses the mark when applied to the better U.S. universities where it's not only difficult to enter but also difficult to graduate. There are few exceptions to the first part about the Japanese university.

The Japanese university system has one of the highest academic standards for entry of any university system in the world. After Japanese youth have spent so much of their early years in intensive study to prepare for that dreaded period in their lives, the *juken senso* (literally examination preparation war), it abruptly ends. University entrance marks the termination of serious study until entry into a company when job requirements once again bring the young Japanese back to gambare – perseverance.

The four years of a Japanese university, or two in the many junior colleges, other than "making up" for the many years of intensive preparation, are leisurely ones for most Japanese university students. The academic demands in the vast majority of institutions, including the most famous, cannot approach those of the famous, and even a fair number of the not-so-famous universities and colleges in the United States. The quality of too many of the local U.S. institutions of higher education, however, leaves much to be desired. Nevertheless, it really is a peculiar comparison. At the preuniversity level, the average U.S. school is academically inferior to its Japanese counterpart in academic performance. At the university level, exactly the opposite is true. Whereas there is an enormous failure rate in U.S. higher education, calculated at between 35 to 45 percent over a four-year period, the failure rate at Japanese universities is insignificant. Contrary to what the uninitiated would surmise, the minuscule rate of student failure in the Japanese university cannot be attributed to the diligent work by the students. Rather, it is directly related to the lack of academic standards on the part of the university.

With the exception of a minority of students in certain scientific fields at a minority of Japanese universities, the academic demands to graduate are minimal. The student, after so many years of intensive preparation, has come to the stage where he believes it is his right to be graduated whether he attends class, opens a book, or ever checks a reference in the library. In a seemingly paternalistic way, the professor sympathizes by setting minimal requirements and minimal standards for passing the examination or for scoring the only required work, a final paper of little significance.

To this foreign teacher at a university in Japan, there seems to be only a fairly small number of students and professors throughout the land who set higher standards for themselves beyond the general mediocre level expected at Japanese universities. From this group thousands of students, as well as many professors, travel to the United States each year to enter a U.S. university at either the undergraduate or graduate level. The Institute for International Education reported that over 13,500 Japanese students were enrolled in U.S. colleges and universities during a recent year.[5] But for a university professor in a large Japanese university even of the prestigious type, especially but not exclusively at private institutions, to actually fail those students who rarely attend class and turn in a poor final paper would be an act of considerable controversy. Few attempt it.

A Japanese friend, distinguished professor at one of the most famous private universities in Japan once mentioned that 1,200 students were enrolled in his course in political science each term. When asked how they could accommodate so many students in one place, he explained that seating was not a problem. In fact, his course was scheduled in an auditorium with only 500 seats. It was taken for granted that they would never be filled.

The Japanese university is desperately in need of a major reform. The pity of it all is that the student body represents the finest product of a very demanding preuniversity school system. Admittedly many of these students have literally exhausted themselves, especially during that last year or so as a jukensei, a high school preparatory student, or a yobiko student. But to virtually stop studying for the next several years represents an immense waste of potential development. It's the way the system works, it is true, and Japan has prospered in spite of its university system, as a Japanese colleague has pointedly remarked to this non-Japanese. But think how much more Japan could prosper if the many universities had more stringent standards, a reform long overdue.

In a peculiar sense of reasoning, it appears that the academic standards of the Japanese university will not be raised until the academic demands for entry are eased. And that is precisely why the entrance examination itself must first of all be revised to reduce the need for rote memorization of inordinate amounts of factual information and to increase the requirements for deduction, reasoning, and analyzing. This type of examination is as demanding in its own way as the former, but the nature of preparation for it comes under the category of education rather than instruction.

As my Japanese colleague pointed out, Japan has prospered in spite of her university tradition. But the Japanese have also achieved an international reputation as adroit adapters, cleverly applying Western techniques and methods to produce high quality products to be sold throughout the West. The imitativeness ascribed to them was to a considerable extent deserved and understandable in response to the needs of the catch-up phase of her history. But that period is on its way out, and so is the imitative phase of her development. New innovative ideas in high technology are beginning to come from Japan although the adapter psychology remains strong.

This nation is poised to make important original contributions far beyond the Walkman or the two-inch television screen in many areas, but particularly in science and technology, for the benefit of humanity. With a highly educated, motivated citizenry, a huge middle class providing the driving force, and a tiny lower class minimally burdening the economy, conditions are excellent for developing originality, creativity, and innovation in the Japanese classroom. The teaching corps is one of the most academically competent in the world, willing to devote many extra hours at modest salaries under somewhat primitive working conditions. In addition, home support of the school is widespread.

The stage is set. The Japanese, at their sharpest when challenged by competition, are ripe for perhaps their greatest challenge of the twenty-first century, the development of high technology for the betterment of humanity, not only for those living in the developed world but especially for those in the Third World. This means not only sixth generation computers for advanced societies but also new Japanese ideas and tools to improve the quality of life of the majority of the world's population living in inexcusable poverty and hunger during an era of high technology. To harness the immense vitality of the Japanese people, with perhaps the highest mass academic standards in the world, to one of the greatest global problems is the challenge to Japan in the twenty-first century. It is a moment of historical consequence for the Japanese people. Their example could become a new challenge to the United States.

There is one last lesson to be learned from the United States. It may be the most important one. It concerns the attitude of a frontrunner. Japan has never been in the forefront of industrial and commercial development before. She has always considered herself the poor kid on the block. The rich kids from the United States and Europe were expected to take the lead. The poor kid from Japan followed.

Japan is no longer the poor child, although remnants of that mentality persist. Statistics defy that attitude. What this implies is that the Japanese must assume a leadership role in world affairs commensurate with their economic and commercial position. The classroom must reflect this new role. Students should be taught that they, as Japanese, must be cognizant of Japan's new place in the world order and must begin to think and act like leaders, developers, and innovators, not merely followers. That means the classroom must have a much broader perspective. Events must be considered more from an international perspective. New and original ideas in every area must come from the Japanese. The confidence of leaders must be instilled in future generations.

At the same time the smug complacency that overtakes the leader makes the study of history vital to a leader. The complacency of the leading Western nation, the United States, must be avoided at all costs. Japan is now challenging the United States in part because it was motivated to catch up with that country, which itself has become complacent. Once the shoe is on the other foot, the new runner faces the constant threat of those it challenged. The Japanese must never lose sight of the enormous potential of the United States once it shrugs off its complacency to meet the Japanese challenge. For Japan to catch up with the United States, it has had to run harder than the United States. For Japan to remain in the vanguard, it must forever remain diligent.

POSTSCRIPT:
ARE WE A NATION AT RISK?

Risk: chance of harm or loss; danger, peril, jeopardy
— Webster

Are we really a nation at risk, as the highly publicized report to the U.S. government warns? As an American who has lived half of his life in the United States, a bit less than that in Japan, and the remaining years in England, I should like to complete this study by addressing that critical question. However, before doing so a brief description of events leading up to this analysis is in order. My response is formed particularly from the experiences of a recent round-the-world trip.

Our family departed from Tokyo on a small Soviet liner and traveled to an obscure port in the USSR Far East Maritime Province. We then traveled north to catch the Trans-Siberian Railroad westward and spent a week with a local Siberian teacher discussing at great length problems of Communist education. We stopped at Moscow where, as well as in Leningrad and Latvia, I had completed educational field research 20 years ago. We crossed Europe by train for a nostalgic visit to London and Cambridge, visiting some of the same local schools I had used for my study of British education during my three years as a graduate student at the University of London in the 1960s. Finally we traveled across the United States for a major educational research project starting with my own hometown schools in the East. Later I visited the schools in the area where I first began my teaching career in the U.S. public school system.

For six months I crisscrossed the United States visiting schools in ten states from Florida to New York to Oregon to California. Although the major purpose of the research was a study of the teachings about the Pacific War in U.S. history courses and of the attitudes of U.S. teachers and students toward Japan by means of textbook reviews, interviews with nearly 50 history teachers, and applying student and teacher questionnaires, it extended far beyond that scope. I also had the fascinating opportunity to witness contemporary U.S. education in process by spending many days inside schools talking to teachers and students and interviewing administrators about the educational issues of the day. It was a nostalgic return to the U.S. school.

The U.S. schools included in my study were located in large cities such as Washington, D.C., Chicago, and Los Angeles; in middle-sized cities such as Tallahassee, Florida; High Point, North Carolina; Harrisburg, Pennsylvania; and Boise, Idaho; and in small towns and tiny communities such as Laporte, Pennsylvania (population 175); Baker, Oregon; Fruitland, Idaho; Monticello, Florida; Thomasville, Georgia; and my hometown, Berwick, Pennsylvania.

A few of the inner-city schools were large with over 2,000 students, and some rural schools were small with fewer than 500. Some were all white, and others nearly all black including one with 1,614 black students of a total of 1,615 students, the other one being Asiatic. One school was 90 percent Hispanic. Several schools could be classified as America's finest and most famous public high schools where over 90 percent of the graduates go on to higher education. Others were at the opposite end with less than 10 percent of the graduates continuing to higher education, most of them entering a local junior college with a higher percentage going into the armed forces.

Ten months after leaving Japan, we returned home. Fresh from those many experiences I settled down to prepare this manuscript and resume my teaching duties. I also renewed my long-standing ties with many Japanese friends both from the academic and industrial world as well as with local folk, subjecting a number of them to my ideas for their response. I have also had to begin planning my annual study trips to the Philippines and Malaysia where some of my students go for thesis work on education in developing countries.

Now, it is from this rather broad comparative perspective that I finally attempt to answer the question in my own mind: Is our country at risk? Risk, according to Webster, means endangered, imperiled, in jeopardy. Is our country in jeopardy? Are we imperiled? My simple answer: I think not. The United States is not endangered, as is implied in our government's report, *A Nation at Risk*, by her competitors such as Japan. Rather, we are being challenged by Japan and others to look at ourselves, look at others, learn from their strengths and weaknesses, and undertake the necessary in-course corrections on our voyage into the challenging twenty-first century.

If our leaders, our school administrators, and our teachers could travel around the world visiting foreign schools, and then travel around the United States visiting our own schools, they would more fully understand what U.S. education is all about by comparing our schools with others, a major purpose of comparative education. Most of them would also probably agree with me that our nation is not endangered from an educational point of view. As one who has had that fortunate and enlightening experience of traveling and visiting, let me share my opinions and conclusions.

First of all, the strongest impression one gains coming out of the U.S. school scene, and then looking at it from abroad, is the glaring differences between our best and our poorest schools in our two-tiered system. There are, I can testify, first-rate public schools in the United States. Let no one be misled by the critical reports. Our best are not only very good; they are uniquely good from any comparative perspective. It is the unique character of our good schools that, unfortunately, cannot be evaluated with international studies comparing our students with those of other nations on computerized tests, but that keeps us in the forefront of high technology.

What makes our good schools different from the good schools of many other countries, including those of Japan? It is not the academic performance as measured by formal paper-pencil examinations. It is, rather, the atmosphere, the attitudes of both students and faculty, in which our advanced level studies are being undertaken. What distinguishes our elite students, that is, our good students, from the Japanese elite students concerns the role of examination preparation. Their best students are feverishly studying massive amounts of information in an intensely competitive situation. There is little time for any other activity but the dreary process of poring over mock tests, memorizing huge amounts of data, and experiencing immense anticipatory anxiety as the shiken senso, the examination war, approaches.

In order for the American to appreciate fully the atmosphere in which the Japanese university-bound student takes the dreaded entrance examination, and to compare it with the U.S. experience, a description of our university's test has relevancy. First of all, the typical Japanese student takes three or four different private university examinations. Many will also take the Unified Entrance Examination for National Universities. Some will take a total of six or seven entrance examinations during the same season, each one except the Unified Examination costing about $100, in order to increase their chances of success. In addition, because the examinations are usually two-day affairs, the thousands of students living far from the test site must travel to the university, reserve at least three nights in a hotel for each examination and meet other expenses. Some mothers come along for the events. It amounts to several thousand dollars for many a jukensei during the season with no assurance, of course, of success.

Each of the 3,000-plus students who applies for our examination (we take only 350) usually arrives on campus in one of a terribly crowded fleet of buses added for the two-day morning and evening rush to accommodate the influx. Parents, mostly mothers, will be directed to a special waiting room for the long days. Using a number code each applicant finds his way to a specified seat assigned to him weeks before by mail. Because the applicants do not know each other having been randomly assigned, there is almost no talking in the room. They simply sit quietly, staring ahead in anticipation. There is clearly a tense strained atmosphere.

Ten minutes before the first examination begins, the proctors, all university faculty and staff, enter the room carrying the materials. A short greeting is made with some attempt to "break the ice," rarely successful in such a situation. A detailed explanation of the procedures to be followed for the next two days is given. Any questions? Rarely. Revealingly, seldom is there one student among the 3,000-plus who forgets to bring the proper type of pencil and eraser for the computerized tests.

At the precise stroke of 8:40 a.m., the 3,000 students, in many classrooms, all arranged in perfectly straight rows will be told to open their pamphlet to page one. After carefully reading aloud the written instructions, "Dewa hajimete," they begin. All bend forward as one and begin the reading of an essay in, of course, complete silence. At the half hour a proctor quietly writes on the board, "Twenty minutes left." Then ten minutes, and then five. Almost simultaneously in every room, the chief proctor on the precise minute, because all proctors' watches are carefully synchronized, instructs the applicants to stop. The theme papers are collected and the students are given a ten-minute break. The doors are opened to change the air.

Upon return, at the appointed moment the classroom becomes absolutely quiet as the test papers are distributed and, like clockwork, exactly the same procedure is followed in every room. This time the students will also receive a computerized answer card because they must now answer questions about the essay they have just read, a novel form of testing for them all. At precisely 10:50 a.m., the test papers and cards are collected. A ten-minute break follows. And so it goes through various tests in social studies, natural science, and Japanese. At the end of the first day at 4:30 p.m., all applicants, totally exhausted, are dismissed to return to jam the buses that take them off to the train station either to return home, to a relative's home in the city, or to a hotel.

The next morning at eight o'clock, the buses come rolling on to campus for day two of the examination and a repeat of the procedure of the previous day. This time the tests include humanities, written English, and much to the horror of the students, a lengthy oral English listening test, and an SAT-type test. By now a few students have found or made friends. Most, however, spend the two days alone often eating a box lunch in their seats during the 45-minute noon break. Many simply stare out the window during other breaks. It's a lonely experience among the crowd. Some, of course, do not return the second day convinced they had failed the first day's tests and simply give up.

By the time the second full day of examinations is completed, the applicants are literally worn out. It has been a grueling experience. And it will be repeated in a few days or a week later at another university and then again as the examination season in late February and early March passes by. One new colleague from the West, experiencing the entrance examination for the first time in Japan, summed up his feelings as the weary applicants were filing out the door after the second day in a state of total exhaustion: "It's inhumane!"

But perhaps the most trying moment is still to come. All applicants will be told the date the test results are to be published, about two weeks later. During that period we run the answer cards through our big computers and prepare our acceptance list in a secretive operation that rivals a clandestine military operation. We must by all means safeguard the fairness and objectivity of the selection system.

On that fateful day, in addition to mailing individually the thousands of success and failure letters, we erect on campus a long sign board where the coded numbers of all successful applicants are posted. Hours before the appointed time those who live in or near this area, some with their mothers who have been through an "examination hell" as well, come drifting on to campus. As the staff begin to unroll the long sheet with the numbers, the whole crowd is by now on tiptoe, feverishly trying to find that special number. It is one of the most unforgettable moments of Japanese education when the screams of joy begin bursting through the crowd as the successful applicants jump for joy. Equally unforgettable are the many more who quietly turn away, often the girls with tears running down their cheeks, heading back to the bus stop. As they pass by, one can only quietly hope they will get accepted somewhere else. Thus marks the end of another entrance examination period for us. It's a memorable experience for this foreigner no matter how many times one goes through it. Imagine what it must be like for these young Japanese.

The university-bound student in the United States seldom experiences the pressures that nearly all university-bound students in Japan undergo because of the university entrance examination, before, during, and after the event. And that is precisely what makes our system unique. In the first place the SAT, the closest instrument the Americans have to a university entrance examination system, is administered at some local high school serving an area usually within commuting range of all applicants. That means many local students are taking the examination together. There is a great deal of talking among applicants and some "horsing around" amid few signs of tension. After all, few of them have considered the test seriously enough to study for it.

Once inside the auditorium or gymnasium, after proper identification, students are usually seated at random with the proper interval between seats. There is often much confusion amidst a fairly relaxed atmosphere. The local teacher in charge, familiar to many local students, will often sprinkle his introduction with humor. Many questions are asked, some rather humorous: "My name is O'Brien. What do I do with the apostrophe on the computer card?"

Because the schedule is rather loosely set, there is no precise moment for the examination to begin. When the monitor completes the introduction and all questions are exhausted, they begin the approximately three-hour examination, including short breaks. Even then, some students do not return promptly on time after the ten-minute break. Once assembled, the next examination is begun after the monitor finally gets the group settled down. This is seldom a precisionlike operation.

At the end of three hours, the examination ends with little fanfare. The students joke around on the way out. Many will give little thought to the results for the next month or so since the examination scores will come through the mail four to six weeks later. And even then, there is no notice of pass or failure, just the scores. If the student feels the score is low, he'll sign up to take the next SAT the following month or so. After all, the only thing he or she has to lose is the $10 application fee.

In addition to the relaxed atmosphere of the examination itself, a variety of factors are incorporated in the final university decision. They may include high school grades, perhaps a local test or an essay, and an interview, not just the one examination score as in Japan. And few, if any, high school teachers use the SATs as a threat to motivate students to study. In fact, most students make no specific effort even to prepare for the SATs other than their regular class studies. And that work is not usually based on the SATs because teachers have no prospectus of the SAT to teach from. A Japanese student finds it incomprehensible that the few U.S. high schools that offer a special SAT-preparatory course have few takers when the whole Japanese school system is, in one sense, SAT preparatory, that is, preparing for university entrance examinations.

The atmosphere surrounding the Japanese university entrance examination in comparison to that of the American is mirrored in the high school classroom of the jukensei students bound for the university in their respective countries. The Japanese student is engrossed in preparation dreading the examination season; the U.S. student is simply studying for his regular classes with no great concern about the date of the next SAT. The atmosphere in the highly academic U.S. high schools is decidedly relaxed, quite informal, with a great deal of interaction and spontaneity between student and teacher both within the classroom and without.

The uniqueness of good U.S. schools is that, in spite of their informal atmosphere, in spite of the lack of tense anticipation of examinations, and without the rigidity of a formal classroom setting, these graduates lead our nation, nay, the world, into space, to the moon, out for an untethered stroll in space, and into technological leadership. Even though our SAT scores have declined, although a reverse course may now be underway, Americans still wrote 38 percent of the world's scientific and technical articles in a recent year.[1] Our technical secrets are the most sought after in the world. Americans, mostly native born and educated, have won more than half of all Nobel Prizes awarded in science since World War II in spite of the discouraging reports of the trend toward scientific and technical illiteracy among our young people.

Our vitality is surely as "vital" as ever. Our good schools, in which we once took great pride as the foundation of our great experiment in democracy, are at this very moment educating the vanguard that will, it is predicted, lead America into the twenty-first century as the foremost nation in high technology. We will be out in front, perhaps barely, but we will be there. Our good students are being prepared for the university in an atmosphere in which rote learning for examination preparation does not engulf their entire lives, as such preparation does in Japan. That is what makes our good schools unique. Perhaps that's why we are in the forefront of technological innovation.

As long as our good schools produce the kinds of graduates they do today, we would be wise not to tamper too much with them. Of course, they can always be improved. Every school in the world can be improved. Many of our capable students could do better. But our good public high schools should be encouraged to continue their fine tradition in producing many highly literate and, most important, inquisitive graduates. With good schools like that, and they are found in every city, our nation is not at risk.

Yet you also come away fresh from visiting many schools in the United States convinced that something very important is missing in U.S. education. Not only are some of our best students not working as hard as they could to further levels of academic excellence, the average student has far too little demands placed on him to learn the basics. And the slowest students are, understandably, completely lost in our secondary schools because they can barely read and write, let alone multiply and divide. No wonder 25 percent of our high school students quit before graduation. No wonder some of those who don't quit but can't read disrupt the classroom, fight in the hallways, and sell drugs on the school grounds.

Those who criticize our schools fail to appreciate the distinctions among the schools in our two-tiered system. Our good schools should be recognized for what they are, uniquely good. Our poor schools should also be recognized for what they are, uniquely poor. In three major cities of the United States, I had the opportunity to visit both types located approximately one-half hour from each other. Although they're both U.S. high schools located in the same city, they exist in two different worlds.

Nothing can be more enlightening about U.S. education than visiting one of our good public schools and one of our poor public schools, both situated in the same community. Even to a former U.S. public school teacher, and a seasoned educator who has visited schools all over the world, the experience of visiting our best and our worst schools in the same city over a two-day period can be disconcerting to say the least. To a foreign visitor, it must be overwhelming to witness such a situation in a democratic supereconomic power like the United States.

The physical conditions in our bad schools are appalling; those in the good schools, luxurious from any international comparison, far surpassing the Japanese school. The library facilities, the resource centers such as audio-visual, the lounges, the classrooms, and even the bathrooms in our good schools are far superior to those in our bad schools. As I say, even as an American looking back at the American scene from Japan, it seems unreal.

To walk into a very good school in the suburbs of one of our cities, where there is a sense of orderliness, where the rooms are well lit and in good repair, where there is relative calm in the main office, where there is a remarkable degree of camaraderie among faculty, staff, and students in and outside the class, is a reassuring experience. In one such very good public school, I happened to walk in on a class underway in, of all places, the school's planetarium where the students were located throughout the room calculating the height of the dome with handheld devices. I could envision these students ten years later in our space program. How can our nation be at risk with schools like that?

On the way into the building I met a senior reading a novel on the lawn. He informed me that he planned to go into architecture after graduation that year. I asked him if he was studying for the SATs. His simple answer: Not really. He had taken the preliminary SATs the year before and didn't do too badly. He thought he'd do all right without "boning up" this year. "No big problem." After all, 90 percent of the graduating classes over the previous five years had gone on to higher education, the overwhelming majority to four-year colleges and universities.

The next morning I visited an inner-city school in the same community where I went through a security post at the door. An armed policeman assigned on a fulltime basis to the school was standing nearby. After receiving a permission slip I was able to go down the badly worn hallway to the main office. Amidst considerable noise and confusion with students and teachers coming and going, many shouting back and forth, I was invited to sit down and wait for the history teacher to come for our interview. The well-worn leather sofa I sat on was torn through the seat.

Suddenly a teacher came bursting through the door with two students in tow. All were shouting. The policeman followed them in. Right before me the assistant principal for discipline interrogated the highly excited students about an incident around the water fountain on the second floor.

The students vehemently denied their alleged roles in the ruckus. After they were told to report back to the office after school, they stomped out of the office in a huff. One wonders how their teacher handled them in the next class, if they went to it, which is doubtful.

Even on the way to the classroom, where I learned that 30 percent of all female students had an abortion or a baby by the age of 16, and that absenteeism was rampant reaching as high as 25 percent on any given day, we encountered a rather difficult shoving match by three students in the hallway. Breaking up the confrontation required considerable courage in this average-sized teacher with boys much larger than average. It was all in the course of a day's work at one of our poor schools. Strangely enough, with all the problems of that school, the building had unbelievably been remodeled six to eight years previously when many classroom walls had been removed so that two classes could be held in the same long room. That is, one class in history faced one way, and another class in geography faced the opposite direction. Apparently the open classroom fad was in vogue at the time of the rebuilding. It was an unreal classroom situation, but it was all too real having taken place in our nation's capital.

One of the most vivid recollections I hold of my 50 interviews with history teachers and many with administrators, both from our good and bad schools, is of the personal characteristics of the teachers and the heads or deputy heads of the schools. Perhaps I just happened to meet 50 well-spoken, fairly keen teachers and dozens of administrators. The fact remains that the teachers and administrators from the poor schools were similar in sophistication, in awareness, and in manner as were those from the good schools. If I had held the interviews away from the schools, I could not have judged which came from which type of school. The history teachers were one of the more encouraging elements in my recent research on U.S. education. Under extremely difficult conditions these teachers and administrators in our poor schools are making a herculean effort to teach their students something of value. Their efforts go unrecognized and little appreciated.

When our leaders talk about our nation at risk and say that "the educational foundations of our society are presently being eroded by a rising tide of mediocrity that threatens our very future as a nation and a people," they fail to recognize the nature of the problem. Our good schools are very good and should be maintained as such. Our bad schools are very bad and must be improved. When our leaders call for more money for education, they miss the mark. Our good schools are well supplied and well equipped, and the teachers have far better facilities than those in virtually any Japanese school. Our bad schools are poorly supplied and poorly equipped, and the teachers work under appalling conditions far more difficult than those in any Japanese school. That is the heart of the problem.

Instead of higher salaries for master teachers, more funding should be better directed to all teachers in our poor schools. They deserve a bonus. What we must do financially is to maintain the level of funding of our good schools to keep them good. New money must go into our bad schools, into their libraries, the classrooms, and even into the toilets. These schools are America's Achilles' heel.

Again, the Japanese can show us the way. Although there are inevitable differences among their schools from any aspect, in no respect do their best differ from their worst as ours do. Our best are as good as theirs, and in unique ways, even better. Our worst are considerably worse than theirs, again in unique ways. And we have so many more troubled schools than the Japanese, relative to our respective populations.

We are not, to repeat, jeopardized by the Japanese. Rather, we are as a nation being challenged by them because they have been able to motivate their students, both the bright and the average, to study diligently for the examinations and to teach their very slowest how to read, write, and calculate at a level that permits them to be gainfully employed. For example, the Japanese became alarmed with a record 2.6 percent unemployment rate. Their schools are producing, across the board, graduates who can be gainfully employed.

The Japanese challenge is not in how we educate our talented people. They really can't show us much there. Our best will challenge their best in the future and in all areas. In general, our best are more creative and imaginative than theirs. They will continue to look to us for the most innovative ideas. They will continue to come to our universities by the thousands for advanced specialized studies in all disciplines.

Where we can't match them, though, is in the education of the average and the below average student in the basics, from the first grade onward. Of course, they don't have to contend with minorities who have language problems as we do, but that still does not excuse the inexcusable standards of our schools for the average and particularly lower achievers. And even though many of our states and communities, partly in response to the widespread adverse publicity from the *Nation-at-Risk* report, have begun to initiate new programs to improve the general standards of our schools, they fall far short of those of the demanding Japanese public school.

The challenge from Japan is in their example, to wit: virtually every child in every community can learn to read and write and multiply and divide; essentially every graduate from the secondary school can gain minimum knowledge and skills for gainful employment. Most Japanese, of course, go far beyond that. We as a nation, nevertheless, should set these standards as our national goal. To this American, that is the challenge to our industrial society from the Japanese school.

Notes

CHAPTER 1

1. Asahi *Evening News*, Tokyo, February 27, 1985.
2. "U.S. Economic Performance in a Global Perspective," New York Stock Exchange, Office of Economic Research, 1981, p. 12.
3. *Japan Times*, Tokyo, February 28, 1985.
4. *Japan Times*, April 12, 1984.
5. Special Report, *Business Week*, May 23, 1983.
6. *Time Magazine*, October 22, 1984.
7. *Japan Times*, September 6, 1983.
8. New York *Times*, January 8, 1984.
9. Asahi *Evening News*, Tokyo, December 14, 1985.
10. *Japan Times*, November 10, 1985.
11. Philadelphia *Inquirer*, January 1, 1984.
12. *Japan Times*, March 13, 1980.
13. New York *Times*, December 25, 1983.
14. *Fortune*, June 18, 1979, pp. 104-20.
15. See Ivan Hall, Mori Arinori, Harvard University Press, 1973.
16. *Time Magazine*, September 10, 1984.

CHAPTER 2

1. Tsunoda, de Bary, and Keene, comps., *Sources of Japanese Tradition* (New York: Columbia University Press, 1958), p. 53.
2. *Sources of Japanese Tradition*, p. 50.
3. *Japan Times*, October 13, 1984.

CHAPTER 3

1. *A Nation at Risk*, p. 16.
2. Ibid.
3. Asahi *Evening News*, May 5, 1985.
4. Mombu Tokei Yoran, *Ministry of Education Statistical Handbook*, 1985, p. 34.
5. Shozo Muraishi, *Perspectives on Early Reading, Orthography and Reading*, 5th World Congress on Reading, 1974.
6. Kiyoshi Makita, *Dyslexia and Orthography*, 11th Annual Study Conference, United Kingdom Reading Association, England, 1974.

7. Daniel Resnick, *Standards, Curriculum & Performance: A History and Comparative Perspective*, A Report to the National Commission on Excellence in Education, August 31, 1982.

8. *A Nation at Risk*, p. 31.

9. *Newsweek*, January 9, 1984.

10. Mombu Tokei Yoran, *Ministry of Education Statistical Handbook*, 1985, p. 35.

11. *National Association of School Principals Bulletin* 67 (April 1983): 75.

12. New York *Times*, June 30, 1985.

13. Kiyoshi Makita, "The Rarity of Reading Disability in Japanese Children," *American Journal of Orthopsychiatry* 38, 1968.

14. See *Educational Forum*, January 1977.

CHAPTER 4

1. Mombu Tokei Yoran, *Ministry of Education Statistical Handbook*, 1985, pp. 44 and 48.

2. *A Nation at Risk*, p. 31.

3. *National Assessment of Education Progress*, Spring 1983.

4. *Toyo Keizai Data File* (Oriental Economist Data File), Toyo Keizai Shimposha, 1983, p. 184.

5. *A Nation at Risk*, p. 27.

6. Dallas *Times Herald*, "A Special Report on American Education," December 11, 1983.

7. Yomiuri Shimbun, Tokyo, September 26, 1984.

8. *Japan Times*, November 14, 1985.

9. *National Assessment of Education Progress, Newsletter*, Spring 1983.

10. Ibid.

11. Yomiuri Shimbun, Tokyo, January 19, 1984

12. *A Nation at Risk*, p. 26.

CHAPTER 5

Chapter 5 has no notes.

CHAPTER 6

1. *Kyoiku to Joho* (Education and Information), Ministry of Education, June 1984, p. 39.

2. *A Nation at Risk*, p. 29.

CHAPTER 7

1. Education Commission of the States, *The Information Society: Are High School Graduates Ready?* (Denver, CO: 1982), p. 2.
2. *A Nation at Risk*, pp. 28-91.
3. Ibid., p. 19.
4. UPI Report, December 13, 1983.
5. *The Information Society: Are High School Graduates Ready?* p. 37.
6. *Time Magazine*, January 23, 1984.
7. Asahi Shimbun, March 1, 1984.
8. *Japan Times*, December 29, 1984.
9. Asahi *Evening News*, February 15, 1985.
10. New York *Times*, December 4, 1983.
11. Asahi *Evening News* (The New York Times News Service), February 28, 1985.
12. Philadelphia *Inquirer*, November 14, 1983.
13. *Times* Educational Supplement, London, November 15, 1985.
14. Philadelphia *Inquirer*, October 3, 1983.
15. New York *Times*, October 23, 1983.
16. Asahi *Evening News*, February 15, 1985.
17. *Japan Times*, May 11, 1983.
18. *U.S. News and World Report*, November 7, 1983.
19. *Time Magazine*, December 9, 1985.
20. *Japan Times*, October 24, 1985.
21. *A Nation at Risk*, p. 30.

CHAPTER 8

1. *A Nation at Risk*, p. 30.
2. Asahi Shimbun, January 28, 1982.
3. *A Survey of the Health and Working Conditions of the Teachers of Tokyo* (Tokyoto Kyoshokuin no Kinmu • Kenko Oyobi Futan Jissai Chosa), Tokyo Teachers Union, 1981.
4. *A Nation at Risk*, p21.
5. *Open Doors*, International Student Census, IIE, 1983.

POSTSCRIPT

1. "Science and Engineering Education for the 1980s and Beyond," a report by the Department of Education and the National Science Foundation.

Acknowledgments

Grateful acknowledgment is made to the following for permission to reprint previously published material:

Kyoiku Shuppan Publishing Company for Figures 3.1, 3.2, 3.5-3.7
Gakko Tosho Publishing Company for Figures 3.3 and 3.4
Nihon Shoseki Publishing Company for Figures in Chapter 5
Shinko Shuppansha Keirinkan Publishing Company for Figures 4.16, 4.17, and 4.18
Tokyo Shoseki Publishing Company for Figures 4.1-4.15

Index

About the Author

Benjamin Duke is a professor of comparative and international education at the International Christian University in Tokyo where he has been teaching for the past 25 years. Before that he was a public school teacher in the United States. Professor Duke holds the Ph.D. from the Pennsylvania State University and the Ph.D. from the University of London, England.

Dr. Duke's research and teaching has concentrated on education in Asia. His earlier book, *Japan's Militant Teachers: A History of the Left Wing Teachers Movement*, focused on postwar education reforms in Japan. Other publications such as *The Karachi Plan: Master Design for Education in Asia*, "Democratic Education: Divergent Patterns in Japan and America" (*UNESCO's International Review of Education*), and "Why Noriko Can Read: Some Hints for Johnny" (*Educational Forum*) reflect his broader studies in comparative education.